IN THE STEPS OF JOHN WESLEY

By the same author

THE ROMANTIC MOVEMENT AND METHODISM
NEW HORIZONS
THE LIGHT ON THE MOOR
CARAVAN TO BETHLEHEM
THROUGH THE YEAR WITH WESLEY
JOHN WESLEY'S PRAYERS
SELECTED LETTERS OF JOHN WESLEY
THE GLORIOUS COMPANY (2 volumes)

1. A famous portrait of John Wesley painted by John Michael Williams, R.A. in 1742. It now hangs at Didsbury College, Westbury-on-Trym

IN THE STEPS OF JOHN WESLEY

by

FREDERICK C. GILL

LUTTERWORTH PRESS

LONDON

First published 1962

PRINTED IN GREAT BRITAIN
BY EBENEZER BAYLIS AND SON, LTD.
THE TRINITY PRESS, WORCESTER, AND LONDON

List of Plates

MAP

Contents

Acknowledgements

I AM INDEBTED to many friends and correspondents who have most generously loaned photographs, handbooks and other material and given me local information. It has not been possible to include every item to which they have drawn my attention, but I greatly appreciate their kindness. It has been interesting to hear from some who are descendants of Wesley or of families associated with him, and I am grateful to others who gave me help in many of the places visited. I wish to thank especially Dr. Frank Cumbers and Dr. J. Alan Kay of the Epworth Press; the Rev. Max Woodward of Wesley's Chapel; the Rev. W. Le Cato Edwards (Warden of Epworth Old Rectory); the rector of Epworth; the Master of the Charterhouse; Lady Ridley; Mrs. Katharine Trevelyan; Mrs. Edward Goffey; the Rev. and Mrs. A. C. Blain for hospitality in the Isle of Man and the Rev. and Mrs. W. J. Jenkins in Bath; the Headmaster of Truro Cathedral School; Miss J. Godber, M.A. (County Archivist of Bedford); the Curators of the following Museums: Wesley's Chapel, Tolson Memorial, Dr. Johnson's House, Whitby, Bristol, St. Ives (Cornwall), Douglas and Jersey; the Wardens of the New Room and Charles Wesley's House, Bristol; Miss D. Worthington (*The Shropshire Magazine*); Miss M. Wight (Worcester Archaeological Society); Miss D. A. Musson (Friends of Gainsborough Old Hall); the Bursar of Lincoln College, Oxford; Dr. Elmer T. Clark for a copy of his *Methodist Album*; Mr. Arthur Gaunt (Author of *Pennine Ways*); Mr. J. Tait; Mr. A. J. Chatterton; Mr. W. E. Tait; Mrs. A. Lord (Madeley Vicarage); Mrs. A. Rainford, J.P.; Mrs. N. Venables Kyrke, J.P.; the rectors of St. Giles, Cripplegate; St. Giles-in-the-Fields; St. Mary's, Dublin; the vicars of St. Gennys; Stanton Harcourt; Stanton; St. Michael's, Oxford; Christ Church, Macclesfield; Bunbury; St. Mary's, Islington; the ministers of Yarm and Arbroath Methodist Chapels; the Rev. G. H. Crossland, M.C.; Dr. Stuart Bolton; Mr. B. le Messurier; Mrs. Gertrude Jolley; Mr. F. G. Sawyer; Mrs. Norman; and Mr. E. F. Guiton.

I would particularly like to acknowledge the considerable

help given to me by the Rev. T. Shaw and Mr. John Pearce in Cornwall, the Rev. R. Lee Cole, M.A., B.D., in Ireland, the Rev. W. Llewelyn Jones in Wales; and to the following for their assistance and for information drawn from their books: the Revs. J. Henry Martin (*John Wesley's London Chapels*), Wesley Swift (*Methodism in Scotland*), Robert A. Haire (*Wesley's Visits to Ireland*); to Miss Joan M. Anderson for her booklet *Early Methodism in Bedford*; L. J. Meyler's handbook *John Wesley and Pembrokeshire*; Dr. T. W. Woodhead's brochure *Buxton Wesley Chapel*; Dr. Frank Baker, author of *The Methodist Pilgrim in England*; and the Rev. Robert H. Gallagher, Secretary of the Wesley Historical Society (Irish Branch) and author of *John Bredin.*

Many people also gave assistance in obtaining photographs and these include: the Rev. T. A. Bradshaw, B.A., Mr. John Rosewarne, the Rev. Norman Goldhawk, the Rev. J. Henry Martin, Mrs. N. Ruttle, Mr. Dennis Willis, Mr. Greenaway, Miss Margaret Baker, Miss Margaret Stewart, and Mr. A. R. Cheers. I am also indebted to my sister for transport in the West country; Miss Joan Robinson, J.P., for her kindness in typing the manuscript; my wife, as always, for her unfailing help; and finally Mr. Michael Foxell who (with Dr. Cecil Northcott) suggested the writing of this book, for his generous interest and encouragement. If I have failed to acknowledge any other indebtedness, I offer apologies and my warmest thanks.

FREDERICK C. GILL
September 1961

PLATES

The publishers wish to thank all those who have gone to a great deal of trouble to obtain the photographs to illustrate this book. A large number were especially commissioned, and the publishers acknowledge the following sources: E. W. Tattersall (Nos. 1, 3*b*, 5*a*, 13*a*, 14*a*, 15*b*, 17*b*, 28*a*); the Rev. Le Cato Edwards (2*a* and *b*, 3*a*); A. F. Kersting (5*b*, 6*b*, 7*a* and *b*, 9*a–e*); Thomas Photos (4*a* and *b*); Margaret Baker (6*a*, 8*a–c*, 16*a* and *b*); Mr. Greenaway (11*a*); M. E. Foxell (10, 11*b*, 12*b*, 17*a*, 18*a* and *b*, 19*a* and *b*, 20*b*); Margaret Stewart (26*a*);

National Building Record (21*a* and *b*, 28*b*, 29*a*); West Bromwich Central Library (22*a*); H. Turner (22*c*); E. H. Law (22*b*); A. Gaunt (28*c*); Eagle Photos (14*b*); *Lancashire Life* (27); Margaret Hicks (15*a*); W. Llewelyn Jones (29*b*); Studio St. Ives (20*c*); The Rev. Norman Robb (30*c*); The Rev. T. A. Bradshaw (30*a* and *b*); W. H. Hoult (25*b*); Gertrude Jolley (24*b*); A. R. Cheers (26*b*); North Eastern Evening Gazette Ltd. (23*b*); Dennis Willis (23*a*); Messrs. Stansfield and Burton (24*a*); Annie L. Dobson (25*a*); B. Matthews (Photo Printers) Ltd. (13*b*); John Rosewarne (20*a*).

Introduction

MANY volumes have been written on other aspects of Wesley, but apart from Dr. Frank Baker's useful guide *The Methodist Pilgrim in England* (limited to five key areas) and local handbooks, there is no comprehensive account of surviving Wesley landmarks and relics. This book is an attempt to fill the gap and deals topographically with his journeys. It begins in Epworth, takes in Oxford and the Cotswolds, traces his London associations, follows him into the west, moves through the Midlands and northern areas to Scotland, includes the Isle of Man and the Channel Islands, and finally takes us through Wales to Ireland where Wesley paid his last (and twenty-first) visit, at the age of eighty-six.

He was the greatest traveller of his day within these islands, covering during the course of his life nearly a quarter of a million miles, for the most part on horseback until in later life he used a carriage. Others, like Pennant and Cobbett, were mere ramblers in comparison. No other equalled Wesley's mileage. Not only in distance, but in the repetition and regularity of his itineraries, and in the number of years that he travelled—until his eighty-seventh year—he outstripped them all. "I must be on horseback for life," he said, "if I would be healthy."

It has not been possible to include every place he visited, though every area is covered. And items like "Wesley" trees and "Wesley" chairs are so numerous, and pious sentiment has gathered round so many, that it is often difficult to know which are genuine. Probably no other in our history has left behind him such a quantity of traditional relics and reminders. As an old man he had become a public figure so widely venerated that people gathered at cross-roads to see him pass, holding up their children for his blessing, and after his death even locks of his hair were preserved and treasured by succeeding generations.

Wherever he went he was welcomed with warmhearted hospitality and there are many surviving manor houses, vicarages and farmhouses, as well as inns and cottages, where he stayed.

Over the years he established a close friendship with those who entertained him, returning often to their homes, and in some cases their descendants still occupy the same properties.

It is fascinating to trace the lost pattern of the past, but increasingly difficult in our rapidly changing English scene where bomb damage and bulldozers have obliterated many familiar features, and modern architecture and re-planning are transforming the shape and character of our towns and countryside—a shape and character undisturbed for generations, for until recently a man in his old age could look out on the unchanged landscape he had known as a child. Even while I have been writing this book some places mentioned have been altered, or have disappeared almost before the ink was dry. It is wise, therefore, to note and record what remains before it is too late, and, in this, the growing number of local Wesley Historical Societies, as well as other antiquarian groups, are doing useful work. Individual churches can help not only by carefully preserving their records, but by exploring Methodist origins, particularly of the eighteenth century, in their own localities.

Interest in Wesley grows with the years and is by no means confined to his followers. My correspondence and journeys have disclosed to a surprising degree how deep is that interest and how widespread is Wesley's influence outside his own denomination. But this should not surprise us, for Wesley was no sectarian and belongs to us all—"incomparably," says a Presbyterian, the Reverend Kenneth Slack, "the most influential English figure in the religious story of the world." Yet occasionally one hears, even within Methodism, the careless remark: "Why go back to Wesley?" The answer is that, like a tree, no great movement can live if cut from its roots, but needs constantly to refresh its spirit by remembering its origin and returning to the source of its strength.

As for Wesley—in challenging the tight-laced orthodoxy of his day he literally meant what he said, that he took the *world* as his parish. It was no empty or defiant boast, nor was it the impulsive outburst of a fanatic, for no man was ever less fanatical, nor was it the cry of a frustrated spirit cold-shouldered by his equals, but a calm and confident assertion that his path lay beyond parochial boundaries, God only knew to what uncharted ways. Just as Francis of Assisi shattered the complacency of an introverted Church and blazed new trails for Christ, so Wesley laid aside convenience and convention. Both

2. The Old Rectory at Epworth which was rebuilt on the same foundations as the original house after the disastrous fire of 1709 and has recently been completely renovated by the World Methodist Council. It is open to visitors and is used as a retreat for study and fellowship

Left, the stairway leading to the attic rooms and "Old Jeffrey's Chamber"

3. The late seventeenth-century dresser in Susanna's kitchen at the Old Rectory, Epworth

Below, Epworth. The Red Lion, where Wesley stayed, and the village cross, which replaced the old Butter Cross, from the steps of which he preached

were rebels of the spirit—the black-gowned preacher and the brown-robed friar—and both took to the open road.

But Wesley was no wandering evangelist—no peripatetic preacher creating a sudden diversion, here today and gone tomorrow, whose work evaporated on his departure. He returned repeatedly to the same areas—Cornwall, Northumberland, Lancashire, Ireland—and built up in each and elsewhere a solid leadership and a compact fraternity.

We can forgive the writer of the florid Preface of an old but fascinating book *Wesley his own Biographer* because of one sentence in which he refers to Wesley's most natural and striking attribute, namely his unflagging vitality and extraordinary buoyancy: "He enjoyed the profoundest tranquillity whilst creating around him the most intense excitement." And he adds: "John Wesley marches through the ages and through the world, his chosen and appropriate parish." What was his secret? Wesley himself gives the answer, in the words of Thomas à Kempis: "He rides easily whom the grace of God carries."

CHRONOLOGY OF JOHN WESLEY

1703	*June 17*	Wesley's birth at Epworth
1707	*December 18*	Charles Wesley born at Epworth
1714	*January 28*	Entered Charterhouse
1720	*June 24*	Entered Christchurch, Oxford
1725	*September 19*	Ordained deacon
1726	*March 17*	Elected Fellow of Lincoln College
1728	*September 22*	Ordained priest
1735	*April 25*	Death of his father
	October 21	Sailed for Georgia
1736	*February 5*	Landed in Georgia
1737	*December 2*	Returned to England. (Landed February 1, 1738.)
1738	*May 24*	Meeting in Aldersgate Street. His evangelical conversion
1739	*November 11*	His first service at the Foundery
1742	*July 30*	Death of his mother
1744	*June 25*	His first Conference
	August 24	His last University sermon
1751	*February 8*	His marriage to Mrs. Vazeille
	June 1	Resignation of his Fellowship
1778	*November 1*	Opening of City Road Chapel
1781	*October 8*	Death of his wife
1784	*September 1–2*	His first ordinations
1788	*March 29*	Death of Charles Wesley
1790	*July 27*	Wesley's last Conference
1791	*February 23*	His last sermon
	March 2	His death, in his eighty-eighth year
	March 9	His burial at City Road

CHAPTER ONE

THE HOME OF THE WESLEYS—WROOT—EPWORTH—THE OLD RECTORY—THE TALE OF A CLOCK—I LOOK FOR A GHOST—ST. MARY'S—THE BUTTER CROSS—WESLEY MEMORIAL CHURCH—A FAMOUS TOMBSTONE

It was a bright October day when I drove into Epworth, one of those late autumn days of golden sunlight so welcome after a stormy summer. There was water in the dykes and low-lying fields, and the absence of cloud made a glittering landscape. There was water everywhere—by the roadsides and intersecting the wide unfenced land, black and sluggish in the ditches, bright and vivid where it caught the sunlight. As I crossed the endless bridges, with only a windmill or farmstead to break the horizon, and followed the long flat road which twisted among the waterways, I could understand why Samuel Wesley travelled between his two parishes by boat; also the strange and alien character of his parishioners, isolated as they were in the Isle of Axholme, hemmed in by water, with their insular habits and the cultural and social limitations imposed by their physical detachment from the broader stream of English life. The wonder is that Epworth ever achieved distinction, for it has no natural grace or beauty. But like Haworth, that grim and stony village among the moors, it was a cradle of genius, and from the sombre heart of the Fens came a fire that cleansed and exalted the nation's life.

But before I came to Epworth I turned aside to the small village of Wroot, where Wesley had acted as his father's curate. He had left Oxford in the summer of 1727 for that purpose and had taken up his residence in the village, which was surrounded by bogs, with a thatched parsonage in a farmyard and a small brick church, both of which have disappeared. The inhabitants, according to his sister Hetty, were "unpolished wights, as dull as asses, with heads as impervious as stones". The parish numbered only two hundred people and was inaccessible for many months of the year except by boat. In this obscure village

Wesley had often lived as a boy, for here his father resided at times for economy's sake, to escape his creditors, and after his Epworth rectory had been destroyed by fire.

The name Wroot is of Danish origin—"Wroot out of England", as they used to say, when a single causeway, often submerged, was its only approach, and packhorses picked their way by the stony paths at the water's edge. A letter from the rector to his son John in 1727 vividly describes it:

> I am *hipp'd* by my voyage and journey to and from Epworth last Sunday; being lamed with having my breeches too full of water, partly with a downfall from a thunder shower, and partly from the wash over the boat. . . . I wish the rain had not reached us on this side of Lincoln, but we have it so continual that we have scarce one bank left, and I cannot possibly have one quarter of oats left in all the levels. . . . We can neither go afoot nor on horseback to Epworth, but only by boat as far as Scawsit Bridge, and then walk over the common.

How often this road from Epworth to Wroot has seen the coming and going of the Wesleys! It was along this road that Wesley had come to meet his father or had passed him as they interchanged in their work between the parishes. It was on this road that marks the old causeway that Hetty, clinging to her father's coat, seated behind him on his horse, had been brought home in tears, and afterwards, when locked in her room, had escaped by the open window into the night to her lover. As I passed along it there was no sign or hint of the ghosts of the past; all was bright in the morning light, and the former life and tragedy of that lonely road were as if they had never been.

Only a ruined doorway remains of the old parsonage, almost opposite the present vicarage, and broken walls that once sheltered all that warm and eager life, with a tumbledown stable that held Samuel's horse, and an overgrown farmyard and garden where Susanna fed her chickens and pigs.

When Wesley refused his father's offer of the parish, it was given to Johnny Whitelamb who married Wesley's crippled sister Mollie. Whitelamb had been his father's protégé—a charity schoolboy of Epworth adopted by the rector to help as his amanuensis and to serve in the house, and afterwards sent by him with great generosity to Oxford. For forty years Whitelamb was vicar of Wroot, though unhappily his wife died within twelve months of their marriage. As I made my way to the church which stands outside and a little above the village—an undistinguished brick building of later date—I thought of those forty years in that obscure and limited sphere. Only his grave remains, with its weathered and tumbled headstone badly in need of repair. Apart from this, and the overgrown garden of Susanna, Wroot is disappointing to the Wesley pilgrim, but it is strange there is no local memorial.

Epworth today, though a thriving township, is no larger in population than in Wesley's day, when it numbered two thousand, and still keeps its old pattern. There is the long straggling street, the tree-lined path up to the parish church, the grave of Wesley's father from which Wesley preached when denied his father's pulpit, and the long high wall round the Old Rectory garden. I lunched at the Red Lion (Plate 3*b*) where Wesley often stayed after his father's death. Outside the window was the Market Square from which the coach had carried off John and Charles Wesley as schoolboys to London and where Wesley frequently preached—the last time as an old man of eighty-seven.

The handsome rectory (Plate 2*a*) still stands which replaced the one destroyed by fire in 1709, when Wesley was providentially rescued. This early eighteenth-century building of fine brick, after many structural changes at different periods, has recently been splendidly restored to its original form. All Methodists will rejoice at its purchase and transformation, and in its present use as a shrine of world Methodism. The World Methodist Conference held six years ago in Lake Junaluska gave warm approval to the scheme and generous financial help came from America. Its aim is to provide hostel and conference accommodation as a living centre of Methodist fellowship and activity and a national memorial of the greatest figure of the English Church.

This bold enterprise means that along with the Wesley Memorial Church, Epworth will be uniquely equipped to serve the interests of both British and World Methodism, and that the town will become more than ever a place of pilgrimage. Behind the scheme there has been both courage and imagination, and it is good to think that more than any previous generation modern Methodism has had the energy and vision to conceive and make it possible.

Yet Epworth on this, my first visit, and before the restoration of the Old Rectory, gave no outward inkling of its history. There was "no sense of a conscious past", to borrow a phrase of

Henry James. Unlike other places which have harboured genius it seemed not so obviously haunted by it and there was no brooding air of immortality. Perhaps it is the nature of the area, which jealously guards its secret. It certainly has not commercialized its fame, and the shops were strangely empty of Wesley postcards and souvenirs. The little Lincolnshire town slept in the afternoon sun as if blissfully unconscious of the greatness it had cradled or of the Movement which has carried its name to the ends of the earth.

It required a second visit for me to absorb the spirit of Epworth. Through the kindness of the Warden, the Rev. W. Le Cato Edwards, I stayed at the Old Rectory, now newly-restored largely through his initiative. For three days I wandered round the town, talked with its inhabitants, and slept in a room adjoining the former study of Wesley's father—scene of so many family conflicts, and opposite the steep and narrow stairs to the haunted garret.

But what would Wesley make of it now—the cream paint, the bathrooms, the modern amenities! For this gracious house has been more than restored; it has been magnificently renewed, and with such comfort and conveniences as the Wesley family never dreamed of. Yet it remains the authentic structure with the same rooms, with walls and windows restored to their original place—for it had been much altered; and entering through its welcoming door we meet an atmosphere of comfort and relaxation. It conveys an immediate impression of harmony and serenity, as if the old torments and tragedies that it once knew were forgotten and all that remained was an abiding beatitude and peace.

This substantial Queen Anne house with its fine front and its fifty windows was erected by Wesley's father on the site of the thatched rectory which burned like matchwood on the night of the fire. Despite his poverty and improvidence he built it well and in excellent taste, but it cost him a crippling four hundred pounds and we may well wonder how he came to build so commodious a house which at the time must have seemed reckless extravagance. The former rectory was described in 1607 as "consisting of five baies, built all of timber and plaster and covered with straw thatch, the whole building being contrived into three stories and disposed in seven chief rooms—a kitchinge, a hall, a parlour, a butterie, and three large upper rooms and some others of common use." It had been partly destroyed by a previous fire in 1702, for the rectory suffered two disastrous fires. This was the house in which Wesley was born on June 17, 1703 and from the window of which he was rescued, though the popular picture of that event is somewhat imaginative.

Over the front entrance of the present building is the Wesley coat of arms, in white, purple and gold, showing a castle superimposed (signifying security) and twelve scallop shells, which dates from the Middle Ages when one of the Wesleys went to the Crusades. The use of the shield which goes with it—a scallop shell and a purple cross—was granted by the College of Heralds to the Methodist Conference in 1948.

Much of the furniture is of Wesley's period, some of it owned or used by him or his family, and a collection of Wesley relics and documents is being accumulated. In the large entrance hall is a massive and magnificently carved sideboard which belonged to the family and which may well have stood in the place it now occupies, for there is no other wall space that can take it. It was sold to the Red Lion on Samuel Wesley's death where it remained for a hundred years, then went to Squire Adrian Peacock of Bottisford, and afterwards belonged to a Methodist family in Cheshire from whom it was purchased and brought back to its original home.

Above it is an attractive portrait of Wesley's mother in her younger days which deserves a wider reproduction—it is so much more fascinating than her familiar bonneted profile. The profile, by the way, might be that of Wesley himself, especially if we compare it with Romney's portrait or with the medallion in Westminster Abbey—it has the same calm look of neat, buttoned-up efficiency. But in this coloured portrait we see the lively and attractive daughter of Dr. Annesley, full of grace and charm.

An interesting item is Wesley's grandmother clock with its slender case and small brass dial. At one time it came into the possession of a farmer, John Crosby, who said one day to one of his labourers, John Vause, "Johnny, does ta want a clock?" "I want one, Maister," he answered, "but I can't afford to get one." "Well," said his master, "thou shalt have one of John Wesley's." And Johnny agreed to work for a week and take this clock in payment. In time he removed to Thorne and the clock passed to his son-in-law with whom it remained for over forty years. It was made by Markwick of London and still keeps perfect time.

Through double doors on the left of the entrance is the parlour where several of the windows still have their original glass. To the right of the vestibule is the schoolroom where for six hours a day Mrs. Wesley taught her children, but which has no sign of its former use and is devoted to small retreats and conferences. Opening from it is Susanna's famous kitchen, but do not imagine you will find the old-fashioned kitchen of her day when it was full of family life, the clatter of clogs, the sound of children or packed with villagers for her cottage meetings. All is bright, stream-lined, austere, but this is the room, full of old memories, with its tiled floor, its great open stepped chimney, its window looking out into the yard, a fine old dresser (imported since), and, hanging on the wall, the charred fragment of a wooden beam from the old burned down rectory.

Returning to the entrance hall, we pass through a door into an inner vestibule opening into the dining room and with a handsome staircase. On the first floor are the main bedrooms, light, airy, well-proportioned, though with no indication as to how they were allocated among the Wesley family. Our main interest is in the study, at the end of the corridor, and in the garret above. The study is surprisingly small for a busy rector in a large house. It is directly over the kitchen, with its original fireplace, and with a powder closet opening from it, much used in those days of wigs. Here for twenty-six years Wesley's father wrote his sermons, worked laboriously at his *Dissertations on Job*, and wrestled with his domestic problems. Here John Wesley helped him. And here on more than one occasion there were stormy family scenes—with Hetty over her marriage, with his wife when money was scarce and debts were piling up, and with John himself over a tactless sermon he preached in his father's church.

Outside the study and opposite the bedroom in which I slept were the narrow stairs leading to the attics and to the haunted "Jeffrey's Chamber"—Old Jeffrey being the name given to the family ghost. Few ghost stories are better authenticated. Strange rappings were heard when the rector was at his prayers. There was the sound of breaking bottles and jingling coins, and the sight of the hand-mill turning itself and a trencher twirling of its own accord. Hetty was the one most affected, possibly because she was the most impressionable and was undergoing deep emotional stress at the time; but even her matter-of-fact mother felt the ghost brush past her on this attic staircase, with the sound of clanking chains. The rector primed his pistol, got a mastiff, and called in watchers. Robert Brown the manservant saw "it" in the kitchen, resembling a rabbit, and ran after it with the fire tongs. Some think it was the work of a poltergeist, though we are reminded that the local inhabitants were not without talents for plaguing people whom they did not like. It cannot, however, be lightly dismissed and remains an unsolved mystery.

Climbing those narrow stairs (Plate 2*b*) we come nearest of all to the hidden life of the old house, for it was here that Hetty sat each night on the bottom step outside the study with her father's candle, waiting for him to emerge. Even today, with the crooked stairs well-lit, we cannot climb them without a thrill, but we find no ghostly atmosphere in the now bright, cream-walled attics, where once the children and servants slept. And Jeffrey's Chamber is no longer stacked with fruit and grain. Save for two immaculate beds almost lost in the length of it, a dressing table, and a floor matting of reeds plaited in strips by local industry, it is as bare as the deck of a ship. It is forty feet long and its most striking features are the eight stout ship's timbers bent to an angle which support the roof. The beams throughout the house mostly seem to be ship's timbers and older than the building itself. The floors of this upper storey are made of lime and cow hair, and are as hard as cement. But why, oh why, was the garret not left as it was, full of eerie shadows and dark corners?

From the rectory we turn to the parish church with its broad stone-flagged avenue of limes above the Market Square. Founded in the thirteenth century and badly damaged in the Civil War, it underwent a wholesale renovation in 1868, including a new altar and pulpit. The old communion table was sold, but was eventually secured by the Wesley Memorial Church, and the original pulpit is believed to be in America. The bells, too, are later than Wesley, dating from 1813.

This is the church of Wesley's childhood, with its ancient parish chest, with two handsome seventeenth-century chairs within the communion rail, one of which belonged to Susanna, and with the octagonal font where most of the Wesley children were baptized. A massive door of solid oak with a great iron handle opens into the vestry where the rector showed me the small silver chalice, made by William Fawley of London in 1697, presented to Samuel Wesley by his patron, the Marquis of Normanby, bearing the inscription: "Epworthiae. In insula de Axholm, A.D. 1706", and from which Wesley at the age of nine received his first Communion. The costly mazer bowl, formerly owned by the church, was sold some years ago to the British Museum for a thousand pounds. Possibly there is other church plate still buried in the King's Head Croft, where some of it was formerly unearthed, hidden, no doubt, in the Civil War.

The registers date from 1538 when registration was first ordered by Thomas Cromwell, but there is a gap between 1601 and 1710; the entries of John and Charles Wesley's baptisms are therefore missing. The pages covering the years 1538–1601 were discovered in bad condition in the church chest and in private houses, and have now been carefully repaired and rebound. It is possible that later pages disappeared in the rectory fire. There are entries, however, relating to Wesley's family, including the marriage of his sister Mary, and his father's burial. But most interesting are those in Wesley's own hand, 1727–29, when he was acting as his father's curate. It was astonishing, however, not to find an appropriate memorial of Wesley within the church nor indeed to discover any notice or leaflet relating to its close association with Methodism.

Samuel Wesley's grave can be found to the right of the south porch. Its original brickwork was replaced with stone in 1872, with two fragments of iron in the stonework marking the spot where Wesley stood to preach. The graveyard is also altered, for it was recently reported that four hundred of its mouldering tombstones had been removed by tractor and dumped into a rubbish pit, but the old rector's tomb remains undisturbed.

The rectory glebe is also much changed for it was larger in Samuel Wesley's day, but after his death twenty-six acres of it were lost, and attempts to recover them were ineffectual. It is said they were seized by a money-lender to whom he was in debt.

Mr. G. H. Archer, the last Deputy Steward of the Manor, gave me interesting details of the old Butter Cross from which Wesley preached, which, according to the Manorial records, was taken down in 1803 as a nuisance, and a new Cross was erected a few yards to the north of the old site. It is therefore unlikely that Wesley ever saw the present Cross or preached from it, though some of the original stones may remain. Queen Street was then only a glorified footpath, and the new Cross was brought into Market Square itself. More recently there was an outcry when its removal was proposed to relieve traffic congestion.

On the main road, in a fine setting, is the Wesley Memorial Church of good Gothic design with a slender spire and in spacious and well-kept grounds. The entire lay-out of church, school and manse is dignified and impressive. Inside is the old communion table which formerly stood in the parish church, from which over so many years the Wesley family received Communion, and which for a far longer period has served generations of villagers.

We have already mentioned the Red Lion, the upper part of which is mostly unchanged. Along the narrow bedroom corridor are rooms numbered 4 and 5, one of which, or possibly both, were used by Wesley on his several visits.

In 1742, seven years after his father's death, Wesley paid his first return visit to Epworth. It was a Saturday and he put up at the Red Lion, but it was a poor homecoming. There was no open door or welcoming hand. "I went to an Inn," he wrote, "in the middle of the town, not knowing whether there were any left in it now who would not be ashamed of my acquaintance. But an old servant of my father's, with two or three poor women, presently found me out."

But worse was to follow. The next morning he visited the curate, Mr. Romley, whose parents had been close friends of his, and offered his assistance, which was coldly refused. In a way it was understandable, for he and Romley temperamentally were poles apart. Did the ghost of the old rector rise before Romley, with his perversity, his debts, his clever sons and lively daughters, or of his wife, that determined woman who, flouting all canonical rules, filled her kitchen with the riff-raff of the village? Was the memory of the Wesleys a byword in the place, for their imprudence and improvidence? We may be sure that, locally, Wesley was tarred with the family failings, and that, whatever he was in Oxford, here in Epworth he was the son of his father, and was meeting Romley against the background and small talk of a market town.

Romley made matters worse by preaching a tactless sermon,

and Wesley, who was present, listened to a blistering tirade against religious enthusiasm. Afterwards his travelling companion gave notice to the people coming out of church that "Mr. Wesley, not being permitted to preach in the church, designs to preach here at six o'clock". Little did the curate realize the far-reaching results of his resistance, and Wesley, with unerring instinct, turned the occasion to good account. Later, on the walls of a thousand vestries, we find the familiar reproduction of the scene—of Wesley in gown and bands, with open Bible and outstretched hands, appealing to the multitude.

So successful were these tombstone sermons that Wesley altered his itinerary. He remained for eight days, preaching each night in the churchyard, and with such effect that in a neighbouring town a genial magistrate, confronted with a wagon-load of Methodists, refused a conviction. "Carry them back," he said, "and let them convert all the scolds in the town." And Whitelamb proved a better ally than Romley, for Wesley preached twice in his old pulpit at Wroot to crowded congregations.

Six weeks later he was back again and the tombstone services were resumed. It was on this occasion that he was refused the Sacrament in the parish church. No blame attaches to Wesley and it was irregular and inexcusable on the part of the curate. Wesley, indeed, showed great courtesy, for when he found that his open air crowds desired Communion, he said, "By all means, but it would be more respectful first to ask Mr. Romley, the curate's, leave." The latter replied: "Pray, tell Mr. Wesley, I shall not give *him* the Sacrament; for he is not *fit*." This was the height of madness, as well as of unkindness, and that night in his room at the Red Lion, Wesley wrote:

> There could not have been so fit a place under heaven, where this should befal me first, as my father's house, the place of my nativity, and the very place where, according to the straitest sect of our religion, I had so long lived a Pharisee! It was also fit in the highest degree, that he who repelled me from that very table where I had myself so often distributed the bread of life, should be one who owed his all in this world to the tender love which my father had shown to his, as well as personally to himself.

Epworth drew Wesley like a magnet; six months later he was back again, and yet again within three months. On each occasion, to the embarrassment of the curate, he worshipped in the parish church, but Romley's trouble was psychological, and after a mental breakdown he ended his days, five years later, in a madhouse. Always Wesley loved Epworth. In his seventy-fifth year he walked alone in the churchyard, brooding on old memories, under the limes and by his father's grave. "I felt," he said, "the truth of 'one generation goeth, and another cometh'," and quoted the poet:

> The natal soil to all how strangely sweet!
> The place where first he breathed who can forget?

"Epworth," he said, "which I still love beyond most places in the world."

CHAPTER TWO

OXFORD—LINCOLN COLLEGE—CHRISTCHURCH—ST. MARY'S AND ST. MICHAEL'S—THE CASTLE—FINSTOCK—SCENE OF WESLEY'S FIRST SERMON—STANTON HARCOURT—THE COTSWOLDS—OLDEST RECTORY IN ENGLAND—A WESLEY CAFÉ—THE WEAVERS' HALL

OXFORD in those days was very different from now—a mile in length, barely as much in breadth, with its north and east gates still standing, with no Cowley and other sprawling suburbs, and with cobbled streets with a central kennel in which the residents dumped their refuse. Wesley in after years looked back with nostalgia to his time there. "I love," he said, "the very sight of Oxford."

Many of the colleges were under scaffolding on the days we came. In court after court the stonework was being renewed and a costly renovation was in process, including the front quadrangle of Lincoln of which Wesley was a Fellow. Founded in 1427, a small college, slow in growth, by his day it had already completed its chapel and inner quadrangle (Plate 4*a*).

According to tradition the rooms he occupied are in the front quadrangle where in a blocked-up window we see his bronze bust—a copy of that by Roubiliac in the National Portrait Gallery. The rooms (which are in private use, but can be visited by arrangement with the Bursar) are on the first floor up No. 2 staircase, and were restored in 1928 by the generosity of American Methodists, when for the opening ceremony Wesley's pulpit was brought from the College Chapel into the quadrangle which was crowded with distinguished guests. There is now, however, some doubt, as we shall see in a moment, as to whether these were the actual rooms used by Wesley.

Bishop John Hamilton of America, who had been mainly instrumental in their restoration, said it was "the privilege and honour of the American Methodists to restore the rooms" and that they had been restored as nearly as possible "in the manner in which such work was best done in the times in which they were built, and furnished in the style of the period in which Wesley lived." The bishop added: "We bring honour to Lincoln College today because it was here that he received encouragement and support. Leaves of absence from the duties of his office were frequently granted him, and his salary continued through the twenty-five years." It was this assistance made possible by the College that enabled him to travel and to erect at Bristol the first meeting-house for his followers.

The Rector of the College, Mr. J. A. R. Munro, in acknowledging this generous restoration, underlined the bishop's words. "It was that endowment which provided for him an independent livelihood . . . and instead of burying himself in a country vicarage, to take, in his own words, the whole world for his parish." But for this Fellowship, therefore, Methodism might never have been.

The rooms are not only improved, but a good deal more comfortable. Not every feature could be reproduced; in all such reconstructions there is a margin of conjecture. According to Mr. Munro "the walls, chimney flue, the oak floor, the small windows, one in the little lobby, one in the bedchamber, and a third long ago built up and now occupied by Wesley's bust, are perhaps all that survive. The three big windows of the sitting-room were opened only a hundred years ago. . . . The American Committee has judiciously left them untouched."

In what then does the restoration consist? The rooms since Wesley's day have been put to different uses by various occupants. At one time, before the building of the new College Library, they were lined with shelves stacked with books. "Not a stick remained of the eighteenth-century fittings." Generations of tenants had plastered the walls with canvas and disfiguring wallpaper. The mean fireplace needed replacement. Today the original Tudor style of the rooms is complete. The lovely linen-fold panelling, though brought from elsewhere, is antique. The furniture consists of an old English mahogany writing table, two Chippendale arm-chairs, a handsome secretaire bookcase with latticed doors, and a Queen Anne walnut bureau bookcase, with two Persian rugs and an eighteenth-century clock (Plate 4*b*).

A copy of Romney's painting of Wesley hangs on the wainscoted wall. Romney completed the original when Wesley sat for him four times at the age of eighty-five. Wesley, we are reminded, was probably the most frequently painted male

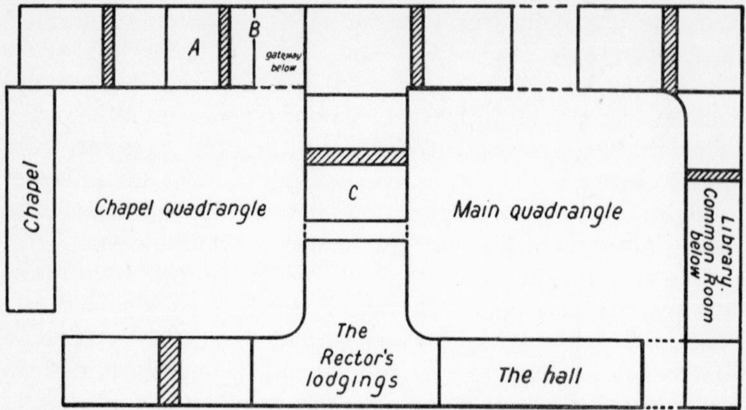

A plan of Lincoln College, Oxford, in the eighteenth century reproduced from *The Young Mr. Wesley* by Dr. V. H. H. Green whose research indicates that Wesley lived on the first floor in rooms (A) from 1726 to 1737 and rooms (B) from 1737 to 1751. (C) shows the position of the rooms known as John Wesley's Rooms which were restored in 1928.

celebrity of the century, and he sat to most of the famous artists of the period. (The Reynolds portrait was probably lost in a fire at Dangan Castle.) This Romney portrait, copied by W. D. Hamilton, shows Wesley two years before he died. The original was sold at Christies in 1873; it was bought by Messrs. Agnew in 1907 and later became part of the late Mr. J. R. McFadden's art collection in Philadelphia. At one time it changed hands for forty thousand dollars.

Since these words were written, however, Dr. V. H. H. Green, Fellow and Senior Tutor of Lincoln, has raised a doubt as to whether these rooms were ever occupied by Wesley. In his recent book, *The Young Mr. Wesley*, full of fascinating and well-documented detail of Wesley's university life, he says that the rooms used by Wesley (at different periods) are the two first floor sets in the corner furthest from the chapel, on the Turl side of the Chapel Quadrangle and *not* in the front quadrangle. The rooms nearest the corner were in his possession from 1737 until his resignation in 1751 (they can be visited by appointment and during vacation). As to the rooms at present ascribed to him, which have been restored, Dr. Green says: "It seems impossible to say with absolute certainty who was living in them between 1729 and 1736, but it was certainly not John Wesley."

The rooms now designated by Dr. Green are less spacious and impressive than the restored rooms, but in age and atmosphere are no less characteristic and, indeed, as will be seen from the plan, are so near to the latter (which overlook both quadrangles) as almost to adjoin. If we accept Dr. Green's conclusions, then it was here that Wesley first gathered his Oxford Methodists—the Holy Club, received his pupils, and began the planned and meticulous daily discipline to which he held for the whole of his life. And up these narrow stairs (which serve both sets) came not only his friends, jubilant and exhilarated, but also the poor and the penitent, the shivering girl in her rags on a winter's night, the simple janitor who out of his poverty thanked God for everything.

Dr. Green draws his conclusion after deep quarrying in the College archives and in material hitherto unpublished, including Wesley's Oxford diaries, and he provides a plan of the College as it was in the eighteenth century showing how the rooms were then allocated. If he is right—and we have no reason in view of the evidence to suppose otherwise—let us hope that the College will indicate clearly which rooms really belonged to Wesley. In any case, the existing Wesley rooms are a fitting and gracious memorial, commemorating, as Dr. Green points out, Wesley's connection with the College rather than his residence in a particular set of rooms. And he expresses the hope that one day there may be an endowment for a Wesley Fellowship at Lincoln as a further reminder of Wesley's long association with the College. That perhaps would be the finest memorial of all.

But how did the tradition arise concerning these rooms? John Morley, who used them, says in his *Recollections*, "For many terms I was lodged in Wesley's rooms." One day he told John Bright that when at Oxford he had occupied the same rooms as John Wesley, and Bright replied: "Well, Morley, precious little good it seems to have done you."

Dr. Green's book gives other interesting details showing how full and varied was Wesley's life in Oxford. He met his friends in the manner of the day at the local inns and coffee-houses, played billiards, backgammon and tennis, took a hand at cards in the Common Room, was interested in music and dancing, occasionally went shooting and hunting, and was not above visiting the theatre, local horse races and Bawtry Fair.

From the ivy-clad quadrangle we turn through the passage to the chapel—small and intimate, its seven stained-glass windows casting a mellow light into its shadow, and full of music, as we entered, from its sweet-toned organ. We notice the black and white tiled floor, the inlaid stalls with their carved ends, the shallow vaulted roof, and the brass candle-holders (fitted with electric bulbs). Wesley's pulpit, to the left of the altar, is solid and square on four clawed legs, with four straight steps up to it at the back. Wesley was twenty-two when six months after his ordination he was elected a Fellow of Lincoln, and here in this chapel and pulpit during the twenty-five years of his Fellowship he worshipped and preached.

In the College Hall his portrait looks down from behind the high table, and though the Hall has undergone several restorations it still reflects the atmosphere of an older day with its three lines of tables with their massive silver candelabra and its richly decorated open stone fireplace. The panelled Senior Common Room remains unchanged and the College records contain entries relating to Wesley, including his letter of resignation of his Fellowship on his marriage.

After Lincoln College, Christchurch—where the three Wesley brothers began their Oxford careers—is lavish and spacious, and we look in vain round its immense quadrangle for the rooms they once occupied, which are not identified. But in its Great Hall, up the magnificent stone staircase with its fan-vaulted ceiling held by a single pillar, we find just inside the door another copy of Romney's portrait of Wesley, which is considered on good authority to be a replica by the artist himself. And in the chapel, which is also the cathedral, both John and Charles Wesley were ordained by Bishop Potter.

On seven occasions Wesley preached the University Sermon in the University Church of St. Mary the Virgin, though not from its present pulpit. The church, full of historical associations, still bears the marks of the scaffold erected for the trial of Archbishop Cranmer. Wesley won his first convert here—Robin Griffiths, son of the vicar of Broadway. And he preached here his sermon on Scriptural Christianity which so offended the authorities that he was no longer invited to its pulpit. A century later Newman was its vicar, and here Pusey, like Wesley before him, with his sermon on National Apostasy produced a new spiritual awakening.

St. Michael's Church adjoining the former Bocardo—the northern gate of the city where Latimer and Ridley were imprisoned before they were burned at the stake nearby—should

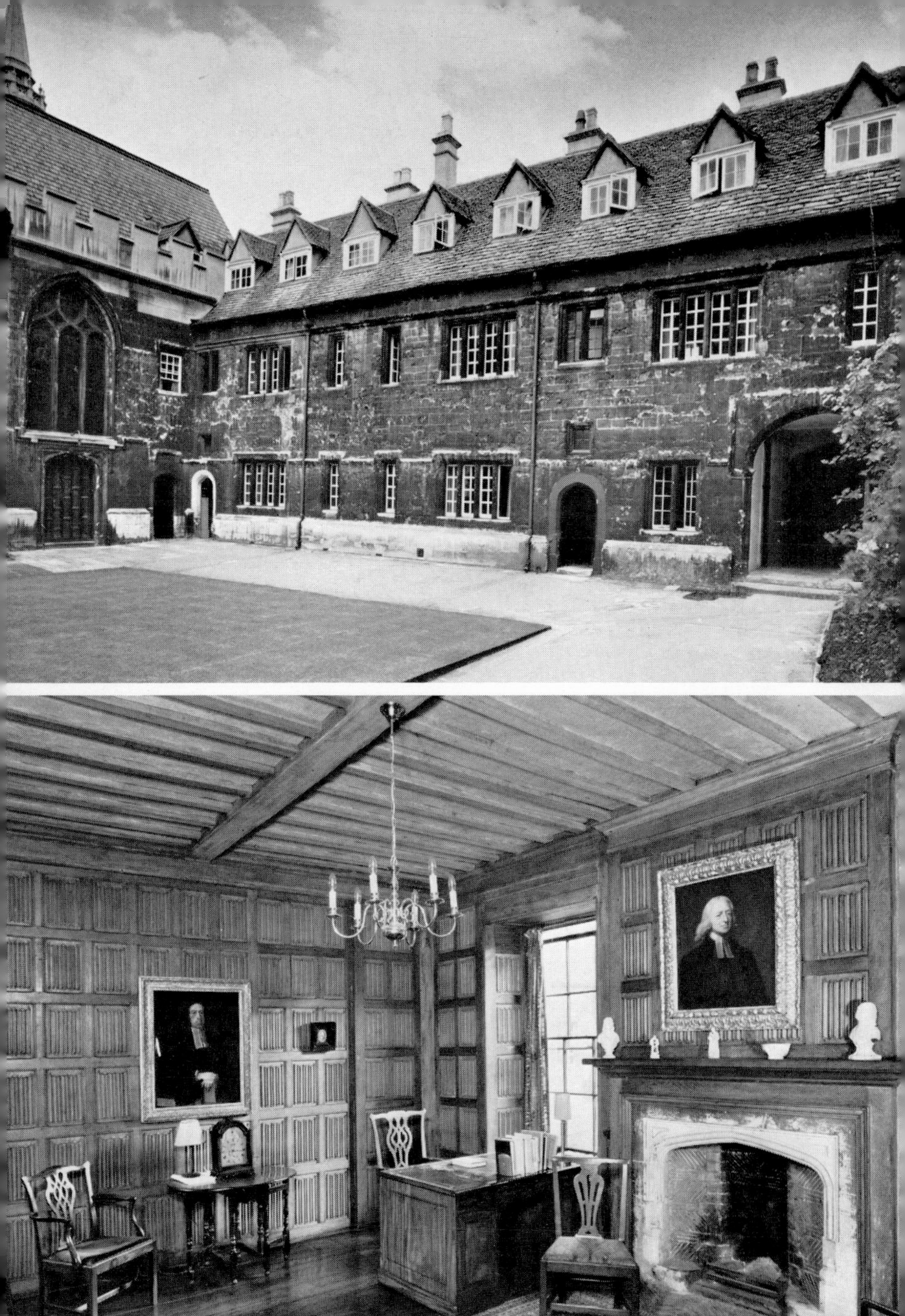

4. The Chapel Quad, Lincoln College, Oxford. Wesley occupied rooms above and to the left of the archway, and did not use the rooms, shown *below*, magnificently restored in 1928 and now preserved in his memory

5. Wesley's Chapel in City Road, exterior and interior

also be visited. Since 1487 the church had been closely linked to Lincoln College and Wesley's first duty as a Fellow was to preach there in 1726 when the College attended in state. A notice on the fifteenth-century pulpit records the occasion. But in the drastic restoration of the church in the last century many features familiar to Wesley disappeared. He also preached in St. Ebbe's, St. Martin's, St. Aldate's, St. Thomas', and All Saints'. The Bocardo, used as a prison, mostly for debtors, was almost daily visited by Wesley and his followers. It was demolished in 1771, though traces remain of the dungeons and of an underground passage in the cellars of No. 35, Cornmarket Street and the Northgate Tavern.

St. George's Tower (the Castle), which served as the county jail, is all that survives of a six-towered Norman fortress. Members of the Holy Club made it their duty, with the approval of the bishop, to visit it daily, to hold services, administer Communion, teach the prisoners to read, to write their letters, and provide after-care. This was no spasmodic work of piety, but a well-planned and comprehensive social service, and with a fund established to sustain it. The prisoners were neglected and no one cared until Wesley met their need. In prison welfare he was a pioneer.

His first Oxford chapel was in New Hall Street (the site of it is probably Nos. 33 and 34). He described it as "a lightsome, cheerful place, and well-filled with rich and poor, scholars as well as townsmen". His grandfather had been a student of New Hall Inn, now demolished, and the present Wesley Memorial Church in the same street continues the work of a Methodist Society which has existed here for over two hundred years.

While in the neighbourhood I went to Wood Green on the Woodstock Road where Wesley preached outside Holy Trinity Church and stayed in a thatched cottage opposite the Manor Farm. An aged inhabitant took pains to help me, but burst into loud guffaws when he learned Wesley's date. "Ho! Ho!" he chortled. "Naw, oi weren't yer then!"

One of Wesley's most frequent correspondents was Nancy Bolton who lived with her brother, a Witney brewer, at the Manor Farm House, Finstock, a hamlet near Charlbury on the edge of Wychwood Forest. It was built in 1660 and Dr. Stuart Bolton tells me that until recently it was still occupied by a

JW—C

member of the Bolton family. The house is well preserved, with its unspoiled exterior, Tudor casements and doorway, and three lovely lozenge windows in its gables. Wesley, when he stayed there, preached in the kitchen and people came from miles around.

From Witney, well known to Wesley through his friendship with the Bolton family, who formerly lived at Blandford Park, I made my way to Stanton Harcourt and South Leigh which in his time formed a single parish. South Leigh Parish Church is memorable because it was here that he preached his first sermon. The small stone-flagged church remains little changed, though its medieval frescoes were not uncovered until 1872 and the slender pedestal of its wine-glass pulpit in which he stood is also later—the work of Sir Ninian Comper. Wesley came as a young deacon, newly-ordained, from Oxford. He would see the same clock on the church tower with the words: "Ye know not what hour the Lord may come." An inscription on the pulpit records Wesley's visit. Forty-six years later he wrote in his diary: "I preached at South Lye. Here it was that I preached my first sermon, some forty years ago. One man was in my present audience who heard it. Most of the rest have gone to their long rest." I climbed the stone steps of the plain oak pulpit and thought of Wesley facing his first congregation.

Stanton Harcourt, two miles distant, has a Flemish appearance, but of the great manor house of the Harcourts only its enormous kitchen with a conical roof, and Pope's Tower in which the poet shut himself away from the world to complete his translation of Homer, remain. The parish church has the oldest rood screen in England—thirteenth century, along with a Norman nave and doorways, and a chancel lit with Early English lancet windows. There are also the magnificent Harcourt tombs. This is probably the Oxfordshire village church where Wesley acted for a short period as curate at a salary of thirty pounds a year, which, he says, enabled him to keep his horse, at a time when, hard-pressed for money, he would otherwise have been obliged to sell it. Dr. V. H. H. Green, however, in *The Young Mr. Wesley* says that the curacy referred to "was almost certainly at Pyrton, near Wallingford", but whichever identification is correct, it was at Stanton Harcourt that he preached his famous sermon: "By grace are ye saved, through faith," which he repeated the same afternoon in St. Mary's, Oxford, before the University. This was the sermon which, eighteen days after his Aldersgate experience, sounded the note of revival.

The old vicarage, part of which is now the Harcourt Estate Office, is still referred to as Wesley's Cottage. When John Gambold, afterwards a Moravian bishop, was vicar here, it was a meeting place of the early Methodist leaders. John and Charles Wesley came here often, their sister Kezia sometimes stayed here, and Wesley brought Peter Böhler, the Moravian, here for an important discussion with Gambold. So this picturesque house, though modernized and sub-divided, has a unique place in both local and Methodist history. It has, according to Dr. Frank Baker, three ghosts: a Grey Lady, a Cavalier, and a Dog! Once, they say, it was a pesthouse, but the present friendly vicar opened the door to me upon a gay and bright interior, and where Wesley once sat with his friends in grave deliberation was a fascinating model railway lay-out engaging the rapt attention of a small boy.

During his curacy in these parts Wesley once spent a busy Sunday at Shipton-under-Wychwood church, taking three services and a baptism, a wedding and a funeral. More than once he visited the Bishop of Oxford at Cuddesdon, and he preached in the parish churches of Wytham, Combe, Chislehampton, and, of course, Pyrton. Other churches where he officiated, listed by Dr. Green, include Ascot, Holwell, Buckland (Berkshire), Stanesfield, Bampton, Black Bourton, Ferry Hinksey, Fleet Marston, and Winchendon.

When we come to Stanton and Buckland in the Cotswolds we find the unspoiled countryside of Wesley's youth. The cottages of honey-coloured stone drink in the warm sunlight and in this lovely survival of an older England, which lies off the main road on the slopes of a larch-covered hill, time seems almost to stand still.

In the centre of Stanton is the village Cross with its eighteenth-century shaft on a thirteenth-century base. A charming byway leads to the stone church with its squat tower, a sanctus bell in the turret, a pointed steeple, and a battlemented entrance. The south porch has an upper storey with a niche for the figure of St. Michael, its patron saint. No trace remains of the Saxon church which once stood here. Two of its three wide bays are Norman; it has an old timbered roof, and there are fragments of glass in its east window as old as the stone of the building. It has two pulpits, the one, worn, battered with age, and out of use, being one of the few fourteenth-century pulpits surviving in Britain. It was first used in 1375. The other is seventeenth-century oak work, with panels adorned with roses, and with a handsome canopy. On the three end pews at the rear we can see the chafing marks of the chains where the shepherds attending service tied their dogs.

It was Sunday afternoon and the village slept in the April sun, as peaceful and almost as unchanged as when Wesley knew it. It was here that he came so often in his Oxford days to visit his friend, Robert Kirkham, whose father was rector, but the rectory at the church gate, now a private house, was built in 1820, when the old rectory was burned down. The setting, however, remains: the garden, with its wide lawn and two ancient trees—one said to be six hundred years old—, the approach from the church gate with surrounding thatched barns and houses, and, close by, Stanton Court which is sixteenth century, and Warren House with its dainty dormer windows and a fine plaster ceiling. All these were familiar to Wesley and he often officiated in this church.

The smaller village of Buckland, with hardly a score of houses, is two miles away, with a less picturesque church, the plain high tower of which stands prominently above the road. It has a plain pulpit, and old oak pews, and William Morris supervised the work and defrayed the cost of one of its windows. The Granville family, with whom Wesley was friendly, occupied for a short time the house behind the church, now extended and known as Buckland Manor. The family had aristocratic connections and of the two daughters one, Mary Pendarves, was a widow of twenty-four, well known in Court circles, who later numbered Swift and Johnson among her friends and Fanny Burney as one of her protégées. She afterwards married Patrick Delany, Dean of Down, and became famous as one of the brilliant women of the day.

Wesley found this charming circle, which included the Kirkham family, irresistible. Romance was in the air and Wesley, ever susceptible to charm and wit, was caught up and enraptured in an atmosphere of youthful exuberance and companionship in which piety and gaiety intermingled. Indeed, his heart was almost as strangely warmed as, later, in Aldersgate Street. "My heart burns within me," he wrote to Mary Pendarves, "when I reflect on the many marks of regard you have already shown." For the full story we must turn to his *Letters* or to Mrs. Elsie Harrison's lively novel *Son to Susanna.* In that bright Cotswold atmosphere there were picnics, rambles, dancing on the rectory lawn, and the church bell calling to evensong. They were the happiest days of Wesley's youth—a golden interlude, perhaps the happiest, certainly the most carefree, of his life.

On one occasion he walked from Oxford to Stanton by way of Shipston and Stow, stayed for a week with the Kirkhams, and saw the Granville girls every day. On another, he and his brother met the two sisters at Burford and travelled with them by coach to Oxford. "Neither the dirty way nor the rattling wheels," wrote Mary, "could spoil such a happy occasion." It is likely enough that he could have married her, that had he come to the point she would not have refused him; some of his friends expected, even encouraged it. The correspondence presents a fascinating puzzle. But though so closely drawn together, after four years their ways led apart—hers to a gay and brilliant world, and his to sound the trumpet of revival.

Buckland has the oldest rectory in continuous use in England, dating from 1450. It was probably the abbot's lodging on his visitation and may have served as a hostel for pilgrims to the neighbouring shrine of Hailes. The present rector, the Rev. Michael Bland, takes great interest and pride in its history, and no wonder! He showed me the main room which reaches in height to the roof of the building, with a great half-timbered wall on one side, so that it looks like an old moot hall, with its stone flags and medieval windows. The oldest portion of the house is the stone balustrade of the stairs, part of which is thought to be Saxon. The rectory, apart from its modern amenities, is much as it was when Wesley slept there. A photograph in the standard edition of the *Journal* incorrectly shows the Granvilles' house as the rectory. Wesley was equally at home in the former Broadway vicarage which is now the Lower St. Patrick's Tea Rooms, opposite the Lygon Arms, and when his friend, Robin Griffiths, son of the vicar, died, he preached his funeral sermon in the (old) parish church of St. Eadburga.

Group Captain P. W. Lowe Holmes, of Stanton, gave me this story which has come down in his family from about 1781 when Wesley was the guest of one of his ancestors, whose sons did not share their father's enthusiasm for the preacher and determined to curtail his visit. They drew lots as to which of them should hide in Wesley's bedroom and disturb his slumbers. The following night a sepulchral voice called from the chimney: "John Wesley!" But Wesley was not so easily roused. However, the voice persisted until he awoke, sat up, and replied: "Yea, Lord. Here am I." A reply came in solemn tones: "The Lord hath need of thee in Birmingham." Silence followed, and tradition says that the preacher came down the next morning with his bag packed and after breakfast "sped on his way, to the mystification of his host and the uneasy relief of the conspirators".

Cheltenham in Wesley's day was a one-street village. The doubling of the population at the turn of the century, and the influx of visitors, led to a mild property boom, and the straggling village became a thriving resort. Wesley saw it in its early development, before Sarah Siddons stayed at Birch Farm which was near the present Town Hall or Dr. Jenner had opened his free dispensary in the Lower High Street, and fifty years before Tennyson lived with his mother in St. George's Square and F. W. Robertson was a curate at Christchurch. A pillared market stood in the centre of the High Street, opposite the Plough Hotel, then a dormered hostelry, and the street was full of thatched and gabled cottages. The old church of St. Mary's is now screened by business premises, and the one-time village street, now lined with shops, is the town's busiest thoroughfare.

Wesley preached in the market and on the bowling green of the Plough and met with opposition from the rector, a Dissenting minister, and footmen of the visiting gentry. Ten years later he had "half a houseful of hearers", but for all they understood, he said, he might have been talking Greek! At Gotherton (Gotherington) and Tewkesbury he found people of "quite another kind". Messrs. Sharpe and Fisher's ironmongery premises in Albion Street occupy the site of the chapel he used, opposite the ancient Pate's Almshouses which are the only reminder of how the street looked in his day.

In every place he seemed to find one bright and eager heart; in Cheltenham it was Penelope Newman who kept a bookshop and who became one of his numerous correspondents. She was young and under his influence her energy ran into new channels; she evangelized the neighbouring villages and married one of his preachers.

Winchcombe is the only town I know in Britain which has a Wesley café (Plate 15b). It stands in the main street bearing on its gabled and half-timbered front a dubious effigy of Wesley, and a tablet placed there by Mrs. Dent of Sudeley Castle recording that he stayed there. The building, which is six hundred years old, was at one time a grocer's shop, and apart from the conversion of the ground floor into a café with a tea bar, is substantially the same—a typical Winchcombe house with rambling back premises and a patch of old-world garden. In the café is the familiar picture of Wesley preaching in Epworth, and a small bust of the preacher (by Sir Enoch Wood) presented by Mrs. W. F. Scott of Oxford.

John Staite lived here in Wesley's day, and Mrs. Pullan and her son, the present occupiers, took me up the twisting stairs to the bedroom in which Wesley slept and where his host, when too infirm to leave his bed, held his Society class. But the gabled room, except for its age, bears little evidence of its former associations. Mrs. Davies of Bradford-on-Avon, a descendant of John Staite, says the house was sold by her grandmother in 1913, that she possesses the brass candlesticks which accompanied Wesley to bed, and that a tray he used passed into the ownership of Mrs. Green of Winchcombe. Most interesting of all is the hymn which Wesley presented to his host: "Our souls by love together knit," with a chorus: "A Saviour let Creation sing." Enclosed in a wooden frame it later belonged to the Rev. John Willis, but its present whereabouts are unknown. Mrs. Willis and Mrs. John Sexty, the one blind and the other lame, went from door to door soliciting money to start a Sunday-school, and as they went these old pilgrims sang this jubilant song.

Just below the Manse is a handsome private residence, formerly Methodist property, known as The Great House, where it is said that Wesley visited and preached. Services were held there to which people flocked from as far afield as Hawling, Guiting and the Swells, bringing their meals with them. Well-known Methodist families like the Rattenburys and the Blebys had local associations.

Wesley was often at Stanley. He was invited to preach in Gretton church, but the invitation was withdrawn and he preached in Mr. Stephen's orchard, which still exists, close to the fountain. As a boy I remember driving in a wagonette to annual Good Friday gatherings there. He stayed with the Eden family in Broad Marston who built a chapel for his use which has since been converted into a cottage. And he preached at Honeybourne, also in the parish churches of Broadway, Quinton and Pebworth, and at Coombe Hill, in a farmhouse now derelict, just off the main Tewkesbury to Gloucester road, on the overgrown highway behind the Methodist church.

In Cirencester I looked for the Weavers' Hall in Thomas Street near the town centre, though the local inhabitants seemed strangely unaware of its whereabouts and no name or tablet marks it. No date can be given of its origin, but it was used by the Weavers' Guild as far back as 1483 and though now divided into two dwellings it preserves its medieval front, picturesque in its simplicity, with an arched doorway and small upper windows. Its whitewashed stone passage opens upon an old-fashioned garden through which the stream still runs where the wool staplers dipped their wool, and an old wool factory stands on the opposite side of the street. Wesley preached here in 1787 when it was in regular use for Methodist services. I sat by Mrs. Wakeman's fire in that part of the building which she occupies and thought of the long story of the years, when for three centuries before Wesley the building hummed with life, and when at his coming its upper room was crowded.

At Gloucester Wesley stayed at the Bell Inn, the birthplace of George Whitefield. He preached seventeen times in Painswick and often on Minchinhampton Common, where a hillock is known as Whitefield's Tump. His first sermon in Stroud was from a butcher's block in The Shambles, which was then the market, near the parish church. He preached in the Roundhouse—an octagon, in Acre Street, which is now used by the Salvation Army. It was here that he reproved some women in his congregation for excessive snuff-taking. For two or three days he lay ill in the house of Ebenezer King, a well-to-do tallow chandler, in Middle Street, and Sarah Face who cleaned his shoes there was proud of the fact to her dying day. Castle Street Methodist church has a communion chair which he used. Up to 1823 Stroud Methodists kept to Wesley's practice of regularly attending the parish church for Communion. He also preached at Wallbridge, Randwich, and in the little lost neighbouring towns—villages now—stranded in their lovely valleys. At Brimscombe the New Inn was a centre of Methodist hospitality and sheltered the first local Sunday-school. Its landlady was Mrs. Sarah Butler, who was strict with her customers, allowed no bad language and rationed their drinks.

CHAPTER THREE

LONDON—THE FOUNDERY—HOXTON SQUARE—SPITALFIELDS—GREAT ST. HELEN'S—NEWGATE—ST. SEPULCHRE'S—ALDERSGATE—LONDON'S OLDEST CHURCH—CITY ROAD—FIRE !—WESLEY'S BURIAL BY LANTERN LIGHT—TRIBUTE OF A ROMAN CATHOLIC—FIVE THOUSAND BURIALS—THE FOUNDERY CHAPEL—WESLEY'S HOUSE—HIS STUDY—HIS SILVER SHOE BUCKLES—WESLEY'S BEDROOM AND PRAYER ROOM—MANY RELICS

BOMBS and bulldozers have changed the face of Wesley's London, but his chapel and house remain, well-preserved, in City Road. The site of the Foundery—his first headquarters—is in Windmill Street, behind City Road, near the Ardath Tobacco Company's premises. Nothing remains of the original building which figures so prominently in early Methodist history. It was a derelict arsenal when Wesley acquired it, and mouldering to decay with the rain pouring through the roof when he relinquished it.

When the arsenal transferred its operations to Woolwich, Wesley, in need of larger premises, purchased and reconditioned this old foundery, providing on the ground floor a galleried chapel to hold seventeen hundred people, with a large room behind accommodating three hundred which was used for a variety of activities. No less than sixty-six class meetings met there every week, in addition to the 5 a.m. preaching services, and two weekly prayer meetings. It was fitted at one end with desks, as a day school, with two masters and sixty scholars. At its other end was a sales counter which served as Wesley's first bookroom. It was also used as a dispensary—the first free dispensary in London.

Above it were Wesley's private apartments, in which his mother spent the last years of her life and where she died.[1] An

[1] Her grave is in Bunhill Fields (opposite Wesley's Chapel), on the side of the left-hand path, not far from Bunyan's tomb. This famous Nonconformist burial ground also holds the remains of Defoe, Watts, and Blake.

adjoining house accommodated four or five preachers and his domestic staff, with an almshouse attached with a dozen inmates. "I myself," says Wesley, "as well as the other preachers who are in town, diet with the poor, on the same food and at the same table." It was a settlement almost on the Franciscan model. In addition there were stables, a garden and an open yard.

The bell in its turret which called worshippers to the five o'clock preaching was preserved for a time at Friars Mount in North London and afterwards found its way to Radnor Street Chapel, recently demolished, but has since disappeared. The pulpit is at Richmond College, and a chandelier went to Bowes Chapel in Yorkshire. Its other interesting relics are preserved at the City Road Museum.

Charles Square, which lies off Pitfield Street, in the same neighbourhood, was a favourite preaching place. Old trees remain, but new flats have replaced many of the dilapidated Georgian houses, in one of which John Newton lived. It was recorded when Whitefield preached here, that, "the houses of the gentlemen living in the Square are filled with their acquaintances from the City, as though they had come to see bears and monkeys."

Hoxton Square, two hundred yards beyond, remains a picturesque relic of old London, despite its shabby frame of faded dwellings. It was originally Hogsden Square, where pigs were sold, and the huge poplar in its centre is said to be the oldest tree in London. Here lived well-known and influential families, among them Thomas Marriott, a baker, whose son was one of Wesley's executors. Wesley speaks of retiring to Hoxton for a few days when he had contracted a cold, and it was in this square that Methodism opened its first theological college, with Dr. Jabez Bunting in charge. These ancient streets and squares, now lost in a dreary agglomeration of shops and warehouses and which formerly stood on the fringe of the city, were the scenes of Wesley's regular preaching and pastoral work.

The birthplace of his mother is in Spital Yard, off Spital Square, near Bishopsgate, in a maze of warehouses—a three-storied house where Dr. Annesley lived with his large family after his ejection from the living of St. Giles, Cripplegate. Among those who came here were Defoe, Dunton the bookseller, and Wesley's father, attracted by Dr. Annesley's lively daughters, one of whom was painted by Lely. The house is now a Methodist Community Centre with two deaconesses in residence, but, though recently restored, its front entrance has gone, and access is only possible by a door at the rear in Stothard Street.

One of the earliest Methodist chapels was in Spitalfields, acquired from the Huguenots who occupied this part of London when they fled from France in 1685 and where they flourished as silk weavers and built no less than eleven chapels. It is now part of Messrs. Truman's brewery at the corner of Grey Eagle Street where the old bricked-up windows can still be seen. Wesley's *Journal* has many references to this building. Eighteen hundred people were present at the first Covenant service he held there, and he continued to visit it to within a month of his death. It had two flourishing Sunday schools, the printed rules of which said:

> The scholars must all come clean washed, and combed, at half past nine o'clock in the morning, and at two in the afternoon. When the scholars are dismissed, they must go straight home, without loitering in the streets; and if any be seen running, jumping or playing at any game, or in other respects misbehaving themselves, they will be admonished for the first offence, punished for the second, and excluded for the third.

Great St. Helen's Church is in this neighbourhood, at the end of a quiet tree-lined square which offers a welcome contrast to the roar and racket of the surrounding streets. Wesley preached more than once from its seventeenth-century pulpit, but in 1738 after an evangelical sermon to a crowded congregation he was told: "Sir, you must preach here no more," and fifty-five years passed before he was invited to preach there again. Charles Wesley and Whitefield also preached there. Another old London church which preserves a surprising immunity from the surrounding ugliness and din is St. Ethelburga's, in the same area, where Wesley preached in 1785.

At All Hallows Church in Lombard Street he preached for the first time without a manuscript. Forty years later, after a charity sermon there, he recalled the incident: "That was the first time that, having no notes about me, I preached extempore." He preached there on at least seven occasions.

If we turn westwards past St. Paul's into High Holborn we can peer through the iron railings near the City Temple at the derelict church of St. Andrew, which was burned down during the war,[1] and recall that it was here, after preaching on Christian charity, that Wesley wrote: "O hard sayings! Who can hear them? Here, too, it seems, I am to preach no more."

Years earlier Wesley's father had been ordained here and served as a curate. His parents had begun their married life in curate's lodgings in the neighbourhood which in those days was picturesque with gabled houses. A pretty sketch exists of the church at that time.

When Wesley was a gownsboy at Charterhouse, at his father's request he waited on Dr. Sacheverell, the vicar, to request a recommendation to Christ's College, Oxford, but he met with a cool reception. "When I was introduced, I found him alone, as tall as a maypole and as fine as an archbishop. I was a very little fellow. . . . He said, 'You are too young to go to the University. You cannot know Latin or Greek yet. Go back to school.' I looked at him as David looked at Goliath, and despised him in my heart. I thought if I do not know Greek and Latin better than you I ought to go back to school indeed. I left him and neither entreaties nor commands could have again brought me back to him."

From this point, looking east, we see St. Sepulchre's—the largest parish church in London, with its fifteenth-century tower which in the Fire of London was a blazing inferno, and its massive three-storied porch. Its fascinating history is given by the vicar, the Reverend G. H. Salter, in his book *A Watcher at the Gate for Thirty-Eight Reigns*, full of thrilling detail and generously illustrated. In this church on Christmas Day, 1778, Wesley preached at the age of seventy-five, having taken three other services elsewhere, the first at four o'clock in the morning.

John Rogers, who was once vicar here, was one of the first Protestant martyrs. The Saracen's Head, a famous inn now demolished, stood opposite where we see Snow Hill Police Station. In Cock Lane, a few yards north of the church, the house still stands—No. 20, which was the scene of the famous ghost, and in Green Arbour Court—a former slum, now occupied by the Continental Express Limited—Oliver Goldsmith lived in poverty. The old Fleet Prison, familiar to Wesley and famous for its irregular marriages, was close by in Farringdon Street where the Memorial Hall stands, and Newgate Prison

[1] Since rebuilt in conformity with Christopher Wren's original design, reconsecrated October 1961.

which he frequently visited has been replaced by the Central Criminal Court. On one of his visits he found fifty-seven prisoners under sentence of death. "While they were coming in," he records, "there was something awful in the clink of their chains." Sometimes he was refused admission. "So we are forbid to go to Newgate for fear of making them wicked; and to Bedlam for fear of driving them mad!"

Among those he visited was the notorious Dr. Dodd before his execution. This popular London preacher of brilliant gifts, but of a wild and extravagant nature, had offered a bribe of three hundred pounds to obtain the lucrative living of St. George's, Hanover Square, and was convicted of forging a bond in the name of his former pupil, Lord Chesterfield. Wesley had never met Dodd, but thirty years earlier they had corresponded, and he had been among Wesley's opponents. Now the doomed man sent for the man he had reviled. "At the third message," says Wesley, "I took up my cross and went to see Dr. Dodd in the Compter,"—a waiting jail in Wood Street. Four times he went altogether, the last visit being to Newgate.

The handbell which was rung by the church bellman at midnight outside the cells of the condemned on the eve of their execution is preserved at St. Sepulchre's, from which Shakespeare in all likelihood took his phrase "the fatal bellman". On the morning of the execution the condemned were brought across the road to the church, when the bell was again rung, followed by a grim silence as the bellman exhorted the crowd to pray and the criminals to repent. Each prisoner was then presented with a nosegay and took his place in the cart for the journey to Tyburn, from which come such expressions as "in the cart" and "going west". Methodists comforted and accompanied the victims, and included pioneer prison visitors like Sarah Peters and Silas Told, and sometimes Wesley himself or his brother.

While in the neighbourhood we must not overlook St. Luke's in Old Street, now partially demolished, with the curious obelisk on its clock tower. This large galleried church, built in 1733, with its high pulpit and magnificent altar, had close links with Wesley, for it was here he brought his members from the Foundery and later from City Road for Communion, and he refers to it more than once as "our parish church". The parish magazine indicates that there is still close co-operation with the City Road minister. But the church is scheduled for demolition on account of serious subsidence and its activities have been transferred to St. Giles's, Cripplegate, which is being restored. Its pulpit, from which Wesley often preached, is temporarily stored in St. Luke's tower. Let us hope it will find a new and appropriate home. The tower itself with its obelisk steeple—the oddest in London—is likely to be preserved.

From St. Luke's it is no great distance to St. Giles's down Golden Lane past the new area of lofty multi-coloured flats which have completely transformed the neighbourhood. The bombed area round St. Giles's has now been cleared in preparation for the building of the new Barbican high-density urban development, and the church of St. Giles's was reopened in 1960 for public worship. Wesley preached here on two occasions, Cromwell was married here, and Dr. Annesley was once its vicar. The church holds the remains of Foxe, Frobisher, and Milton (Foxe and Milton were buried in the chancel). From the churchyard—one blessing of the blitz—we can see the dome of St. Paul's, as if across open fields, though this view will soon be obliterated by new buildings.

It was in a room in Aldersgate Street that Wesley felt his "heart strangely warmed", where a tablet, on Barclay's Bank at No. 28, marks the probable spot. And if we walk down the street and cross to Little Britain we shall find at No. 12 the site of the house of John Bray, the brazier, also marked with a plaque, where the Wesleys often stayed. Down this street and to this house, where Charles Wesley lay ill at the time, Wesley came singing with his friends to break the glad news on the night of his evangelical conversion. Hall House occupied the site of No. 28, entered from Nettleton Court which in those days lay at the rear, but the area, bombed during the war, is now a car park. Adjoining the building are some stables and a railway goods yard behind the King's Arms. But Maidenhead Court remains with its old-fashioned atmosphere, at the side of Barclay's Bank, and we can see the round-headed doorway, now walled up, which formerly opened into the vaulted passage that appears to have led into Hall House. The passage is now used by the bank employees as a place in which to hang their coats. All is conjecture, but an old local tradition says that this doorway and passage were the entrance to the historic meeting room, and the late Mr. P. J. Lupton claimed that a room in Hall House was the scene of Wesley's experience. On the same side of Maidenhead Court a second doorway and passage led into Nettleton Court. Some years ago a good deal of interest was roused by the discovery of portions of an eighteenth-century Tate and Brady's Psalter under the floor of the stable loft in the railway yard, and a careful survey was then made of the area and of the interior of the premises now occupying it. It was clear there was at no time access to the left from Nettleton Court and so it was concluded that the stables were not the scene of the meetings of the Aldersgate Street Society but that in all probability Hall House (No. 28 Aldersgate Street) was the authentic site.

Aldersgate—one of the four original city gates—spanned the street a little to the south of St. Botolph's, with a central carriage way and a postern on each side. It was pulled down in 1761. Milton lived in Aldersgate Street (1640–45), on the east side. Dekker, in his *Seven Deadly Sins*, makes Candlelight enter London "at Aldersgate, for though the street be fair and spacious, yet few lights in misty evenings used there to thrust out their golden heads".

The oldest parish church in London and perhaps the loveliest —St. Bartholomew's the Great—goes back to Rahere and the foundation of his famous hospital. Standing in its own quiet enclosure with its beautiful west gateway and cloistered aisles, it is the original choir of the old priory founded in 1123. The rector in Wesley's day was Richard Thomas, a convert of Howell Harris, and who was present at two of the early Conferences. When Wesley was preaching a charity sermon here on one occasion, the church and its entrances were so crowded that it was only with difficulty that he was able to get to the pulpit.

But to return to City Road. When the lease of the Foundery expired Wesley secured a site in Royal Row (now City Road). Finsbury Square was a developing area and City Road was a prosperous thoroughfare running out to the green fields of Islington. He was fortunate (and far-seeing) in acquiring a main frontage, though the Chapel today, which faces Bunhill Fields, is marooned in a wilderness of warehouses. The new mammoth blocks of flats, however, and the redevelopment plans of Old Street will bring an influx of new residents into the area. A condition attached to the lease required the new chapel to be built a hundred and twenty yards back from the road, to allow houses to be erected in front, and with only an archway for entrance. Happily this condition was later withdrawn, but

6. Wesley's grave in the small cemetery behind the Chapel in City Road

Below, the Foundery Chapel which contains some of the original benches, and the organ on which Charles Wesley played

7. Wesley's house, City Road. Over the chimney-piece of his study, *above*, hangs the well-known portrait by Frank O. Salisbury. Wesley is known to have used the arm-chair and on the left is his walnut bureau

Left, Wesley's walnut table and candle-stick in the little Prayer Room which has been called "the Power house of Methodism"

this accounts for the spacious forecourt which gives the Chapel its fine setting.

On an April day in 1776 Wesley led his two thousand members from the beloved but crumbling Foundery to the stone-laying of the new building, when in pouring rain and at a crowded ceremony he laid the first stone.

It is interesting to glance at the original proposal which was "to build an elegant chapel such as even the Lord Mayor might attend without any diminishing of his official dignity; that it should be wholly supplied by ordained clergy of the Established Church, except on week-days, and that the Liturgy should be read at Sunday morning and evening services". And Holy Communion was to be celebrated every Sunday. This restriction of the pulpit to Anglican clergy was not popular, but was persisted in until the Trustees, faced with declining congregations, waited on Charles Wesley with a polite request that he should preach there less frequently and open the pulpit to the itinerant preachers.

The building of the Chapel laid a heavy financial burden on Wesley who toured the country in search of funds, and for many years it was an anxious liability. It was completed in 1778, and in 1779 Wesley occupied the house he had built on the right of the forecourt, which is preserved much as he left it.

In its early years the Chapel had only two rows of seats in its large gallery, behind which was a level platform where the rest of the gallery congregation had to stand. The gallery entrances had two wicket gates at the foot and at the top of each staircase, with four gatekeepers who were each paid four pounds a year, and these gates were in use for fifty years.

Three times the building has been mercifully preserved from fire. Two years after its erection Wesley was awakened at 2 a.m. by a blaze in an adjoining timber yard. He rose at once, gave the alarm and called his household to prayer. A century later a policeman on night duty noticed flames coming from under the Morning Chapel. Dense fog and hard frost hampered the fire brigade who with lanterns worked frantically at the frozen water cocks. The roof and fine Adam ceiling were destroyed and the Chapel was ankle-deep in water and ice, but the main structure and pulpit were saved. In the last war the building was ringed with flame in an air attack and only narrowly escaped destruction.

It was the scene of early Conferences and many historic

occasions. It was here that Wesley on a cold December morning went to the early service (at 5.30) and found no preacher present. Then the fat was in the fire! Discovering that the three preachers in residence had sat up late the previous night, he gave orders that in future all in the house were to be in bed by nine.

When Wesley died his body lay here in state and was viewed by ten thousand people, and for fear of unmanageable crowds his burial behind the Chapel took place by lantern light at five o'clock in the morning. Those who attended were each given a biscuit in an envelope engraved with his likeness, and the Chapel was draped in black cloth at a cost of forty-one pounds.

From the old account books we learn that Wesley received thirty pounds a year, his brother sixty pounds, and the travelling preachers twelve pounds in addition to their accommodation and expenses. Some items make interesting reading: "Newspappers, 13/–. Lamplighter, four weeks 6s. Letters for week £2 15. 8½d. Shaving the preachers at Conference £7 5. 3d. Expenses of a hogs head of cider, from Guernsey, a present to Mr. Wesley, £1 9. 5. Paid Mr. Moore for a cold bath £1 15s. Hairdressers bill £1 1s. for the quarter."

The property has changed, though not substantially, in the course of the years (Plate 5*a*). Its present portico and spacious vestibule are later additions, giving it a broader and more handsome front. Wesley's old house, tall and narrow, is the same, but there was no manse, as now, on the opposite side of the forecourt. In those days there were stables, and an old cottage to the left of the Chapel in which Dr. Coke opened a bookroom. The forecourt consisted of a broad railed path with iron gates.

The Chapel had a mahogany double-decker pulpit, fifteen feet high, which has been reduced and its lower desk removed. Wesley used the masts of ships—the best seasoned wood then procurable—massive pine pillars given to him by George III from Deptford dockyard, to support the gallery. These were later replaced with marble columns, the gift of Overseas Methodism, each with a plate giving the name of the donor, and the square gallery was made oval. Some of the old masts are preserved in the vestibule. The windows, unlike today, were plain, and there was no organ. The building accommodated fifteen hundred.

In 1864, when the lease expired, the freehold was purchased for nine thousand pounds and the property was extensively improved (Plate 5*b*). Its present ceiling is a replica of the original. Because the building rested on timber piles in marshy ground it became necessary in 1880 to reinforce the foundations in concrete, and further improvements followed. The original chancel arch remains, though the choir stalls are a later addition, but we can kneel at the same Communion rail. The Chapel, however, is no longer the plain structure that it was, but rich in memorials including fine windows given by daughter churches, the Salisbury windows, and a carved Communion screen of Manx craftsmanship based on the ancient runic cross at Kirk Braddan—a gift from the Isle of Man.

It was a Roman Catholic, Father Maximin Piette, who wrote: "I found myself in the quiet interior of the chapel. Here I discovered a far more impressive atmosphere than I had experienced in the immense vastness of St. Paul's Cathedral, which I had visited the night before." St. Paul's impressed him as a Pantheon, but in the rich interior of Wesley's Chapel "the busts and other memorials were as welcome as old friends coming to meet me at the end of a long journey".

This unspoiled shrine is one of London's treasures, to be sought out by every tourist. It has its own distinctive atmosphere—immediate, memorable and satisfying. It is no cold repository of history or museum of the dead, but warm and alive with a sense of vital continuity, its gracious interior reflecting not only the memory of the past, but the spirit of a living enterprise.

In the Prayer Room—now the Foundery Chapel—which replaced the original Morning Chapel and which is entered from the right of the vestibule, the atmosphere is no less impressive, only more intimate (Plate 6*b*). For here are the old forms brought from the Foundery, the lectern used in the Foundery bandroom, along with the original offertory plates, and, in a glass case, the pewter Communion plate which was in use there. But most fascinating of all is Charles Wesley's pipe organ, an exquisite instrument of the period—the same as one made for Handel, and as sweet-toned as when Charles Wesley played on it.

To the rear of the Chapel is the beautifully maintained graveyard. Over five thousand bodies lie buried in the Chapel precincts, and recent excavations showed that the ground below is honeycombed with vaults and bricked-in tombs full of lead coffins. The last burial was that of Dr. Jabez Bunting, in 1854, four years after the closure of the graveyard, when special permission for the interment was obtained from the Home Secretary. Bunting was buried in Wesley's grave, where Wesley rests like a prince among his preachers. It was a common tomb for the preachers who died in London. "I should like," he had said, "to be buried here, and on the morning of the Resurrection rise with all my children round me."

The tomb (Plate 6*a*) bears a lengthy epitaph "To the memory of the Venerable John Wesley, M.A., Late Fellow of Lincoln College, Oxford, This great light arose, By the singular providence of God, To enlighten these Nations, And to revive, enforce, and defend The pure apostolical doctrines and practices of the Primitive Church. . . . Gloriously triumphing over death, March 2nd, An. Dom. 1791, In the eighty-eighth year of his age."

Within the apse of the Chapel is a marble tablet to his memory, bearing in its centre a carving of the globe, signifying that the world was his parish, and including the words: "A man in Learning and sincere Piety scarcely inferior to any. In Zeal, Ministerial Labours and extensive Usefulness Superior, perhaps, to all Men Since the days of St. Paul. Regardless of Fatigue, personal Danger and Disgrace He went out into the highways and hedges Calling sinners to Repentance, and Publishing the Gospel of Peace." In the forecourt of the Chapel is his statue in bronze by Adams-Acton, provided in 1891 by the children of Methodism, showing him with one hand holding an open Bible and the other raised in blessing, facing the crowded traffic of City Road.

Wesley's House is well restored and preserved. The marvel is that so narrow a building could be the scene of so much activity, with but two front windows on the ground floor, and three on each of its three upper stories. Yet here he received celebrities like Dr. Johnson and John Howard, and there was a constant coming and going of preachers and visitors. To the right of the narrow hall is the parlour with a small dining room behind. But it is on the first floor, in Wesley's personal apartments—his study, small bedroom and tiny prayer room—no more, for each floor holds but three rooms, that we come nearest to him. We climb the same stairs that he used when he returned from his journeys, and up which he groped, weak and feeble, for the last time before he died. To enter these rooms is an experience not to be missed and not to be hurried over.

The front room is his study (Plate 7*a*) where he wrote much of his voluminous correspondence, transcribed his *Journal*, edited his books, and administered his wide activities. Here is the handsome walnut bureau at which he sat, with its secret drawers, its candle shelves, its broad mirrors which reflected the candlelight as he wrote—the bureau which his wife in an angry moment rifled in his absence provoking such bitter scenes.

Here is his Chippendale bureau and his bookcase—he had excellent taste in furniture. We notice the chair which he used at his first Conference, at the Foundery, and his travelling clock. Against the wall is his long case clock made in 1693 by Claudius du Chesne, which still keeps good time and tells the day of the week, month and year and the phase of the moon. An unusual item is the three-legged cockfighter's chair, with its reversible back, secret drawer, shelf, and pen and ink well, given to him by a converted bookmaker. In a corner is what at first sight appears to be the ghost of Wesley himself, where on a tall stand is draped his long black travelling cloak of brocade, with neck-bands, crowned with his three-cornered hat, his silver-buckled shoes showing beneath the cloak (Plate 9*a*).

There is an interesting story behind these shoe buckles, which at one time were in the possession of the late Dr. W. E. Orchard, and I am grateful to Miss Katie Gliddon—a descendant of the family involved—for the following account. When Wesley preached at Trewhinney, near Mevagissey in Cornwall, he stayed with James and Mary Lelean. The latter was a descendant of a Huguenot family which had settled at Helston. When Wesley was attacked in the neighbourhood by an angry mob Mary Lelean sheltered him and dressed his injuries. On his departure he wondered how he could express his gratitude. "Silver and gold have I none," he said, then removed the silver buckles from his shoes and gave them to her as a parting gift. The buckles remained in the family as a treasured possession and eventually came to the two daughters of Joseph Lelean, one of whom married Dr. Orchard, and they were bequeathed to him. He was then minister of King's Weigh House where he wore them beneath his preaching robes. On his death they passed to his stepson, the Rev. Lelean McNeill Hewitt of Mirfield who presented them to the Wesley Museum. Thus they carry a rare heritage of rich associations—of Wesley and

Cornwall, of Huguenot exiles, and of King's Weigh House and the Mirfield Community.

Behind the study, opening from the narrow landing, is Wesley's bedroom, of surprising smallness and simplicity. He seems to have liked small bedrooms. Here there is hardly room to swing the proverbial cat, for it measures only fourteen by eleven or so feet. This brings to mind the familiar deathbed picture which shows the dying preacher surrounded by no less than eighteen people and a child—an impossible company in such small space. The room, the door and the bed are correctly portrayed, but otherwise it is an artist's dream. The official account of his death names eleven people only who were present. Wesley had been taken ill on returning from Leatherhead and only with difficulty could he climb those steep stairs to his room, where two weeks later he died. In his last moments there came a knock on the door. It was his younger nephew Samuel.

The bed, though of the period, is not the original. There are two glass-fronted wall cupboards, a chest of drawers, an armchair, and his bedside table with a pewter candle-holder.

From the bedroom we pass to the still smaller prayer room beyond (Plate 7*b*), which is six or seven feet wide and eight feet long, where Wesley night and morning said his prayers. As he wrote in the Introduction to his published *Sermons*: "Here then I am, far from the busy ways of men. I sit down alone; only God is here. In His presence I open, I read His Book."

The only furniture is a chair, a prayer stool, a fine Queen Anne table on cabriole legs, and a metal candle-holder. The room has its original small fireplace, and a single tall window through which he would have a wider view than now and could see his deserted Foundery. Everything here suggests quietness and peace. One can almost feel the deep calm of Wesley's spirit. Perhaps here as in no other place we come nearest to him.

There are numerous other exhibits (Plate 9) on the second floor which, along with the top storey, housed his preachers and other inmates. It must have been a much used and crowded house. There is an old Bible, obviously damaged by fire and water, which was found a hundred years after the rectory fire, buried in the garden at Epworth. There is Wesley's academic hood, three pairs of his reading glasses, a bronze candle lantern from his carriage, his nightcap, his teething rattle, and his last quill pen. We notice also his mother's needle case, his spurs, his silver spoons and sugar tongs, his cup and saucer, a fork used by him, some china pepper pots and his silver cuff links; also a cane, a science notebook compiled when he was an undergraduate at Oxford, and his visiting card with its plain inscription: "Mr. John Wesley". And the showcase which holds them rests on the table which stood in the kitchen at the time of his death. In addition to a number of interesting specimens of china and pottery—plaques, cups and Staffordshire ware—in the glass-fronted cupboards beside the chimney, there is to be seen a huge Wedgwood teapot made specially for him as a gift by Josiah Wedgwood himself and used daily by Wesley and his preachers.

His muffler is included, his pearl-handed fruit-knife, his travelling desk—a small black box with metal handles, and, against the wall, his fine tallboy. And we can examine the curious electrical machine which he used in his Dispensary, for he was a pioneer in electrical treatment of ailments. By turning the handle of this primitive contrivance glass cylinders are revolved producing a current. And it still works. Mr. Raymond Kemp, the curator, offered to try it out on me, but refused to test it himself! Dr. Wesley Hill devotes space to it in his interesting book *John Wesley, Physician.*

The room at the rear on this floor is devoted to Charles Wesley and contains his bureau, study chair, and hymns in his handwriting. The storey above is now used as a flat. In some of the rooms there are fine portraits of Wesley, including an unfamiliar one of him in his youth, the origin of which appears to be unknown. There are also old and interesting pictures, one in particular showing the old Foundery.

More than once I have wandered through the house alone, lingering here and there to catch its spirit, sitting at Wesley's desk, pausing at his bedside table, kneeling in his prayer room. No effort was needed to recall the past; its atmosphere was all around me. And Wesley himself seemed very near and his spirit still alive. But when I looked through the windows out of which he had looked, it was upon a different world. The London he knew had gone, the pattern had changed, and the traffic of City Road, down which at nightfall he came riding homewards, spoke of a new and noisier age.

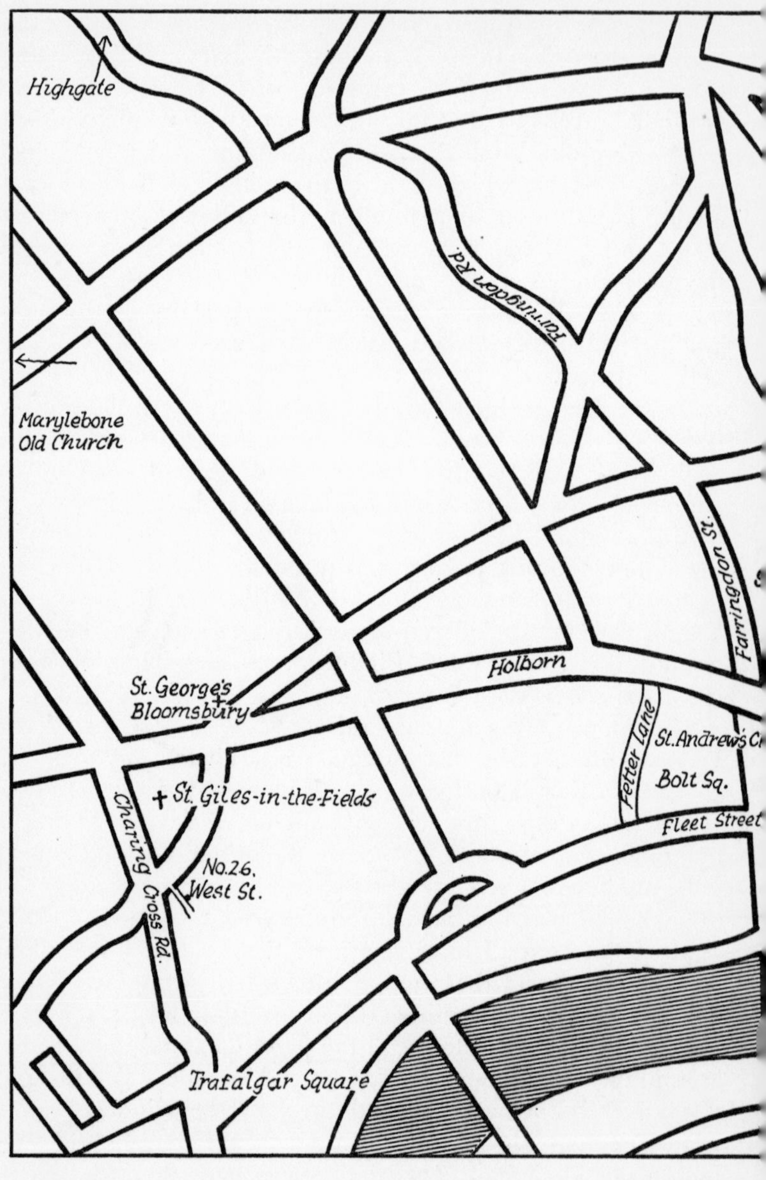

Obviously Wesley would not recognize the London of today, for although during his lifetime the city had spread considerably—to the west new and fashionable estates had engulfed large areas, to the north-east Finsbury Square and Hoxton Square had been built, the New Road (now Marylebone Road) had been driven through meadows to by-pass the congested City, and two bridges, Westminster and Blackfriars, crossed the Thames (the first to be built since London Bridge six centuries before) and thus opened up the villages to the south for development—it was still only a short ride from his house in City Road through the market gardens and fields that surrounded the villages

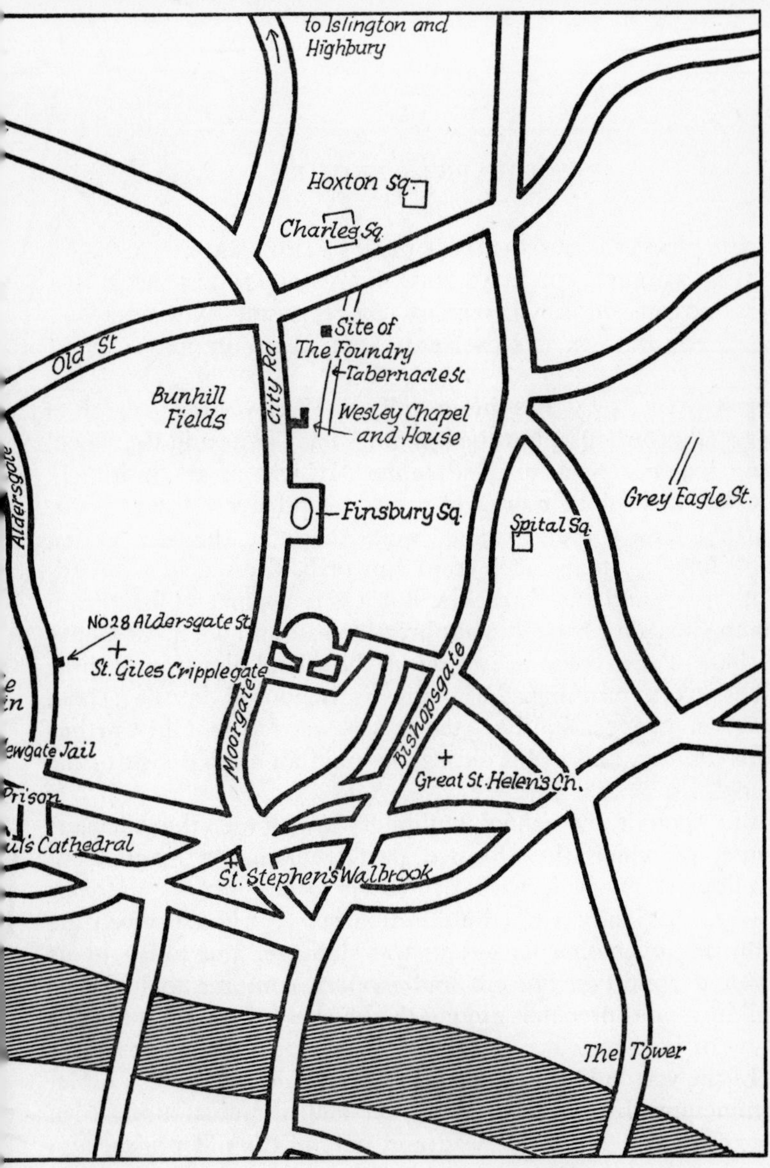

of Islington and Highgate. The vast docks were not constructed until shortly after Wesley's death, and the railways did not reach London until the 1830's*—two factors which were to cause a great expansion in the population—and many more changes were to follow with the years.*

And yet there are places which John Wesley would still recognize—his house in City Road, churches where he preached, old squares where he visited friends, Charterhouse, and the façade of West Street Chapel. This map indicates the whereabouts of these places in modern London to assist the Wesley pilgrim.

CHAPTER FOUR

THE CHARTERHOUSE—LITTLE DEAN'S YARD—DRURY LANE—WEST STREET—THE ROAD TO TYBURN—OLD MARYLEBONE—ISLINGTON—HIGHBURY FIELDS—DR. JOHNSON—A PADDINGTON INN—IN THE EAST END—THE ABBEY MEMORIAL

THACKERAY has immortalized Wesley's old school of Charterhouse, but the buildings have gone and the school has removed to Godalming. It was near Smithfield Market with its memories of martyrs, and lively scenes of St. Bartholomew's Fair. Wesley went there at the age of ten travelling by stage-coach from Epworth, dressed in a broad-cloth gown and knee breeches. But it was a spartan life: "From ten to fourteen I had little but bread to eat, and not great plenty of that." For exercise he ran round the school playground three times every morning. His name is honoured in the school song, on one occasion he acted as a steward at an Old Carthusians' dinner, and in his old age he paid an annual visit to the school.

But though the school buildings have gone, the Charterhouse, of which they formed part, remains—a magnificent Trollopian survival, with pensioners occupying its gracious rooms. Originally a Carthusian monastery, it has survived the centuries, overcome its serious war damage, and today in its restored condition ancient and modern combine to make its buildings and precincts among the loveliest of their kind in the heart of London.

In the vestibule the first thing that catches the eye is a tablet commemorating Wesley. The great Hall remains, along with the fifteenth-century gateway and part of the old priory, also the chapel where Wesley worshipped as a boy. In the Charterhouse museum is a snuff-box given to him by Mrs. Puddicombe of Dartmouth, wife of Dr. Puddicombe, when he visited them.

Wesley's older brother Samuel at the time was usher of Westminster School and lived in Little Dean's Yard. It was largely through his influence that the first infirmary was established in London, which afterwards became St. George's Hospital. He kept a kindly eye on his two younger brothers, one of whom, Charles, was a pupil in his own school. And cheerful letters went back to Epworth: "Jack is with me and a brave boy, learning Hebrew as fast as he can."

On Samuel's appointment as headmaster of Blundell's School, Tiverton, the two brothers made their London home with the Rev. John Hutton who lived next door to Samuel in Westminster and took in Westminster boys as boarders. One of the earliest Methodist Societies met in his house, and Mr. Lewis H. Hutton of Polstead, a descendant of the family, has a record in his possession reaching back to those days of his family's close association with Wesley. The Wesleys' growing association with Moravian doctrines offended the Rev. and Mrs. Hutton, and Charles transferred his lodging to John Bray's house in Little Britain. Mrs. Hutton wrote to Samuel at Tiverton: "Mr. Charles went from my son's where he lay ill for some time and would not come to our home, where I offered the choice of my two best rooms, but chose to go to a poor brazier's in Little Britain, that the brazier might help him forward with his conversion."

Charles Wesley was so ill that he had to be carried to Bray's house in a chair, and, in his own words, the hospitable Mr. Bray was "a poor ignorant mechanic who knows nothing but Christ, yet by knowing Him knows and discerns all things". It was to his house that Wesley himself came, borne triumphantly by his excited friends on the night of his Aldersgate experience, and until the acquisition of the Foundery it became the London home of the two brothers.

Rivington's bookshop, The Bible and Crown (no longer in existence) in St. Paul's churchyard, was another of their haunts. Rivington had set up as a religious bookseller and published several of Wesley's first books. Meanwhile, a son of the Huttons, James, also set up as a bookseller. A tablet in Little Wild Street marks the site of his shop, The Bible and Sun, where the Fetter Lane Society first met, with which Wesley was closely associated. Of Fetter Lane itself, as it was then, nothing remains and the old meeting-place has gone, but it was here, on the advice of Peter Böhler, that James Hutton had founded the Society of which John Wesley became a member and later the leader—a Society which was strangely prophetic of that which later formed the body of Methodism for its members included two barbers, a poulterer, a clog-maker, a wine-cooper and John Bray. Here the roots of Methodism developed, succoured by Moravian teaching, and from here in July 1740, following a doctrinal dispute, Wesley led his band of devoted followers to his new quarters at the Foundery. No wonder pilgrims in search of memories of Wesley come to Fetter Lane, though no stone that he knew is to be seen.

We turn next to the Drury Lane area, where Wesley established a cause in an upper room in Short's Gardens, between Drury Lane and Neal Street. We cannot locate the site, but from this modest building sprang the flourishing social and redemptive work of the West London Mission. It was still the Drury Lane of Nell Gwynne: of orange girls, linkmen, pickpockets and vicious characters, and of playhouses and pleasure gardens. Wesley lost no time in raising his standard in this cosmopolitan neighbourhood.

Half a mile further on, down Long Acre and St. Martin's Lane, where Covent Garden spills its produce over the crowded pavements, and the offices of film corporations display their tiled and glossy fronts, beyond St. Martin's and the Ambassador's theatres, we come to No. 26 West Street. Take a good look at this unpretentious building (dingy when I first saw it, but since redecorated), which you might so easily pass by. You will notice in its arched windows and plain front the outline of a converted chapel (Plate 10). How many who pass it are aware of its history! You will be looking at the ghost of a once crowded and famous sanctuary.

Wesley took possession of it in 1743 and it became the Mother Church of West End Methodism. The reason why no tablet marks the building is because recently its memorial plaque was torn from the wall, out of mischief or as a souvenir, and has not been renewed. The only legend the building bears today is "Selmer", for it is a warehouse of a firm of musical instrument manufacturers. The property, which belongs to the neighbouring church of St. Giles, was originally one of the several Huguenot chapels in the area. It was erected about 1680 and was called La Tremblade, and was later sold to the Vestry of St. Clement Danes, who leased it to Wesley at thirty pounds a year.

The rector of St. Giles, the Rev. G. C. Taylor, has given me further interesting details. No. 26 consists of the chapel and the chapel house—the latter rebuilt at the turn of the century, so it is not the house that Wesley knew. The chapel was bought by trustees of Elizabeth Palmer in 1728 with £500 she left for the maintenance of twelve poor widows of St. Clement Danes' parish. It was repaired in 1759 and the lease to Wesley was renewed several times. In 1799 Sir Thomas Barnard leased it, spending £1,000 on it, as a mission centre known as the Free Chapel, with the rector of St. Clement Danes in charge. In 1830 it was let to the Irish Society when Anglican services were held there in Irish. The rector of St. Giles opened it in 1836 for Sunday afternoon services, and from 1842 to 1887, the Rev. R. W. Dibdin, senior curate of St. George's, Bloomsbury, worked there. Later the freehold was purchased for £5,000 by public subscription and from 1888 until it was bombed in the war it was known as All Saints' Mission, Seven Dials, serving St. Giles as a chapel of ease. In 1952 its shattered roof was renewed and it was later let to its present occupiers, Messrs. Selmer, who built a first floor at gallery level.

This historic building, the pride of the early Methodists, for years was thronged with worshippers. Wesley's first service there was so crowded that it continued from 10 a.m. to 3 p.m., the congregation being admitted in relays. It was served by Anglican clergy and because it was consecrated, Methodists for the first time received Communion in a building of their own. As the chapel only accommodated two hundred, communicants waited in groups of two hundred at a time, until six hundred, sometimes even a thousand in succession, had been served. On one such occasion there were eighteen hundred communicants. "Never," writes the Rev. J. H. Martin, "had Peter Fenouillet's Communion cups been so used." And rarely has Methodism seen such crowded Communion services. These simple silver cups, originally a gift to the Huguenot Chapel, and used for forty years at West Street, are preserved at Kingsway Hall.

Many other notable services have been held here. It was here that John Fletcher hurried straight from his ordination in the former Chapel Royal at Whitehall to assist Wesley in a crowded Communion service. The Naval and Military Bible Society was founded here in 1779. Charles Wesley preached here during an earthquake panic, and both he and his brother regularly ministered here. Whitefield thrilled the congregation with his oratory, and the saintly Fletcher captivated his hearers.

It was here that Wesley preached a fortnight before he died.

The whole building, now changed within beyond all recognition, partitioned and divided, is full of memories. Here, we read, "John Wesley's coach once stood and Charles Wesley's little horse ambled on with the absent-minded poet. John Fletcher hurried along to help Wesley. George Whitefield came to charm the worshippers. . . . The Countess of Huntingdon and her aristocratic friends drove up to these doors. . . . To this place came men and women seeking rest for their souls. Anxious, eager faces are around you. . . . The whole street is hallowed by the feet of penitent or of rejoicing worshippers."

The original chapel house was used by Charles Wesley and was at one time the home provided by Wesley for his sister Mrs. Harper. In Frith Street, Soho Square, which is close by, his sister Hetty lived and died.

West Street was given up in 1798 when its activities were transferred to Great Queen Street and later to the present Hinde Street Church and Kingsway Hall. But the building remains, for all its neglect, one of Methodism's oldest shrines. Let us hope it may escape demolition, and that its walls may bear again a generous tribute to its old associations.

In the same neighbourhood is St. Giles-in-the-Fields, near Cambridge Circus, with its paved court and children's playground which give it an agreeable setting, its memorials to Flaxman, Marvell and Chapman, and its handsome oak pulpit with railed stairs twice used by Wesley. This early eighteenth-century church, bright with blue and gold, stood on the main route from Newgate to Tyburn, and the cart bearing the condemned was halted here and a bowl of ale was provided for the malefactors, from the Bowl Inn (where Endell Street now is), and on later occasions from the Angel Inn beside the church. In pre-Reformation days it was given at the great gate of the leper hospital of St. Giles. A print in the church shows Jack Sheppard drinking from the bowl outside the Angel Inn. And if you look out from the church porch you can recreate the scene. Wesley at least once, and Charles Wesley more than once, accompanied the criminals. After the execution Wesley walked back to St. Giles and preached to the mob. And in this churchyard he read the burial service over some of his members. He preached in the church in 1739, then was excluded from its pulpit, and it was not until 1786 that he occupied it again.

How many Methodists know that on the landing of the south staircase of the church is a green and white painted deal pulpit which is the top of Wesley's old three-decker pulpit rescued from the West Street Chapel? What memories this relic recalls of the glorious past of the chapel!

Marylebone in those days was a country suburb with green fields between Chesterfield Street and Tottenham Court Road. The King's Head on the corner of Wheatley Street, opposite the National Heart Hospital, stands on the site of a four-storied Georgian house where Charles Wesley lived and died, formerly No. 1, Great Chesterfield Street (now Wesley Street). The lease was given to him by a friend, Mrs. Gumley of Bath, and he found it richly furnished and "stocked with even small beer". This was the scene of the subscription concerts given by his two musical sons and patronized by the nobility, to which came Dr. Johnson, the Earl of Mornington and John Wesley himself—though the latter somewhat reluctantly. "I was a little out of my element," he said, "among the lords and ladies. I love plain music and plain company best." The house was in after years the boyhood home of Joseph Chamberlain.

Charles Wesley is buried in the graveyard of Marylebone Old Church, in which church, with its associations with Sheridan, Hogarth, Byron, Browning and Nelson, his parents were married. (Built 1400, rebuilt 1741, demolished 1949.) Its graveyard, which shows its foundations, is now a garden of rest with an obelisk to the memory of Charles Wesley and his family. (His widow, who long outlived him, died in 1822 at the age of ninety-six.)

The Epworth branch of the Wesley family in the male line only survives through Charles Wesley's younger son Samuel. His brother Charles Wesley, junior, who was organist at this old church, lived with his sister in genteel poverty. When he applied for the post of organist at St. Paul's Cathedral, he was told: "We want no Wesleys here." When George III heard of this he sent for him, and said, "Never mind; the name of Wesley is always welcome to me." And once, when he was at Windsor after the King had lost his sight, the King asked him: "Mr. Wesley, is there anybody in the room beside you and me?" He replied, "No, Your Majesty." "Then," said the King, "I will tell you what I think. It is my judgement that your father, and your uncle, and George Whitefield, and Lady Huntingdon, have done more to promote true religion in England than all the dignified clergy put together."

But what a difference today in Marylebone Fields, where

Wesley preached! Just round the corner from his brother's grave is the new headquarters of the Methodist Missionary Society which carries his work to the ends of the earth, and Broadcasting House in Langham Place which every Easter Sunday morning broadcasts Charles Wesley's great Easter hymn. Never in his wildest dreams could Wesley have foreseen the astonishing progress of his enterprise.

One of the liveliest parish churches in London is St. Mary's, Islington, with a strong evangelical tradition reaching back to the Revival. The old church was wrecked by bombs in 1940 and has been rebuilt in modern design harmonizing with its surviving tower. Charles Wesley for a short period was a curate here—his only parochial appointment. The vicar at the time was a Methodist, George Stonehouse—one of his converts—and many of the earliest Methodist meetings were held in his vicarage. When in 1738 the Wesleys found the parish churches closed against them, Stonehouse generously offered them home and maintenance, and Wesley preached there once a month, when in London, until the Parish Vestry objected and Stonehouse was obliged to exclude them from his pulpit. But Wesley still preached in the vicarage and, when that proved too small, in its garden. It was not the present vicarage, but among the buildings at the north-east corner of the churchyard. In 1739 an important conference of Methodist leaders met there. Whitefield preached his first open-air sermon in London in this churchyard; the base of the cross where he stood survives, and an old print exists depicting the scene.

Among the featureless sprawl of suburbs Islington, a favourite rural retreat of Wesley, still retains its distinctive character. No. 25 Highbury Place, facing Highbury Fields, has a double interest. It lies on the right-hand side as you leave the railway station, one of the largest of the long curve of Georgian houses, double-fronted with a coach-house (now a garage) at the side, and bears a tablet: "Joseph Chamberlain, 1836–1913, lived here." Afterwards it was the home of his widow, Mrs. Carnegie. But long before Chamberlain's day, Wesley enjoyed its generous hospitality, for here lived his friend and executor, John Horton, a member of the City Council, and as he rode out of town on his northern journeys this was one of his first halting places. He also came here often for rest and relaxation and to write. It belongs to a manufacturing firm, Messrs. Greenaways, Ltd., whose offices are on the ground floor. Formerly it was occupied by

Dr. Glover and afterwards fell into disrepair and became a tenement. Mr. Greenaway, who acquired the property some twelve years ago, has made an excellent renovation, preserving the original entrance and upper floors, including the handsome lounge with its fine window. The rooms are here which Wesley found so agreeable; also its situation, which is surprisingly open even today, though so near to the City. No wonder Wesley came here to refresh his spirit! Mr. Greenaway has two fine prints of the period showing the neighbourhood as it was, with haymakers in Highbury Fields (Plate 11*a* and *b*).

No record of Wesley's London can omit mention of Dr. Johnson. Wesley's sister, Mrs. Hall, was a near neighbour of Johnson and every Friday "took tay" with Johnson's housekeeper, Mrs. Williams. They were close friends, but, says Johnson, "they never met but they quarrelled." Boswell describes them: "Blind peevish Mrs. Williams and long lean preaching Mrs. Hall." Later Mrs. Hall became a member of Johnson's household. Wesley's uncle, Dr. Matthew Wesley, a physician, had lived next door to Johnson in Johnson's Court. Afterwards Johnson occupied No. 5, Bolt Square, where Wesley visited him and on his last visit found him "sinking into the grave by a gentle decay".

Johnson's house in Gough Square has an interesting oil painting—Hogarthian in style, probably by one of Hogarth's pupils, full of fascinating detail and well worth seeing. It purports to show Wesley preaching a charity sermon in old Cripplegate church with Johnson, Boswell, Goldsmith and Garrick in the congregation and includes the bonneted almswomen, four "dames" (or overseers) of the parish, along with the churchwardens, though it is a poor representation of John Wesley and the identification may be incorrect. An alderman is depicted entering with his lady followed by a footman carrying a cushion. Wesley(?) is standing in the pulpit, with the clerk in the desk below. Mrs. Rowell, the curator, tells me the picture was originally lent by Mr. T. B. Benton and on his death was presented to the museum by his family. An American enthusiast was so taken by it that he commissioned an artist to copy it. The artist said it would not take him long, but to his surprise he found the picture contained so many figures with the features of each so clearly delineated, and with so much other lively detail, that it took him three months.

 JW—E

Interesting letters survive of Johnson to Wesley, including one saying that Boswell wished to be introduced to him in Edinburgh; also to Charles Wesley and to his daughter Sarah for whom Johnson had a great affection. "I will have the first day You mention. Come, my dear, on Saturday next and you can bring your Aunt with you, to Your most humble servant, Sam: Johnson."

Wesley had wise methods of retirement or could not otherwise have carried on his affairs. Another of his retreats was Palatine House, Stoke Newington, the home of Charles Greenwood, "I retired to Stoke Newington and hid myself almost three days," is typical of several references to it in his *Journal*. The house, now dilapidated in the extreme, is No. 109 Stoke Newington Road, used as offices by a firm of demolition contractors. Mr. H. E. Waites, the Borough Librarian, has identified it as part of the old Palatine Estate, which corresponds with a drawing of it in the standard edition of Wesley's *Journal*. Palatine Cottage, which adjoins it, was the childhood home of Anna Sewell, author of *Black Beauty*. Greenwood was a melancholy man, and Wesley was present in this house when he died.

In seeking retirement, Wesley once spent some weeks at the Red Lion in Paddington at the junction of Harrow and Edgware Road. He came here following an illness and prepared nearly twenty volumes of his *Christian Library* for the Press, going into town every Saturday evening and returning on Monday morning. But today the old inn is beyond recognition and it is difficult to reconcile its enormous saloon bar with its older associations, though its chocolate-coloured front has a handsome wrought-iron lamp-holder which speaks of an earlier day.

Wesley preached in other London churches besides those mentioned, some of which have disappeared; there seems hardly one of the older ones of the city which he did not visit, if only to worship. Every parish church drew him like a magnet and from his crowded meeting-rooms he led his members to their parish Communion. Nor, despite his own plain chapels, was he blind to their beauty. His comment on St. Stephen's Walbrook with its fine dome and canopied pulpit is typical, though he never preached there; this church was badly damaged during the war and has now been beautifully renovated.

I found in Hampstead a tradition that he once held a service at

No. 17, Holly Street, a well-preserved eighteenth-century house which at one time was a Baptist chapel. Though modernized with white stucco and a gay blue-painted door, its period character remains, and its large and pleasant music room still gives the outline of the former chapel.

The old Bermondsey Abbey farmhouse—the Grange, where Wesley was a frequent visitor, was destroyed by a bomb explosion. Wesley's host was Robert Smith, a magistrate and master builder. The chair Wesley used there has gone to the City Road Museum, and Miss Phyllis Barnes tells a pretty story of Wesley, while sitting in this chair, taking Robert Smith's little daughter on his knee—her great-great-grandmother—and teaching her a hymn.

An isolated warehouse in a slum clearance area in Dunridge Street, Bethnal Green, bears a tablet: "Headquarters Christian Community, founded 1685, Reorganized by John Wesley 1772." Bethnal Green was a hamlet when Wesley preached in the neighbouring ruined parish church, which is being rebuilt.

His old Snowsfield Chapel, now a Salvation Army citadel, is south of the river, in Crosby Road, near Guy's Hospital. Its successor was an octagonal building and is now a warehouse. One of his earliest meeting rooms was in Bromley-by-Bow and is probably the building there called Wesley House. His first open-air service was on the hillock at Blackheath known as Whitefield's Mount, and the inn—The Green Man—is still there where he and Whitefield took refreshment after preaching.

Did Wesley ever live in Threadneedle Street? He stayed there in the home of Mrs. Vazeille, the banker's widow, where he was brought and nursed after breaking his leg on the ice on London Bridge and to whom he was afterwards married. Mr. L. H. Wulcko has tried to locate the site, but the street has long since been rebuilt, and Wesley's marriage settlement (at the Epworth Press) does not help us to identify it.

It was stated recently in the *Guardian* that Wesley's chapel in Clerkenwell is to be brought nearer to its original form and a start has been made by the removal of the "pepper pot" ventilator put on the roof late in the last century. The portico was added in 1815. The chapel has memorials to John and Charles Wesley.

Near the British Museum is St. George's Church, Bloomsbury, where Wesley preached his first sermon after his Aldersgate experience—a plain church of classical style, with a statue on its tower of George I which was ridiculed by Horace Walpole. In this church Wesley first sounded the note of his new-found enthusiasm with the text: "This is the victory which overcometh the world, even our faith."

The National Portrait Gallery has two well-known portraits of Wesley, by Romney and Nathaniel Hone, and a life-size marble bust—the work of Roubiliac.

In addition to those already mentioned there are other collections of Wesleyana in London (Plate 8). The largest is at the Epworth Press and includes several of Wesley's diaries, his christening robe, and his preaching bands, which show that he was a small-necked man. The size of the collection can be judged from its two hundred page catalogue. There is also his Field Bible which is brought out each year and handed by the President of the Conference to his successor. It is contained in a black leather case fastened with a button, and has three curious misprints. Its name derives from its printer, John Field, and it has the autograph of Wesley, who used it in his private devotions. He gave it to Henry Moore, who just before he died asked Mrs. Richard Smith to take it to the Rev. John Scott, President of the Conference, with instructions for it to be handed along with Wesley's seals to the incoming President each year. Scott's daughter, Mrs. John Lidgett, says that Mrs. Smith was so concerned for its safety that she slept with it under her pillow until she could put it into her father's hands.

At Richmond College is the largest collection in the world of inscribed books from the private library of John Wesley, comprising some 290 volumes (Plate 12). Many are annotated in his own hand. In addition, the College library possesses some manuscripts (several in code) of Charles Wesley's hymns, as he wrote them for the first time, with his own marginal alterations. In the chapel is the Foundery pulpit which is in daily use. It bears a brass plate which reads: "In this pulpit the Revds. John and Charles Wesley preached for many years the Gospel of the grace of God. It stood originally in the place of worship called the Foundery, situate in Moorfields, London . . . May the students who now occupy it emulate these HOLY MEN in the zeal and fidelity with which they sought to turn many unto righteousness."

In the entrance hall of the College is a full-length statue of Wesley in marble, by Samuel Manning, which Adam Clarke, who was Wesley's contemporary, declared to be a perfect likeness. It was taken from a bust for which Wesley sat five times to Mr. Wood of Burslem, and a model of it was exhibited in the Royal Academy. It was commissioned by Joseph Butterworth, M.P., but no sooner was the marble bought and the work begun than he died and the statue remained unfinished for nearly twenty years. It was completed by a grandson of Samuel Manning who bore the same name and was offered to Westminster Abbey, but was declined because of "the factious nature of Mr. Wesley". A new donor contributed to the total cost of a thousand guineas, and the finished work was presented to the Connexion who placed it where it now stands.

The Abbey authorities later acted more wisely. Today in the south aisle of Westminster Abbey is the Adams-Acton Memorial showing the profiles of John and Charles Wesley, with the words: "The best of all is God is with us", and below is the beautifully drawn scene of Wesley preaching in the open with outstretched hands. The inscription reads: "I look upon all the world as my parish," and at the foot: "God buries His workmen but carries on His work."

CHAPTER FIVE

BRISTOL—THE HORSEFAIR—SPRINGBOARD FOR AMERICA—WESLEY'S LAST CONFERENCE—CHARLES WESLEY'S HOUSE—KINGSWOOD—THE BEACON OF THE WEST—BATH—BEAU NASH—A SQUINT HOLE—HORACE WALPOLE

AFTER London, Bristol was Wesley's main centre. For twelve years it was his home, and for the first thirty years of the Revival he spent more time there than in any other place. His headquarters were in the Horsefair in the old part of the city—an area of cobbled streets and market squares which was badly shattered by bombs and has since been rebuilt, but with a new shopping centre which has changed its character. Providentially the oldest Methodist preaching house in the world, called the New Room, remains, though now dwarfed by the mammoth blocks of glass and concrete which surround it.

I came there on one occasion on a late afternoon and peered through the railings of the chapel yard, for the gates were locked, and wondered what Wesley would have made of it. In his day its doors were open, its pews were full. I doubt if its gates were ever shut. It was an active community centre, a bookshop, a hostel, a school, a dispensary; the place was alive. But as I peered through the iron railings there was not a bench in its neatly cobbled yard, not a flower, not a symbol of life. Only the building itself, with its old-fashioned air and looking a little forlorn in its new surroundings of stores and supermarkets, bore its silent witness (Plate 13).

It is, however, much more than a museum piece, a precious and peerless relic, a unique and fascinating shrine. There are times when it comes alive—very much alive, and admirably fulfils its purpose as an administrative centre for the Bristol District of the Methodist Church, and it draws a stream of visitors from the ends of the earth. Near at hand also are the fine premises of the Central Hall which carries on Wesley's social and redemptive work.

The New Room, which is the most fascinating and unspoiled of all Methodist shrines, preserves its original form and atmosphere. It was built in 1739, reconstructed and enlarged in 1749, and was the first Methodist building to be licensed for public worship. But because Methodists did not regard themselves as Dissenters, Charles Wesley showed his disapproval by endorsing the licence (now in the care of the Epworth Press): "I protest against this needless useless senseless licence."

After Wesley's death the property passed into the hands of the Welsh Calvinistic Methodists, but in 1909 it was purchased by the late Mr. Edmund Lamplough, carefully restored by Sir George Oatley, and presented to the Methodist Church. The present pews, dating from the early nineteenth century, had already replaced the original backless benches, and the upper part of the pulpit has been reconstructed.

The fine equestrian statue of Wesley in the forecourt is said to be the best of its kind in England and is the only one in the world which shows him on horseback.[1] It is the work of the late Gordon A. Walker, R.A., and conveys a remarkable sense of poise and energy, while the loose rein and the book in the preacher's hand are symbolic. And behind it the little lean-to whitewashed stable still stands against the chapel wall.

The chapel, with its double-decker pulpit and its gallery resting on the slenderest of columns which carry the old brass candle sockets, is unusually attractive in its bare simplicity. What a pity Wesley did not always build like this! Too many of his octagon and pepperpot chapels were hastily built and gimcrack, but here we find reflected his true taste and quality. The building is an epitome of the Revival, a symbol of its grace and a legacy of its spirit. It is hallowed by holy memories and haunted with ancestral voices. It is neither splendid nor magnificent in any ecclesiastical sense; there are no rich decorations or ornate memorials, but every line of it in its flawless craftsmanship and artless and unaffected style, so completely unspoiled, reflects an inner beauty and richness of the spirit. John Betjeman, after praising Rickard's work in Viennese baroque at the Central Hall, Westminster, says, "I rejoice in the preservation

[1] A duplicate of this equestrian statue was unveiled in Washington on May 24, 1961, the gift of Lord Rank on behalf of the Methodist Church in Great Britain to the Wesley Theological Seminary, "in token of the friendship between the two nations and in acknowledgement of the words of John Wesley, 'The Methodists are one people in all the world.' "

of such noteworthy Methodist buildings as Wesley's Chapel and the New Room in Bristol."

To enter the latter is a memorable and moving experience, reminding us that within its walls incidents have occurred of far-reaching consequence not only in Methodism but in the history of the English-speaking world. For Bristol was not only the spearhead of Wesley's advance into the world, but the springboard, through his emissaries, of American Methodism.

The Wesleys, the saintly Fletcher, Dr. Coke and every early leader of the Revival preached from this pulpit. At the square Communion table below, hundreds at a time, sometimes as many as a thousand, have received the Sacrament. The morning Communion Service would last far into the afternoon, the aisles thronged with waiting communicants. (We must remember that parish church Communions were much less frequent then, often not more than three or four times a year.) The chapel also has known crowded watch-night services and been filled week after week by those who came to hear Wesley at four o'clock in the morning.

It was here in a small room that the Methodist class-meeting originated, which became the basis of membership, when a Captain Foy suggested that the Society should meet in groups under a leader, and each member subscribe a penny a week. It was here also that Wesley's second Conference met, consisting of eleven members. Eighteen of his Conferences were held here. At one of them, in 1771, when he called for volunteers for work in America—a memorable moment in Methodist and American history—a young preacher from the Black Country, almost straight from the forge, Francis Asbury, stood up and offered to go. Soon afterwards he left England never to return, and became the first Methodist bishop in America. Today his statue in Washington commemorates him as one of the builders of the American nation.

At the Conference of 1777 those present were astonished at the sudden appearance of John Fletcher, vicar of Madeley, who had been seriously ill, and who came in like a ghost, pale and emaciated. The whole assembly rose as Wesley went forward to meet him. Fletcher, already on the margin of death, began to address the Conference, but weakness overcame him and Wesley knelt at his side and began to pray. The burden of his prayer was that God would spare Fletcher's life, and when he rose from his knees he declared with an emphasis which thrilled

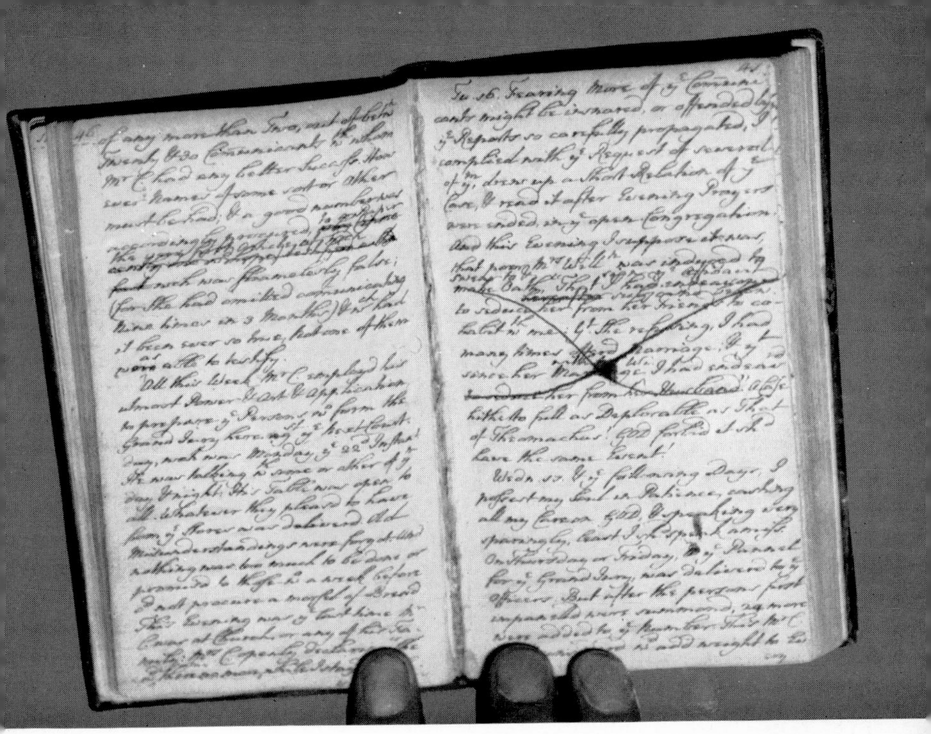

8. Items from the Epworth Press collection. *Above*, a page of Wesley's Journal of 1736. *Below*, Wesley's beautiful silk christening robe, and, *right*, ceramics in the Bottley Collection

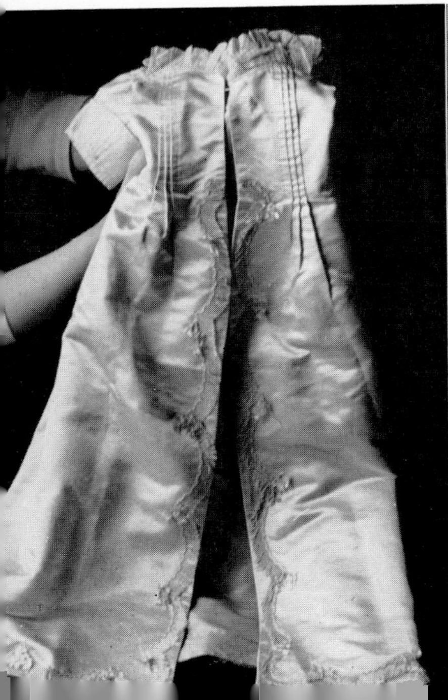

9. From the collection at Wesley's house, City Road. His brocade travelling cloak, a three-cornered hat of the type he much favoured, and the silver buckles which he gave to Mary Lelean, who sheltered him during a riot near Mevagissey. *Below*, Wesley's teething rattle

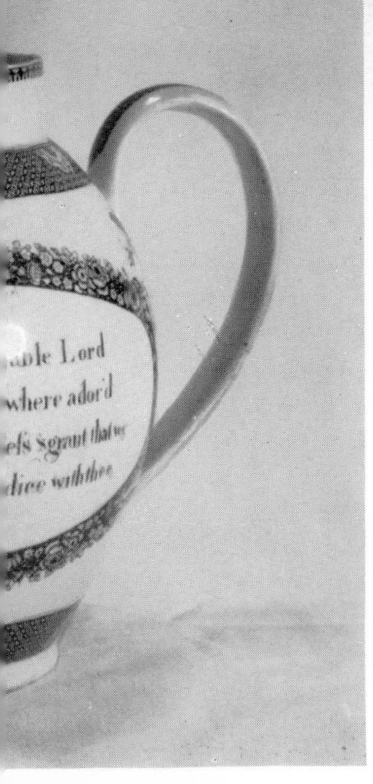

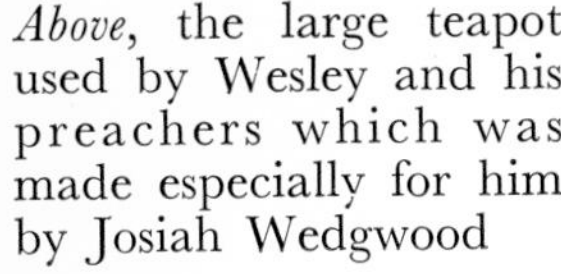

Above, the large teapot used by Wesley and his preachers which was made especially for him by Josiah Wedgwood

Right, top, the electrical machine designed by John Wesley for the treatment of "melancholia". Long before the days of Michael Faraday, Wesley was experimenting with electrical machines for the treatment of various diseases

Right, the bronze lantern from Wesley's carriage

10. No. 26 West Street, London. Now it is used as a warehouse, but formerly this building was the Mother Church of West End Methodism and the pride of early Methodists

every heart: "He shall not die, but live and declare the works of the Lord." Fletcher lived for eight years after this unforgettable scene.

An eyewitness of Wesley's last Conference here, in 1790, has described it. About a hundred and thirty preachers were present. A long table had been placed across the front of the chapel behind which Wesley presided, "with twenty venerable men on the benches, ten on each side, distinguished by their bushy or cauliflower wigs. Mr. Mather as a sort of archdeacon conducted the business. Mr. Valton was the Secretary, with his small quarto ledger." Wesley looked frail and feeble and could not see to announce the hymns, but his spirit was remarkably lively. Two months later he left the city for the last time.

Behind the chapel are the living quarters, used by Wesley and his household, which rather curiously open into the gallery. There is a central common room with a lantern light through which he could observe his preachers in the pulpit below, and with a bare deal table at which those in residence took their meals. Opening from it, and also above, are the bedrooms, the two in the far corner being Wesley's own apartments, one of which has a desk slope fitted into the window for his use. The household included a housekeeper and maids, and often a schoolmaster and orphan children, in addition to Wesley and his preachers who came and went.

In the courtyard behind is a life-size statue in bronze of Charles Wesley, with his right hand characteristically outstretched commending his Saviour. For thirty years this was the scene of his ministry, and for twenty-two years he lived at No. 4, Charles Street in Stoke Croft, not far from the Horsefair (Plate 14*a*). It is one of two tall narrow houses of brick, with two front windows to each of its three floors, well-preserved despite its dingy surroundings, and open to the public, with a Warden in residence. Its front rooms contain their original Adam grates, it is furnished in the style of the period, and the old panelling remains in the hall and adjoining room. In the front attic Charles Wesley is said to have composed many of his six thousand hymns. It was to this house he brought his bride, Sarah Gwynne. The Countess of Huntingdon came here twice a day when he lay ill with smallpox. But the neighbourhood has changed, and the house to which Wesley came so often now stands like a faded dowager, facing a car park in a drab and dreary street.

Among places which have disappeared—built over or reconstructed—are the Brickfields off Cheese Lane where Wesley held his first open air service; the "green at the entrance to Bristol", which is probably the ground in front of Bridgeyate Chapel; the orchard of the Dominican Priory—a favourite preaching spot, the memory of which survives in its name of Quaker Friars; the Wine Street grocer's shop where he first lodged with Mrs. Grenville, Whitefield's sister; Newgate Prison in Little Wine Street which he regularly visited, the Methodist Keeper of which, Abel Dagge, was immortalized by Robert Southey (who was born in the neighbourhood) for his humanitarian devotion; the former Bishop's Palace where Wesley had his famous interview with Bishop Butler who told him he had no business to preach in his diocese; the Lawford Gate Poorhouse which stood in Pennywell Road; No. 6 Dighton Street, the home of Dr. Castleman, where Wesley "ordained" Dr. Coke—his final breach with the Anglican Church; and old St. Werburgh's Church which stood in Corn Street, and St. Ewen's.

The shattered parish churches in which he preached include Temple Church, of which only the tower remains; St. Nicholas, where the curfew has recently been re-instated and now rings at 9 p.m. as previously; St. Peter's and St. Mary-Le-Port. The Theatre Royal in King Street—the oldest theatre in the country—reminds us of Wesley's strong opposition to its opening. He preached in the old parish church in Clifton, where he stayed with a Mr. Dolman during an illness, taking advantage of the hot wells, and prepared his *Notes on the New Testament*. His old King Street Chapel, which he opened in 1791, was demolished in 1954, when the compensation received was applied to the building of a new Methodist church at Filton.

Portland Chapel in Portland Street, Kingsdowne, was built a year after his death largely through the enterprise of Captain Webb, a pioneer of American Methodism. Rich in history and with a beautiful interior, it contains a remarkable number of old Methodist monuments. A small chapel opened by Wesley in Guinea Street, later became St. Mary Redcliffe's parish church-room. He preached in the Paddock at Bedminster, which is now occupied by the Mayor's Paddock Baths, also frequently to crowds on St. Augustine's Quay, and from a horse-block in Baptist Mills which was afterwards used as the foundation stone of the Methodist church at the corner of Mina Road.

St. James' Church—the oldest in Bristol—served as the parish church of Wesley's Horsefair community to which in the early days he brought his members for Communion, and where Charles Wesley's children were baptized, a memorial stone to whom is in the adjoining gardens which were then part of the churchyard. In 1768 Wesley preached in the Lord Mayor's chapel (St. Mark's) in College Green, formerly a thirteenth-century hostel for the poor; a fine painting of this occasion hangs in the Bristol Art Gallery. He afterwards dined at the Mansion House.

Whitefield's Tabernacle survives in Penn Street. It was Whitefield who first drew Wesley to Bristol, and here we can explore the old sanctuary with its fine pews, its memorials of the Wills family, its organ on which Handel may have played, and Whitefield's parlour, study and bedroom, furnished still as in his day.

All this is but an outline of a fast disappearing pattern. The city itself is a Methodist shrine, and not least among its proudest episodes is that of Wesley ministering to its citizens in an age of spiritual need and moral and social degradation, and of his pioneers sailing down the river to win new continents for Christ.

Didsbury College, founded in Manchester in 1842—the oldest Methodist Theological college—was removed to Westbury-on-Trym, three miles from Bristol, in 1942, and includes in its library a large and important collection of early Methodist literature, and the Williams portrait of Wesley shown here as the frontispiece to the book. The Bristol civic archives also contain original material relating to him.

Wesley's first approach to Bristol was through the ancient forest of Kingswood, four miles west of the city—a primitive area with a rough population of miners, squatters, and roving bands of thieves. No field of evangelism was less promising or offered a harsher contrast to Wesley's background. Yet here he wrought his greatest work, and the impact of his influence was little short of miraculous. What Whitefield had told him was true; that the colliers of Kingswood were as pagan as the Red Indians and that here lay a field ripe for harvest.

Wesley wasted no time and already Whitefield had prepared the way. A bronze tablet in the boys' playground of the Rose Green Schools records: "This playground was used as a preaching site by George Whitefield and John Wesley." Whitefield's

Old Tabernacle still stands in Park Road. By 1750 Wesley had four schools in the town, one of which survives—now a well-known public school, Kingswood, in Bath, where it removed in 1857.

The original school, of which Whitefield laid the foundation stone, was in Kennard Road, Kingswood. It was a bold venture to build a school in that labyrinth of lanes and donkey paths, among coalmines and cockpits. Wesley bought a good site—a forest clearing—and built a colliers' school, to which he afterwards added a boarding school. A century later the property was taken over by Mary Carpenter, the philanthropist, who turned it into a Reformatory School. It is now a Home Office Approved School with a Classifying School adjoining. Nothing remains of the old buildings except a red-tiled cottage in the grounds in which Wesley is said to have lived. But despite its new character the place retains strong Methodist memories which are carefully and proudly preserved.

I found both the Principal, Mr. R. H. Adams, and the Warden, Mr. W. W. Hall, interested, and Mr. G. H. Poolman, the carpentry instructor, and a keen Methodist, proved a mine of information. The last part of the original premises to be demolished was the chapel, in 1919, which stood on the site of the present carpenter's shop in which Mr. Poolman talked to me, and in which some of its material is incorporated. It was sixty feet long, thirty feet wide, with four rooms at each end where waifs and strays were housed and where John Cennick, the hymn-writer, lived, who was the first headmaster. A tablet records that Wesley founded his school here. It was in this building that his first watch-night service was held, and it was the lively centre of Kingswood Methodism. Mr. Poolman has a clock and an inkstand made on the premises from its floor boards.

Beyond this building is "John Wesley's Garden", with elms at the side which he may have planted, and beyond is "Wesley's Walk", where he paced up and down under the east wall which still marks the boundary. There is also a chestnut tree on the left of the school yard where the colliers gathered to hear him.

But most interesting of all is the bell which calls the present boys to meals and prayers. It is Wesley's old chapel bell which was dug up many years ago in the grounds. It had been split by frost but was rewelded and after later damage was recast by

Taylor's of Loughborough and re-hung as near as possible to its original site.

The remains of the pulpit are at Kingswood School, Bath. When the Hanham Mount Memorial was created in 1951 by the Kingswood Urban District Council, a replica of Wesley's Kingswood pulpit was desired and Mr. Poolman took it in hand. He went to Kingswood School and found the old pulpit in pieces in a room at the top of the School tower. He brought them away, put them together, and a copy of it was made under his supervision by the boys of the Approved School, and erected as part of the Wesley Memorial on Hanham Mount.

To finish the story—at a centenary exhibition of the Approved School's history in 1952, Wesley's old deal pulpit was again resurrected, and proudly displayed and photographed. For years the boys of the old Reformatory School had scrubbed it every Saturday morning. An old boy revisiting the School noticed it and remembering the many times he had done this chore, remarked: "Don't tell me that you've still got that darned pulpit here!"

The present Institution fosters these old associations, and one of its three Houses is called Wesley House. (Another is Byron House, after Lady Byron, the poet's widow, who took an active interest in Mary Carpenter's Reformatory.) It would delight Wesley, I think, to know that here, where he cared for the colliers' families, boys are still housed and trained, and that the land he acquired in the forest clearing has been so used for over two hundred years. But the present routine can hardly equal his strict regime, and the comfortable dormitories, swimming bath and shower baths are far removed from the spartan conditions of his day.

It is no great distance from the School to Hanham Mount where the town has provided a unique memorial—a sixty-five feet high electric beacon that sends out a green light that can be seen in many parts of Bristol, Bath, and North Somerset. The Mount is also depicted in the civic coat of arms along with a lion holding a lighted torch, symbolizing, among other things, the light of learning in the foundation of Kingswood School. And the motto of the crest is, appropriately: "Face the Dawn."

A rough lane leads from the road to a flagged cross marking the spot where the preachers stood (Plate 14*b*) and to steps up to the observation gallery at the base of the Beacon, at the foot of which in bold bronze letters we read: "Out of the Wood came Light." The Memorial also includes two texts of Scripture, a quotation from Keble, and two bronze plaques, one of which commemorates the persecuted Bristol Baptist preachers of the seventeenth century who preached in the surrounding woods and often swam for their lives across the flooded river. The other refers to Whitefield and Wesley, and the wording begins:

Hanham Mount
On the Mount
at the end of this path
GEORGE WHITEFIELD AND JOHN WESLEY
preached their earliest open-air sermons
in A.D. 1739

Two quotations follow from Whitefield's *Journal* and two from Wesley's, below which are the words: "Church or no Church, we must attend to the saving of souls."

In the garden of the nearby house is the Preachers' Tree—a sapling from the sycamore under which on this spot they also took their stand. In the opposite direction, eastwards from the Beacon, is a flagged path along the length of the Mount—a straight and narrow path, for all is wondrously symbolic, and on a pennant stone beneath our feet we read: "How beautiful upon the mountains are the feet of him that bringeth good tidings." The path brings us to the stone font brought here from Wesley's demolished school chapel and reconstructed by the boys of the Training School. It is ringed round with lavender and rosemary and bears the words: "All the World is my Parish."

In front of it, on the edge of the Mount, is the wooden replica of Wesley's School pulpit made by the Training School boys. Regaining the path, we reach the miniature Wesley Herb Garden in which have been planted "as many as possible of the plants named by Wesley for herbal cures". Saffron, sage, marjoram, thyme, pansies and peonies—all are here, and wild flowers—primroses, pimpernel, violets and wood sorrel. Thus the whole memorial in its conception and variety combines both old and new, is full of lofty symbolism, and is a striking civic tribute to Wesley's memory.

He stayed with the Thurston family on his visits to Thornbury at Kington House, two miles from that town, where the room and bed in which he slept are still preserved. Ralph Grove also entertained him at his house in Castle Street, now the

Castle Hotel. And the main portion of his preaching house, with additions, is now the Public Hall.

Of the "Stinking spaws" of the century none was so lively as Bath, discovered by the Romans, enriched by the wool trade, rebuilt by John Wood and his son who uncovered the Roman bath, refashioned the cobbled streets and with classic vision laid out its handsome terraces. It was a commercial enterprise, deliberately planned and profitably exploited. As the London season ended Bath came alive; the place swarmed with visitors and was full of wits and crooks. Sarah Siddons played to crowded audiences and George Whitefield preached to no less crowded congregations, while beneath its mask of elegance and convention flowed the riotous frivolity and licentiousness of the city's life.

It was on the site of the present Circus where Wesley habitually preached that he encountered Beau Nash, who had been sent down from Oxford, lived by his wits and had established himself, with a fine house and income, as Master of the Revels. As a pantomime king, though not without ability, he so impressed his personality on the tourist community, and with such impudence and audacity, that for fifty-five years his authority went unchallenged. At his death, his faults forgotten, he was honoured with a public funeral and immortalized among the saints with a monument in Bath Abbey.

He was, however, neither vicious nor ungenerous. Once, to teach a young cub a lesson, he invited him to gamble and won from him all that he had, even to the title deeds of his patrimony. When the game was over he confronted his wretched victim. "I have won," he said, "everything you possess." He then extracted from him a solemn promise that never again would he play for money, and with a royal gesture swept his winnings back across the table. "Take them," he said, "and be gone."

This was the man, tyrannical yet paternal, cynical yet magnanimous, who, dressed flamboyantly in gold lace, crowned with a white three-cornered hat, drove like a prince through the streets in a six-horse carriage, with outriders, and footmen sounding French horns. And this was the man who, on a memorable occasion, challenged John Wesley.

It is an oft-told story. A rumour had gone round that the preacher would meet with opposition. On the previous day in

Bristol he had been advised not to preach and had replied with a bold and ringing sermon. Now he had come to Bath to meet the champion, with the promise of the biggest snub of his life from no less than King Carnival himself.

Wesley, when challenged by Nash, asked what authority he possessed. "Are you a magistrate or the Mayor of this city?" "No, I am not," replied Nash. Wesley inquired if he had ever heard him preach and, if not, how could he judge of what he never heard? He answered: "By common report." To which Wesley retorted: "Give me leave, sir, to ask, is not your name Nash?" "Sir, my name is Nash." "Then, sir," replied Wesley with contempt, "I dare not judge you by common report. I trust common report is no good evidence of truth." And at that without another word the discomfited gamester withdrew and thereafter took good care to avoid the sharp-tongued preacher.

This happened in 1739 on the open space now surrounded by John Wood's Palladian Circus of Bath stone built with a grace and symmetry which delight the eye—a magnificent example of eighteenth-century town planning. Among famous men who afterwards lived here are the elder Pitt (No. 7), Livingstone (No. 13), Clive (No. 14), and Gainsborough (No. 24).

But it is in Lady Huntingdon's Chapel (now the Bath Presbyterian Church) that we come nearest to Wesley—the oldest and most interesting building associated with him in Bath. I could almost see the little man in the high pulpit facing the crowded pews, with Horace Walpole peering through the squint hole at the side, and Lady Huntingdon peeping through her private door which opened direct into the gallery from her adjoining house.

The Chapel stands in the Vineyards on the London Road which here spreads itself in noble breadth with wide and elevated side-walks, and is immediately behind Lady Huntingdon's former residence. The Countess, a friend of the Queen, devoted her energy and fortune to works of piety and charity. Though narrow and sectarian, she had a foot firmly and sensibly planted in two worlds: that of Society, in which she was a leading figure, and that of the Revival in which at times she threatened to rival Wesley himself. And her chapels sprouted like mushrooms in every fashionable resort.

In 1766 Wesley was heading for Scotland when he received an urgent request from her to return at once, and although he

11. Highbury Fields in Wesley's day when he came to visit friends at No. 25 Highbury Place (in centre of the row) and, *below*, the same site today

7 If now I have Acceptance found
With Thee, or Favour in thy Sight,
With thine Omnipotence surround,
And arm me with thy Spirit's Might.

8 O may I hear his warning Voice,
And timely fly from Danger near,
With Reverence unto Thee rejoice,
And love Thee with a filial Fear.

9 Still hold my Feet in second Life,
And suffer not my Feet to slide,
Support me in the glorious Strife,
And comfort me on every Side.

10 O give me Faith, and Faith's Increase,
Finish the Work begun in me,
Preserve my Soul in perfect Peace,
That stays, and waits, and hangs on Thee.

11 O let thy gracious Spirit guide
And bring me to the promis'd Land,
Where Righteousness and Peace reside,
And All submit to LOVE's Command.

12 A Land, where Milk and Honey flow,
And Springs of pure Delights arise,
Delights which I shall shortly know;
I shall regain my Paradise.

13 I see it now from *Pisgah's* Top,
Pleasant, and beautiful, and good,
In all the Confidence of Hope
I claim the Purchase of thy Blood.

14 Of Righteousness Divine possest,
O let me grasp the Prize so nigh,
Enter into the promis'd Rest,
Enjoy thy perfect Love, and die.

Hymns for Children.

1 GEntle JESUS, meek and mild,
Look upon a little Child,
Pity my Simplicity,
Suffer me to come to Thee.

2 Fain I would to Thee be brought,
~~Dearest~~ GOD, forbid it not, Gracious
Give me, ~~dearest~~ GOD, a Place gracious
In the Kingdom of thy Grace.

3 Put thy Hands upon my Head,
Let me in thine Arms be stay'd,
Let me lean upon thy Breast,
Lull me, lull me, LORD, to Rest.

4 Hold me fast in thine Embrace,
Let me see thy smiling Face,
Give me, LORD, thy Blessing give,
Pray for me, and I shall live.

5 I shall live the simple Life,
Free from Sin's uneasy Strife,
Sweetly ignorant of Ill,
Innocent, and happy still.

6 O that I may never know
What the wicked People do;
Sin is contrary to Thee,
Sin is the forbidden Tree.

7 Keep me from the great Offence,
Guard my helpless Innocence;
Hide me, from all Evil hide,
~~Self~~, and Stubbornness, and Pride. Anger

12. A page from Wesley's own copy of *Hymns and Sacred Poems* (3rd edition, 1761) showing some corrections he made

Left, part of Wesley's library at Richmond College which possesses nearly three hundred of his books, many annotated in his hand

had reached Yorkshire he abandoned his journey and hurried back with almost indecent haste. But there was good reason. He had recently put forward a sensible scheme for unity among the evangelical clergy which had met with little response, and finding progress barred in that direction, he was now only too ready to co-operate with his temperamental friend, whose chapels had been closed to him, for she was a rabid Calvinist. And also—like a ripe plum—there opened before him the possibility of preaching in her crowded and fashionable chapel in Bath, in which town so far his own enterprise had lamentably failed.

Thus he came for the first time to her Bath chapel, the preserve of the elect, and with all possible speed, his northern journey forgotten. "Many," he records, "were not a little surprised at seeing me in the Countess of Huntingdon's Chapel at Bath." The words suggest warm if not smug satisfaction. "The congregation was not only large, but serious; and I fully delivered my own soul. So I am in no concern whether I preach there again, or no. I have no choice concerning it."

But he was not so indifferent as his words suggest; in fact, he was only too anxious to preach there again and, indeed, as often as he could, and wrote to her to that effect, offering to preach weekly during his stay in the neighbourhood, to which she warmly agreed, signing herself: "Believe me, most faithfully your affectionate friend."

We can hardly blame Wesley, for in this fashionable chapel with its line of waiting coaches his hearers included the Lord Chancellor, Earl Chatham, Lord Chesterfield and many of similar rank. Walpole has described the scene:

> I have been to the opera—Mr. Wesley's. They have boys and girls with charming voices . . . The Chapel is very neat, with true gothic windows . . . Wesley is a clean, elderly man, his hair smoothly combed, but with a little soupçon of curls at the ends. Wondrous clever, as evidently an actor as Garrick. He spoke his sermon, but so fast, and with so little accent, that I am sure he has often uttered it, for it was like a lesson. There were parts and eloquence in it; but towards the end he exalted his voice and acted very ugly enthusiasm, decried learning, and told stories, like Latimer, of the old fool at his college, who said, "I thanks God for everything."

This memory, however, of his Oxford days, is very differently recorded by Wesley. Walpole deliberately makes it appear ridiculous.

The Chapel remains with its eighteenth-century organ, her Ladyship's private entrance, and Nicodemus' Corner, now a boiler room, where the shy and curious behind a grille could see and hear without being observed. I crouched in the coal hole where Walpole once sat with prying eyes. Below the pulpit in this gracious cream-coloured rectangular chapel are the proud symbols of the House of Huntingdon—three massive eagles carved in wood bearing the Huntingdon monogram in crimson and gold. To see these alone is worth a visit. But to me they symbolized even more: the vigour of Wesley as he beat his way through wind and storm, and the sharp-featured Countess who dominated her followers with the eye of an eagle and the heart of a saint.

Wesley's worst trouble in Bath (in later years) was among his own preachers, who complained that Anglican clergy were given priority in Methodist pulpits—which was true and for good reason. And they resented Wesley's invitation to a visiting Irish cleric to preach regularly during his stay. They declared, said Wesley, that "they were appointed by the Conference, not by me, and would not suffer the clergy to ride over their heads". Whereupon he set out in secret from London with his brother and two others, called together his Bath followers, read them a stinging lecture, and dismissed out of hand a faithful but offending preacher, who had led the revolt. "The rules of our preachers," he told them bluntly, "were fixed by me, before any Conference existed, particularly the twelfth: 'Above all you are to preach when and where I appoint'. You seem to have a quite wrong idea of a Conference. It is to meet me in order to advise, not control me. As long as any preacher joins with me, he is to be directed by me in his work." And with this Napoleonic dictum, worthy of a Loyola, he ended the matter, while the Bristol Methodists, out of loyalty and in execrable taste sang an incredible "Hymn to John Wesley" composed by his brother—surely the worst lines he ever wrote:

While others curse and wish him dead,
Do Thou Thy choicest blessings shed,
And crown his hoary hairs.

Near the former residence of Beau Nash, now a restaurant, is King's Meadow where Wesley used to preach, and according to a local guide book, he stayed at No. 2, Broad Street. On Lansdown Hill is Kingswood School, already mentioned.

Among interesting items preserved there are Wesley's bed and other furniture, his pulpit gown, his old Kingswood pulpit, and above all, his "library", many volumes of which are annotated in his own hand.

His old Avon Street meeting room has disappeared and, unfortunately, King Street Chapel, of which he laid the foundation stone, was destroyed by a bomb. If it is true that its Trustees could have acquired the Octagon, a former proprietary chapel and one of the most delightful architectural survivals in Bath, they missed a magnificent opportunity. It had declined into a storeroom, but has since been rescued by the Corporation from neglect and beautifully restored. It would have provided a central site and a superb eighteenth-century setting for Methodist worship.

CHAPTER SIX

INTO THE WEST—A MEDIEVAL FARMHOUSE—STICKLEPATH—ST. GENNYS—TREWINT—THE CATHEDRAL OF THE MOORS—PORT ISAAC—ST. ENDELLION—CARINES—GWENNAP—TRURO CATHEDRAL—A SCHOOL MEMORIAL—METHROSE IN THE RAIN—ROSEMERGY

FROM Bristol to Cornwall—the road that Wesley took so often! As he used to do, we turned aside to Southfield Farm at Brean, near Burnham, which has been occupied by members of the Hicks family for over four hundred years. The present seventeenth-century house (Plate 15*a*) includes walls and foundations as old as the thirteenth century, and the original building is described in Domesday Book, with deeds that go back to 1309. There is the original keystone over the door, and the drawing-room where Wesley preached on more than one occasion. The farmhouse stands high near the coast, with its gate opening upon a walled garden and smooth lawn. Beyond, on the day we came, were orchards laden with golden apples, the surrounding fields were packed with caravans, and in the distance was the shining rim of the sea.

It was from here, two hundred years ago, that Thomas Hicks rode to Bristol Fair, heard Wesley preach and was converted. That was the beginning of Methodism in these parts, since when this gracious house has been occupied by generations of loyal Methodists, and Mr. and Mrs. Stuart Hicks, proud of its history, maintain its fine tradition.

In the same area is the Dragon House, Washford, near Minehead, where Wesley is said to have stayed and preached. At the County Hotel in East Street, Taunton, formerly the Three Cups Inn, the coaching stables have been converted into garages, but the spacious yard remains where Wesley in his Master's gown and cassock had hardly named his text to "a numerous auditory" when "the mayor of the town came in Formality and ordered the Proclamation to be read which immediately silenced the preacher, and they have not been troubled with any of these impertinences since". But the hotel, now a Trust House, newly-painted, with its pillared portico, pink geraniums, and gated coachyard, bears no record of the incident. Another point of interest is an old house called Brynsworthy in Fremington, near Barnstaple, damaged by fire thirty years ago and now an hotel, where Wesley preached from a balcony.

Sticklepath, on the edge of Dartmoor—a picturesque village of white cob and thatched cottages—is little changed. It lay on his direct route to Cornwall and derives its name from the ancient highway which can still be traced up the steep path (or stickle) that climbs the hill called the Mount at the western end of the village. This was the packhorse road which he followed.

The village gave him a warm welcome. Following the suppression of a thatched chantry chapel, and there being no resident vicar, a strong Quaker community had established itself. As Wesley rode into the village he was accosted by a Quaker who asked abruptly: "Is thy name John Wesley?" "Immediately," says Wesley, "two or three more came up and told me I must stop there. I did so. I then found they were called Quakers. But that hurt me not, seeing the love of God was in their heart."

Wesley stayed with a Quaker miller in a thatched cottage, now called Staplers (formerly Black Down), which still has the hooks in its roof from which the wool packs (or sheets) were hung by the wool stapler who later occupied it. The Sticklepath Women's Institute has compiled an interesting local guide which includes a photograph of the cottage. The Gleave woollen mill, now a grist mill, was a stronghold of Methodism when the Pearse family came to it, and a large proportion of the village are Methodists.

The following year Wesley came again, when in addition to a service in the thatched cottage he preached from the White Rock on the Mount, since when the granite boulder has been given an annual coat of whitewash, at one time by the Methodists, and more recently by members of the Men's Club.

A stone in the boundary hedge of the Quaker graveyard by the River Taw records: "In this consecrated ground are interred the bodies of the pious QUAKERS, late residents in this village, who in the year 1743 and after, welcomed and entertained the Wesleys, J. Nelson, and others as they journeyed to preach the GOSPEL. Be not forgetful to entertain strangers. Hebrews XIII, 1 and 2."

The occasion of Wesley's first visit to Devon was the death of his brother Samuel. It was then, in 1739, that he preached his first sermon in Exeter, probably in St. Mary Major's Church, where after the morning service the rector forbade him to preach in the afternoon. "Not that you preach any false doctrine. I allow all that you have said is true. And it is the doctrine of the Church of England. But it is not guarded. It is dangerous. It may lead people into enthusiasm or despair."

Southernhay Green, another of his preaching sites, is now covered with Georgian houses, and the oak drop-leaf table on which he stood is preserved at the Mint Methodist Church. On at least two occasions he worshipped in the cathedral. Bishop Lavington had been one of his most bitter and scurrilous opponents, but a fortnight before Lavington's death Wesley, who was in Exeter at the time, attended the cathedral and records: "I am well pleased to partake of the Lord's Supper with my old opponent Bishop Lavington."

On a later occasion he dined with Lavington's successor. After commenting on the solemn music at the post-Communion in the cathedral, he notes the lovely situation of the palace, the plainness of its furniture—"Not costly or showy, but just fit for a Christian Bishop; the dinner sufficient, but not redundant, plain and good, but not delicate; the propriety of the company—five Clergymen and four of the Aldermen; and the genuine, unaffected courtesy of the Bishop."

Cullompton, Crediton, Tavistock, Crockernwell and Plymouth were among places Wesley frequently visited. He had a large following at Tiverton, but the mayor did not think the town needed him, saying, "There is the old church and the new church. Then there is the Pitt Meeting, the Meeting in Peter Street, and the Meeting in New Street—four ways of going to heaven, enough in all conscience—and if the people won't go to heaven by one or other of these ways, by God they shan't go to heaven at all while I am Mayor of Tiverton."

Devon was never so responsive to Wesley as Cornwall. Dr. W. G. Hoskins says: "In the diocese of Exeter the only friendliness ever shown by the established Church towards Wesley was Bishop Ross's invitation to dinner, and similar hospitality from the vicar of Charles Church in Plymouth."

Wesley's old Devonport Chapel in Ker Street (1776) was

handed over to the Territorial Army just before the war and is now scheduled for demolition under a development plan, but according to Councillor Stanley Goodman, efforts are being made to preserve it as "one of the last remaining significant pieces of eighteenth-century architecture left in the city".

Cornwall abounds in Methodist shrines and there is hardly a market-place in the county in which Wesley has not stood. Nowhere did he make a more lasting impression and the area is full of his memory. A prominent Anglican layman told me: "Down here Wesley is still regarded as a father of the people." I found, as in no other part, the warmest interest kindled at the mention of his name. He paid thirty-two visits to Cornwall and there are five parish churches in the north of the county closely associated with him. Unfortunately there is no guide-book for the Methodist pilgrim in these parts—an omission, let us hope, soon to be rectified by the recently-formed and enterprising Cornish branch of the Wesley Historical Society.

St. Gennys lies on the rockbound coast near Boscastle where the great headlands drop sheer to the sea. The tiny village is a dream of beauty with fields sloping to the cliff tops, and a four-pinnacled church tower peeping out of a hillocked churchyard where the path in places is almost as high as the roof of the church. And the church itself is little changed beyond a new top to the tower—the old tower was blown down in a gale—and a modern pulpit.

Whitefield, during a fortnight's stay in the vicarage, describes an unforgettable scene in the crowded church on a bleak November night when, after his sermon, the vicar, "good Mr. Thompson", went from pew to pew to encourage and comfort many who had been moved to tears. At a similar service on a later occasion four clergymen were present in their gowns and cassocks along with four of Wesley's preachers. And Wesley himself, who was a friend of the vicar, came often and preached. James Hervey came too, author of an eighteenth-century best-seller, *Meditations among the Tombs*, who, in his published *Letters*, describes the vicarage.

Thompson's story is interesting. He had been curate in a neighbouring parish, but, gay and dissolute by nature and not taking too easily to his sacred vocation, he had sought a livelier sphere as a naval chaplain. At the age of thirty-five he was presented with the living of St. Gennys, though as little fitted as ever for that office. One night he had a dream in which with startling clearness he learned the exact hour in which, a month from that time, he would die. He wakened, but only to sleep and dream again, this time of the Last Judgement, where he was called to account for his wasted life. On the following day he informed his parishioners, then shut himself in his room to prepare for the end.

A fortnight passed before he emerged, when he called his flock together to inform them that he was a changed man. On the appointed day, with a small company of friends, he awaited on his knees the fatal moment. But the hour struck and he did not die. Attributing his deliverance to his conversion and the mercy of God, he again addressed his parishioners and appealed to them to follow him in his new way of life. From that time he became an ardent evangelist, accompanied Wesley on his Cornish tours, opened his home to Methodist activities, and influenced neighbouring parishes.

But not everyone approved of his enthusiasm. An old diocesan history records that "one family attends Mr. Thompson's irregular meetings and accompanies him at his circumferaneous vociferations". And Bishop Lavington, on a visitation at Launceston, was so incensed that he threatened to strip off Thompson's gown, whereupon Thompson removed the gown himself, saying that he could preach as well without it.

The present vicar, the Rev. A. L. Parrish—no less hospitable than his eighteenth-century predecessor—showed me over the vicarage which was the scene of Thompson's dream and of Wesley's and Whitefield's visits, and which, with its old-world rose garden and its windows overlooking the sea, lies along the lane by the churchyard. It was smaller in Thompson's day, and had its entrance on the east side which was then the front of the house. Among later additions is a fine music room with a magnificent oriel window, but the old part of the building remains. As we climbed the stairs I thought of Wesley coming here for the last time. He had learned in Camelford that Thompson was dying and desired to see him, and borrowing the best horse available he rode as fast as he could to St. Gennys. On the way a white-headed and ragged man tugged at his bridle, whom Wesley failed at first to recognize. It was John Trembath, a former preacher who had taken to farming and smuggling and had fallen on evil days, reduced to ditch and hedge for bread. Wesley, pitying his distress, arranged to meet him the same evening in Launceston, then rode on to St. Gennys where in a bedroom overlooking the sea he administered the Sacrament to his old friend and parted from him for the last time.

He also preached in the neighbouring church of Week St. Mary, which has a granite tower, and a window showing St. Catherine with her wheel, St. Agnes and her lamb, and St. Cecilia at her organ. On four occasions he took service in Tresmeer church where all that remains of the building he knew is its fifteenth-century tower and Norman font. The other two churches to which he came are North Tamerton with its high-pinnacled tower, lofty arcaded nave and ancient carved bench ends; and Laneast—a lonely Norman sanctuary built in the shape of a cross and containing much fifteenth-century woodwork.

In the parish of Altarnon on Bodmin Moor is Digory Isbell's cottage at Trewint, near Five Lanes, which in 1947 was rescued from demolition through the enterprise of the late Mr. Stanley Sowton, and beautifully restored by Sir George Oatley of Bristol. With its period furniture its appearance is now as when Wesley used it. No tourist should miss seeing it, for even in Cornwall, as a shrine, it is unique. Formerly the mail coach passed its door, for the old turnpike road built in 1760 ran through the hamlet which is now by-passed by the modern A 30 road. But on Wesley's first visit in 1744, there was no road, not even the turnpike, and Trewint stood on the open moor.

A romantic story lies behind this picturesque cottage (Plate 17*a* and *b*). John Nelson, who accompanied Wesley, relates it in his *Journal*. There were three of them altogether and, with only one horse between them, they took turns in riding. They slept on hard boards and lived on blackberries. "Brother Nelson," said Wesley, as he picked them from the hedge, "we ought to be thankful that there are plenty of blackberries; for this is the best country I ever saw for getting a stomach, but the worst that ever I saw for getting food. Do the people think we can live by preaching?"

At St. Ives, says Nelson, "Mr. Wesley and I lay on the floor; he had my greatcoat for his pillow, and I had Burkitt's *Notes on the New Testament* for mine. After being here near three weeks, one morning about three o'clock, Mr. Wesley turned over, and, finding me awake, clapped me on the side, saying 'Brother

Nelson, let us be of good cheer; I have one whole side yet, for the skin is off but one side.' "

In those days they preached on the commons and were seldom offered refreshment. On entering Cornwall, Wesley had sent his two companions ahead, who after a twenty-mile ride, and twelve miles short of their destination, reached Trewint—a cluster of slate-roofed cottages, one of which had a stone porch, and in their predicament they knocked on its door. It belonged to Digory Isbell, a stonemason. His wife Elizabeth came to the door and, when they asked for food, she said, "We have bread, butter and milk, and good hay for your horse." She refused payment and, before they left, they knelt on the floor and, to her astonishment, prayed without a book. Later she told her husband who replied in broad Cornish: "Ef they cum agin, us must be sure an' git um to praich to us an let the nayburs yur um, too."

A fortnight later one of them came again, wet through, and was welcomed. Digory spread the news among his neighbours, "Praicher's cum. Cum vore an' yur um," and the next morning three hundred heard the preacher at the cottage door.

Then Wesley came. Digory doubted if he was real, for rumours had spread that he was dead. "They do say in thaise parts yu baint John Wesley at all—they reckon he died years agone—but I dunnaw." Though he came in April, the moors were covered with snow as in the depth of winter. He arrived wet and weary, having been battered for hours by wind and hail. The cottage was crowded that night to hear him, and in the morning Digory piloted him over the great moor, all the paths being covered with snow, in places too deep for man or horse to pass.

One day when Digory was reading his Bible he came to the story of the Shunamite woman who, with her husband, built on the wall of their house a prophet's chamber, with a bed, table, stool and candlestick, for the use of Elisha. Digory decided to do the same for John Wesley, and he added two small rooms to his cottage. Now a caretaker lives in Digory's stone-porched house, and the two rooms adjoining it with their separate entrance are open to every pilgrim.

The accommodation within is a perfect reproduction. There is the lower room with its floor of Cornish slate—the smallest preaching place in Methodism—where services are still held; and up through the ceiling goes the oak stairway to the little bedroom where Wesley and his preachers slept, with its window looking out upon the moor. Among many interesting exhibits is the book, used as a pillow when Wesley and Nelson shared the same hard bed, a set of beautifully engraved Wesley playing cards, and a gavel made from a tree under which John Wesley preached in Georgia, U.S.A.

The stable used by the preachers is now incorporated as a coal cellar and bathroom in Digory's old cottage, which, though modernized, remains unspoiled. And on the opposite side of the lane is a garden of rest with oak seats and a replica of John Nelson's sundial.

There is no mention of Wesley preaching in Altarnon church—the Cathedral of the Moors—though it has close associations with the cottage. There is a five-stepped horse-block and a sixth-century Cornish cross at its gate, where two streams go tumbling through the village. To the right of the churchyard path is the Isbell tomb with its epitaph:

> . . . They were the first who entertained the Methodist Preachers in this County, and lived and died in the Connection, but strictly adhered to the Duties of the Established Church. Reader, may thy End be like theirs.
>
> From early Life, under the Guidance and Influence of divine Grace, they strengthened each other's Hands in God; Uniting to bear their Redeemer's Cross and promote the Interests of His Kingdom in the Face of an opposing World; thus duly estimating Scriptural Christianity, in Youth, Health and Strength their conduct was regulated by its Precepts: in Age, Infirmity and Death they were supported by its Consolations, and in a happy Immortality they enjoy its Reward.

Legend says that if you run twelve times round the grave you can hear the bells of heaven.

A neighbouring tomb, that of Jonathan Harris, bears a similar record, that "he was a member of the Methodist Society, but strictly adhered to his duty as a member of the Established Church". Until within living memory Cornish Methodists preserved this natural and happy relationship. The vicar of Altarnon says that with a few this attitude continued in his parish until the year 1934. Thus the moorland cottage and the moorstone church are interlinked—the cottage where Wesley preached and slept and the church with its seventy-five richly-carved bench ends for which it is famous, its gracious rood screen, and its quiet graves, by the running stream, of Wesley's devoted followers.

Opposite the bridge leading to the church is a small Methodist chapel which has over its doorway a bust of Wesley by Neville Burnard, a copy of which is in the chapel of Truro Cathedral School. Elizabeth Isbell was a Burnard, and among descendants of the two families were sculptors and stoneworkers famous throughout Cornwall, one of whom helped to build Dartmoor Prison; another was Robert Whale, A.R.A.

From Altarnon we made our way over Bodmin Moor in a Cornish mist, past the desolate Jamaica Inn, to Port Isaac, which Wesley visited twenty times. There can be few places more attractive on a fine autumn morning when from the Headlands Hotel you look out across the green cliffs above Port Gaverne, with the surf swirling and foaming below and the sea blue and white in the sunlight. Years have passed since, long before dawn, our pockets bulging with biscuits, we crept down its crooked street and went out with the lobster boats, up the coast off Bude, and saw the sun rise over King Arthur's legendary land.

Port Isaac is another, even lovelier, Polperro, and despite a blotch of new building in the upper town, remains unspoiled. You can walk down its straggling street and think you are in Italy, with glimpses of the sea down every narrow opening, and its small quayside like a toy piazza. It was here on the Plat that Wesley preached from the top of the seven slate steps at the side of the fish warehouse on your left as you face the sea (Plate 16*b*). The Plat, the steps, the stone buildings, preserve their old pattern. Do the fishermen, I wonder, still sing Methodist hymns here on summer evenings as they used to do? Fine singing it was, each voice taking its part, the sound of it filling the town with music and carried out to sea on the evening air.

Opinions differ as to where Wesley stayed. One tradition says it was at Victoria House (Plate 16*a*), now a greengrocer's shop, facing the Golden Lion, at the narrowest turn of the main street. The story is that he was chased up Fore Street and took refuge there, preached from its first floor window and escaped from an attic over the roofs at the back.

For information I was directed to the "Billy Riggs" of the chapel, but with little result; Mr. Wesley Blake, however, was full of local knowledge. Cornish folk, it seems, are slow in imparting information. Said one, "The only thing you cude du is to go from 'ouse to 'ouse to unquire, issunt ut?" But when they unwrap themselves old memories come tumbling out. So I found with Mr. Provis and others at the quay, one of whom, after much hesitation, unburdened himself of the following rhyme of his childhood:

John Wesley had a thousand bricks,
To build his chimney higher,
To keep the naughty pussy cats
From making (putting) out his fire.

In Port Isaac is the narrowest street in Cornwall—so narrow that only one can pass—and they say the aim of every bandsman is to beat the big drum through it. Wesley must have often passed along it. Wesley House, opposite Wesley Chapel, has no connection with him, other than its name, and neither of the two existing chapels belongs to his day.

Let us look for a moment at his first visit. It was in 1747 and he met with a rough reception. He had been told that Richard Scantlebury was expecting him and, with the street full of a hostile crowd, he knocked on his door, but no one answered. After repeated knocking, the occupier appeared. "Pray, is Mr. T. here?" asked Wesley, referring no doubt to Mr. Thompson, the vicar of St. Gennys, who had arranged for his accommodation. "Mr. T. is not here," was the curt reply, "but, pray, what may thy name be?" "My name is John Wesley." To which Scantlebury answered: "I have heard of thee," and Wesley records: "Perceiving that he had no more to say I turned back to another house."

In 1763 he describes another visit: "I went on to Port Isaac, now the liveliest place in the circuit. I preached from a balcony in the middle of the town. Before I came to Port Isaac the first time one Richard Scantlebury invited me to lodge at his house; but when I came, seeing a large mob at my heels, he fairly shut the door upon me, yet in this very house I now lodged. Richard Scantlebury being gone to his fathers and the present proprietor, Richard Wood, counting it all joy to receive the servants of God."

In Chapel Street is a trim little house, Homestead, with a red painted door and shutters, its narrow patch of garden bright with roses. This was pointed out to me as Scantlebury's house and the door from which Wesley was turned away. But of all the old houses the present Harbour Café, with its crooked roof of cemented slate and its massive sixteenth-century chimney, is the likeliest, where he preached from a window facing the quay, also in Richard Wood's cobbled yard behind, and from which he escaped by way of the roof into Temple Bar. The old house remains, though a coffee bar with red stools now occupies the ground floor.

The town in those days was a thriving port, exporting slate from the quarries at Delabole, and importing coal. The two-mile road over Church Hill, made by convicts from Bodmin Jail, was the route Wesley took out of the town, passing the early Tudor church of St. Endellion where the Port Isaac Methodists, making their way up Church Hill, went regularly to receive Communion. The church, facing the Atlantic winds and with extensive views, has a fine granite doorway, magnificent wagon roofs, and a panel in its tower portrays six bell-ringers in white shirts and red breeches. John Betjeman sings its praises: "Saint Endellion! Saint Endellion! The name is like a ring of bells."

Behind Newquay we find another farmhouse with a prophet's chamber. This is Carines at Cubert where Joseph Hosken was Wesley's host, who added two rooms for the use of his preachers (Plate 18). It lies off the road from Crantock to Cubert where at a road junction we reach the Lantern Café—a picturesque house, formerly a chapel, built by Hosken for the Methodists and bequeathed to them in his will. The local story is that later it was sold to the Church of England for £8! It served as a school and the part now used as a café was the house of the school dame (known in the deeds as Wesley Cottage). For some thirty or forty years it was the village grocery store and the room which was the chapel is now seldom used except for parish council meetings. In 1766 Wesley wrote from Cornwall to John Haime, one of his preachers, who had fought in the Low Countries: "God has, it seems, provided a place for you here. Mr. Hoskins wants a worn-out preacher to live with him, to take care of his family, and to pray with them morning and evening."

At Carines a stone gateway opens into a walled garden with a flagged pavement along the full breadth of which lies the front of the ancient house, with low windows and a white door with a great lion-headed knocker. At a right angle are the two rooms used by Wesley. And outside the garden wall are two ancient elms sprouting new shoots, with the surrounding area neatly cobbled. They are the remains of the trees beneath which he preached. Beside them is a granite post, which was part of an old mounting block, on which, local tradition maintains, he rested his Bible.

We turned next towards Redruth where the land is scarred with derelict tin mines, where streets of slate-roofed houses fill the green valleys, and where, through a tangle of lanes, we came to Busveal and the famous Gwennap Pit. This natural amphitheatre, caused by the filling in of ancient mine workings, has been called Cornwall's Albert Hall and is said to have remarkable acoustic properties. Wesley, who used it on seventeen occasions, describes it as the best natural arena in the country—"a round green hollow, gently shelving down about fifty feet, two hundred feet across one way, three hundred feet across the other. I believe there were full 20,000 people, and the evening being calm, all could hear."

In 1773 he records an even greater congregation: "about two and thirty thousand people; the largest assembly I ever preached to. Yet I found all could hear, even to the skirts of the congregation. Perhaps the first time a man of seventy has been heard by thirty thousand persons at once." In those pre-broadcasting days, it was, of course, phenomenal. Later he described it as "the most magnificent spectacle this side of heaven, and no music on earth comparable to the singing of the multitude". He was eighty-six on the last occasion he preached there.

But its appearance was very different in those days, as shown by old prints, and as we know from its more recent restorations. After his death it fell into disrepair, but in 1806 was restored, since when, every year, a crowded Whit Monday service has been held there. Today it is 116 feet in diameter, 360 feet in circumference at the top, 16 feet at the bottom, and 26 feet deep (Plate 19*a*). Its accommodation therefore is much less than formerly, though still considerable, for I counted no less than thirteen tiers of neatly turfed seats, 3½ feet wide and 18 inches high. It is admirably preserved, and two upright stumps of granite mark the spot where Wesley is supposed to have stood. In 1839 the Chartists rallied there, and in 1951, the Festival of Britain year, Cornish players presented Miss Mitchell's play *The Wesley Tapestry*.

Its approach and surroundings are equally well-laid out and preserved. A gate leads from the lane into the trim enclosure of Busveal Chapel, and a stone-lined path brings us to the ten wide, shallow steps of smooth turf which lead up to the Pit.

Of all Wesley's open-air pulpits, after his father's tomb, this is the most famous. The whole scene—the concentric circles, the soft green turf, the little whitewashed houses, and the grey walls enclosing the quiet sanctuary, all convey a sense of atmosphere and expectancy, as if a great congregation had just left or was about to assemble, and no wonder!—for it has been the scene of remarkable assemblies and exciting incidents and is haunted by hallowed memories.

Returning to Carharrack we noticed an old octagonal building now used as an institute. It would be interesting to establish its origin, for it is a type of building that Wesley favoured for his chapels.

Not for the first time I looked at the Wesley window in Truro Cathedral, above the War Memorial, to the right of the side entrance, which shows him preaching to the miners in Gwennap Pit, with a pit wheel in the background. A printed inscription reads:

> John Wesley, a priest of the Church of England whose heart was strangely warmed in Aldersgate Street, London, on 24th May 1738. As a result of his travels, preaching, enthusiasm and organizing genius, Methodist Societies grew and profoundly influenced the whole religious life of England and nowhere more than in Cornwall which he visited more than thirty times.

The long lancet window includes two other figures of the Revival: Charles Wesley, composer of six thousand hymns, and Samuel Walker, the evangelical curate of St. Mary's, Truro.

When Bishop (afterwards Archbishop) Benson arrived in Truro to re-establish the Cornish Diocese after the lapse of a thousand years, the first thing he did was to go straight to Gwennap Pit with his young son, Martin, to pay homage to "dear John, that marvellous man" and to find inspiration there for his heavy task. He pointed out the two stone posts, and a step between them, which were, he concluded, "the glorious old John's preaching place".

The old Kenwyn rectory, where Wesley stayed, half a mile from the city, afterwards known as Lis Escop—the Bishop's

13. The New Room, Bristol—one of the most fascinating and unspoilt of all Methodist shrines. The exterior, showing the famous equestrian statue and, behind, the little stable. *Below*, Wesley's study

14. No. 4 Charles Street, Bristol, where Charles Wesley lived for twenty-two years

Below, Hanham Mount—the beacon and the stone-flagged cross mark the spot where John Wesley preached to the rough population of miners among whom his influence was little short of miraculous

Palace—is now occupied by the Cathedral School. Wesley describes it as "a house fit for a nobleman, and the most beautifully situated of any I have seen in the county". In its gracious grounds overlooking the city and the river, the old rectory remains, though greatly enlarged and with the School's new buildings around it. When a later bishop (Dr. Morgan) found it too large under modern conditions, it was purchased and presented to the School by Mr. Harold Copeland and renamed Copeland Court.

Passing through the older building I climbed to the chapel on the first floor with its fine bust of Wesley, and the head-master, Mr. S. M. Mischler, provided me with a copy of the framed inscription which, in the handwriting of Bishop Stubbs, hangs beneath it, which after quoting Wesley's own account of his visit, reads:

> In commemoration of this visit and in reverent memory of a great Evangelist and Reformer, this bust of John Wesley is placed on the south wall of this Chapel, being the original wall of the guest-chamber of the old vicarage of Kenwyn. The bust is a copy by Mr. John Harvey of Truro, of that placed over the porch of the Meeting House at Alternon, carved in 1834 by the Cornish sculptor, Neville Northey Burnard, then a boy of sixteen.

So in this quiet chapel the finely-chiselled face looks down upon generations of boys as they worship; and Wesley's memory, and not least his catholic spirit, are graciously and appropriately preserved.

On a wall in the County offices of the Council of Social Services I noticed a map of generous size made up of one-inch Ordnance sheets, with coloured pins and flags, giving aspects of old Methodist history in the County. The Council's genial Secretary, Mr. John Pearce, an active Anglican layman, is well versed in local Methodist history. Wesley's influence, he told me, survives in the area to an astonishing degree, not only in its buildings which cover the countryside, its cob chapels, prayer rooms and prophet's chambers, but in old customs and traditions. Many Cornish families, like his own, come of Methodist stock reaching back to Wesley, and Methodism became part of the natural pattern of Cornish life. For example: if some Cornish people do not take sugar in their tea it may well be because Wesley asked his followers to do without it, as a token of their objection to the slave trade, for sugar came from

Cuba and slaves were engaged in its production. So what originally was a mild form of protest became a family tradition, persisting within living memory—"because Mr. Wesley says so". Mr. Pearce has in his treasured possession a chair which formerly belonged to John Bennetts, an ancestor who frequently entertained both John and Charles Wesley. Also in private hands in Truro is a fine linen tablecloth into which are woven the figures of "Isac & Abraham" which was laid on Wesley's table many times when he stayed in Bristol.

In a downpour we searched for the Manor Farm of Methrose in the parish of Luxulyan, north of St. Austell. Deep in the rain-drenched fields and orchards we found this old building with its grey stone walls and mullion windows and great chimney leaning drunkenly with age. Dr. A. L. Rowse describes it as "the delightful Methrose with its miniature enclosed courtyard and gateway, its one storied hall going up to the roof of the house, its solar and buttery". Here Wesley held a number of his East Cornwall Quarterly Meetings. It is now a farmhouse occupied by Mr. and Mrs. J. B. Higman, direct descendants of the family who lived here in those days, though the house is now divided into two separate dwellings. A coat of arms in one of the bedrooms gives the date 1676.

Inside the gate of the walled courtyard is an ancient font used by Wesley, with its lead lining missing but showing the grooves which held it (Plate 19*b*). And within the house is the small banqueting hall with beams of blackened oak, original panelling, and massive fireplace—the latter now furnished with a Raeburn stove. The house is full of memories. Every shadowed corner seemed to come alive. Here Wesley stood and preached and ate and slept, looked out through those deep-set windows, rode down that narrow lane, and baptized in the font now brimming in the rain.

Further south, at Morvah on the road from St. Ives to St. Just, is Rosemergy—a hamlet beyond Zennor with a cottage which is another (though unrestored) Trewint. Wesley mentions it four times in his *Journal*. John Daniel, a miner and small farmer, lived here with his wife Alice, and we can still see beyond it the remains of a Cornish engine house, reminding us that Wesley was the "apostle of the miners", particularly in this western half of the county, where he had a remarkable following.

A local tradition says that on his first visit to Cornwall he stopped outside this cottage, where he saw Alice Daniel taking honey out of her bee-butt (bee-hive) and asked her for a cup of water. She invited him in and gave him a meal of barley bread which she had just baked and her new honey. Then he spoke to her of things "sweeter than honey" and she called in her neighbours to hear a clergyman who talked as she had never heard any clergyman talk before. The upshot was that the Daniels added two small rooms to their cottage for the use of Wesley and his preachers.

More than twenty years after his first visit, Wesley wrote:

> In riding to St. Ives I called on one with whom I used to lodge, two or three and twenty years ago, Alice Daniel at Rosemerghy. Her sons are all gone from her; and she has but one daughter left, who is always ill. Her husband is dead; and she can no longer read her Bible, for she is stone-blind. Yet she murmurs at nothing, but cheerfully waits till her appointed time shall come. How many of these jewels may be hid, up and down; forgotten of men, but precious in the sight of God!

Two years later he revisited her and preached outside the cottage from the text: "They who shall be accounted worthy to obtain that world, and the resurrection from the dead, are equal unto the angels, and are the children of God, being the children of the resurrection." Doubtless it was on this occasion that Alice Daniel, now bedridden, heard him through her open window (which can be seen on the left of the photograph, Plate 20*a*) with the autumn sunlight flooding her room. Sweeter than honey!—it was still true, despite age and blindness. And could the words "equal to the angels" be more aptly applied than to this blind Cornish saint? That same night Wesley wrote in his *Journal*: "I have always thought there is something venerable in persons worn out with age; especially when they retain their understanding, and walk in the ways of God."

When Mr. John Pearce was lecturing some years ago in Camborne an eminent Cornish Methodist (who has since died) was so moved by the story of Alice Daniel that he purchased the property, giving a good deal of the cliff and moorland to the National Trust. Fortunately the previous owner had refrained from demolishing the house and it is now hoped that it may be restored. A road-widening scheme, however, threatens its existence, but the County Council has been notified of its historic significance, and every effort is being made to secure its preservation. This is the third of such places in Cornwall with a "Prophet's Chamber", the other two (as we have noted) being at Trewint and Carines.

At Trewellard, near St. Just, there is a project to re-erect a fallen pillar where Wesley, on hearing a report of a Calvinistic sermon recently preached there, struck his hand on the granite post and cried "Damnable doctrine!"—the only time, says Mr. Pearce, that Wesley was known to swear!

Another of his preaching sites was under a tree in a field outside Camborne—a place known locally as Knave-go-by—Wesley presumably being the knave—and near Ashton is a natural amphitheatre which he used.

Wesley Rock Chapel, at Hea Moor near Penzance, is famous for its pulpit which is built over the granite stone from which Wesley preached when it stood in a neighbouring meadow (Plate 20*b*). And five miles from Penzance, at Goldsithney is Wesley Cottage where he is said to have slept.

But these by no means exhaust the places in Cornwall to which he came. Falmouth, St. Just, St. Ives, Helston, Newlyn—he visited them all and almost every intervening village. At Falmouth he was roughly handled and a wooden door, indented by stones hurled against him there by the mob, was preserved in a minute chapel above a stable at Buckshead, near Truro, but although we were allowed to search the building it seems to have disappeared. And though at St. Ives his original chapel has been enlarged several times, we can still go through the old door by which he entered, and at its side is a plaque stating that the house of his host, John Nance—a famous name in Cornish Methodism—formerly stood on the opposite side of the lane. St. Ives' museum has a telescope with Wesley's name neatly engraved on its wooden barrel (Plate 20*c*). The story behind it is that Wesley, towards the end of his life, presented it as a token of gratitude to a local family called Bryant with whom he had sometimes stayed. It remained as a treasured possession of the family for nearly two hundred years and was acquired by the museum in 1958 from the Rev. Matthew B. Tanner, who had inherited it from his mother who was herself a Bryant.

Cornwall indeed is a rewarding county for the Methodist pilgrim to visit.

CHAPTER SEVEN

BEXLEY—SHOREHAM—A FAMOUS VICTORY—TUNBRIDGE WELLS—WINCHELSEA—THE SMUGGLERS OF RYE—WESLEY'S LAST SERMON—BRADFORD-ON-AVON—THE WESTLEYS OF DORSET

THE SOUTH hardly attracted Wesley as did the west and north, and counties such as Kent and Sussex could scarcely muster between them as many Methodists as a single town like Macclesfield. But he found his way over the Sussex hills, his coach rumbled through the villages of the Weald, and he preached to the élite at Tunbridge Wells and the smugglers at Winchelsea and Rye.

Shoreham in Kent, and Bexley were favourite haunts. Blendon Hall, the home of the Delamotte family, a mile from Bexley, was the scene of lively Methodist activities. Delamotte was a London sugar merchant and county magistrate whose son Charles had been a member of Wesley's Holy Club in Oxford and had accompanied him to Georgia. The Hall, the earliest rendezvous of Methodism in these parts, was demolished twenty-five years ago, to make way for suburban villas. The Wesleys came there on their return from Georgia, John Wesley hurrying straight from the boat when it landed at Deal.

The vicar of Bexley, Henry Piers, who had passed through a similar experience to that of Wesley, was one of the six Anglican clergymen who attended the first Conference. Wesley's sister Kezia lived for a time at the vicarage which was a frequent retreat of the leaders of the Revival, but no longer exists. Whitefield on one occasion, on his way to the vicarage for week-end services, was met on the heath by a crowd of eight hundred and preached to them on the spot which was by the pond opposite the Golden Lion. But, with growing opposition, the vicar was compelled by his Diocesan to deny the Methodists his pulpit. Whitefield, when excluded, preached in the cobbled yard of Blendon Hall, and to twenty thousand people on Blackheath, taking as his text: "And they cast him out." Long after the

Delamotte and Piers families had left the neighbourhood, Wesley visited the parish and often held services at Welling.

Shoreham, between Eynsford and Sevenoaks, for forty years received an annual visit from Wesley, its vicar, Vincent Perronet, being one of his closest friends and advisers. Each morning he preached in the vicarage and each evening in the parish church. He started the day with a five o'clock sermon, and as Arthur Mee reminds us, with William Blake fast asleep in a house close by. There were riots in the church when Wesley first came. Perronet's son Edward wrote the hymn: "All hail the power of Jesu's name." Wesley came to the vicarage to comfort his friend on the death of his wife, and again of his son. The vicar died at the age of ninety-one.

There was a Methodist curate at Ewhurst Parish Church, in East Sussex—John Richardson, who afterwards became one of Wesley's preachers. The church was crowded under his ministry, but he too was obliged to give up his curacy, and was replaced by a cockfighting parson. Wesley gave him a permanent post at the Foundery and afterwards at City Road Chapel which he held for thirty years. He was the senior of three curates at the Chapel at the time of Wesley's death and read the burial service at his funeral, when, deeply moved and because he suffered from asthma, he faltered painfully at the words "our dear father here departed". He died eleven months later and was buried in Wesley's grave. A tablet in Ewhurst Church records his memory, and electric lighting was installed in the church as a memorial gift by Methodists in 1937.

On November 5, 1769, Wesley wrote in his *Journal*: "In the afternoon we rode through miserable roads to the pleasant village of Ewhurst where I found the most lively congregation that I have met with in the county." Two years later he came again to attend a Quarterly Meeting, and in 1773 he paid a flying visit to Ewhurst churchyard to preach by the grave of Miss Ann Holman, the daughter of John Holman with whom he stayed at Court Lodge, a house which has since been pulled down.

One of the prettiest villages in Kent, Rolveden, two and a half miles from Tenterden, which preserves its long wide street of old houses, was the scene of a legal dispute with far-reaching consequences to Methodism, for it was here that Wesley following an open conflict with a magistrate won an appeal to the King's Bench. It arose out of services held in the half-timbered thatched Layne farmhouse, now known as Wesley House, in the hamlet of Rolveden Layne, half a mile beyond the church (Plate 21*b*). Wesley preached in its large middle room on the second floor, and spoke from the projecting window to the crowd below.

In 1760 a group of Methodists, thinking it more profitable after the labour of the day to gather there than to be at an ale-house, were brought before a local magistrate, Robert Monypenny of Maytham Hall (since rebuilt) and convicted under an old Conventicle act. Heavy fines were imposed which they refused to pay, distraint was made on their goods, and notices of appeal were lodged. The Maidstone Quarter Sessions confirmed the conviction, which was afterwards quashed by the King's Bench. It was a famous victory and Wesley was highly pleased with the result. He at once formed a common fund to help in such cases, to protect the legal rights of his people. And George III was also interested, for when he was asked to stop these runabout preachers he replied: "I tell you while I am on the throne, no man shall be prosecuted for conscience' sake."

The house where Wesley stayed in Sevenoaks, No. 20, London Road, is now a butcher's shop (Messrs. Luck Bros.). He preached to "a large wild company" near the free school, also at Newbourne, two miles from the town. A table which he used at the old King Street Chapel, Canterbury, is preserved in St. Peter's Methodist Church, and Canterbury Museum displays a framed Wesley letter written to an unnamed recipient. At Egham he preached in the church or churchyard. In Gillingham, the chapel he built in Prospect Row, after being used by the Navy as a store, was recently put up for sale.

Nearer London, in Chislehurst Road, Bickley, we find a tiny disused chapel, bearing the inscription "Wesleyan Chapel, 1776, Restored 1867". It is now a carriage builder's workshop, but has its original gable roof and some eighteenth-century brickwork. The land around it, when it was built, was Widmore Common. Wesley preached in this building, or an earlier one on the site, in 1772. He also preached at Reigate Priory (formerly Ryegate Place), which he describes at some length, noting particularly its fine staircase and chimney piece. The property was acquired in 1945 for use as a community centre. But Wesley hardly flattered the residents of Reigate, whom he called "dull as stone".

At Tunbridge Wells he was friendly with the Boone family. Mrs. Boone, widow of Governor Boone of South Carolina, lived in a small elegant house at Mount Ephraim which had been built by Sir Edmund King, physician to Charles II, as his summer residence. Its site is now occupied by the Earls Court Hotel. The property passed to her daughter, Miss Boone, a lady of whimsical eccentricity whose lively and original disposition found an outlet in religion. Though an ardent Anglican, she opened her home to the followers of every odd sect and creed, as well as to the poor and destitute. She was a prominent and highly respected member of local society, "rouged as for a dissipated court and clad in sackcloth as for the conventicle". We are told, "Wesley, Whitefield and their motley followers brought up the rear of a grotesque assemblage, which put religion and gravity at defiance." And to complete the scene there was her pet monkey. The house afterwards passed into the hands of Mrs. Whittaker and Mrs. Tighe, both friends of Wesley.

In the older part of the town (Little Mount Zion) in Newray Lane, a delightful steep cobbled way, is a building occupied as a workshop by the Gas Company which was formerly a chapel used by him, where he preached on five occasions. It was built in 1720 for the Presbyterians and has been used at different times by various denominations. A typical period house, New Bounds, now called Little Bounds, remains at Southborough, formerly occupied by one of his friends, Sir Thomas l'Anson, where Wesley preached in the large parlour and from its balcony. It was in this area that he ruminated on the disadvantages of country life, quoting Horace—"O the happiness of eating beans well greased with fat bacon, Nay, and cabbage too!"—and violently disagreed.

In the oak room of a fifteenth-century cottage which is still occupied, called Tanhouse at Horn's Cross in East Sussex, he preached on a wet day, when the house was "stowed as full as possible". He records that he heard the sound of the Tower guns, fifty miles away. At Eynsford where he spoke from the bridge, a boulder is still locally known by his name.

By far the best-known of the many "Wesley trees" is that in Winchelsea which is a replacement of the one under which he preached his last open air sermon. It stands nearly opposite the New Inn in German Street near the churchyard wall, and its inscription reads: "Under an ash tree that stood on the site of this one John Wesley ended his great open air ministry October 7, 1790."

In a back street running parallel with the main Square we find Wesley's old chapel (Plate 21*a*)—a red brick building with the date 1785 over the door and with a plain cream-painted interior. A flight of wooden stairs leads to the gallery, and, centrally placed facing the door, is the high pulpit in which he stood. In front of it hangs his portrait, and a plaque on the wall reads:

> John Wesley the Founder under the providence of God of the Wesleyan Methodist Church preached in this Chapel in January 1789, and in the following year, 1790, being then 87 years old, he preached in this town his last outdoor sermon from the text: "The Kingdom of God is at hand, repent ye and believe the Gospel."

In this chapel, also, is a collection box made from the wood of the original "Wesley tree", and a large piece of the trunk of the same tree is to be seen at Wesley's House in City Road, London.

Smuggling was the besetting sin of this area, especially at Rye, which not even Wesley's influence could prevent. He wrote a tract called *A Word to a Smuggler*, but "I find," he says, "the people willing to hear the good Word at Rye, but they will not part with their accursed smuggling." Thackeray, in notes he left at his death of an unfinished novel, put these words into the mouth of its leading character: "I would not go on with the smuggling, being converted by Mr. Wesley who came to preach at Rye." So perhaps Wesley succeeded better than he knew.

He preached for the last time in his life at Leatherhead. On the previous day he had dined at John Horton's in Highbury Fields and had preached at City Road at night. Though far from well he rose at his usual hour (4 a.m.) and travelled by coach to Kingston House, Leatherhead, where he held a service in the dining room. The property was pulled down in 1936 to make room for the new Council Offices. A tablet on the wall of the forecourt records the occasion and an old tree is carefully preserved under which he is also said to have preached—the site, which was originally the Fairfields Pit, provided the most natural local arena for the purpose.

The object of his journey to Leatherhead was to visit Mr. Belson, a magistrate, who lived at Kingston House, whose wife had recently died, and this was his second visit within a few weeks. Thus, though he was himself on the brink of the grave, he made his last journey to comfort a friend. A few neighbours gathered to hear him, after which he took tea before going on to spend the night at Mickleham vicarage.

Further west there is hardly a town which he did not visit. We find him in Salisbury calling on his mother who lived there for a time, preaching on Harnham Hill, in The Butts in the Old Sarum Road, in the stables of the Green Dragon, at Fisherton, then a small village on the outskirts, and in a shop in Greencroft Street. Two deeds bearing his signature are preserved by the trustees of Salisbury Methodist Church which relate to land in Church Street where the first chapel was built, which was rebuilt in 1814 and later enlarged into the present building. At a much earlier period he preached in Bemerton church, famous for its associations with George Herbert.

At Wilton, between Pewsey and Hungerford, on a bank in front of Orchard House, a "Wesley stone" marks another preaching spot. The house was formerly known as Bank Farm and its deeds stipulated that the stone should not be removed. He also preached in Pewsey Parish Church, the peculiarities of whose vicar, Joseph Townsend, are satirized in Richard Graves' eighteenth-century novel *The Spiritual Quixote*. Fordingbridge has a local tradition that Wesley preached from behind a wall in Shaftesbury Street near the stables of the Royal Arms which, before their alteration, consisted of a long building used for Methodist services.

He frequently visited the area south of Bath. In the lovely village of Ditcheat with its magnificent church flanked by a marvellous Elizabethan manor, he held a service in the spacious churchyard. It was at Ditcheat that the village stocks were removed by magistrates' order and placed opposite the preaching house for the greater convenience of putting therein any who caused disturbance to the preaching, and because of a butcher with a cleaver who swore he would bleed the Methodists.

Park House, Shepton Mallet, for many years occupied by the Allen family, is of interest as the first headquarters of Methodism in the town. Mr. T. Melhuish who has lived there for nearly half a century gives interesting details. Its large sitting room was used for services and Wesley preached from the end window which still has some of the old crooked sheet panes of the period. On one occasion he was attacked here by a hired mob who stormed the house and broke the windows, and he was obliged to escape through a back bedroom window into the adjoining fields, now the grounds of a convent. This solid stone-built house, screened by laurels, is near the town centre and, apart from its square bay windows, slated roof and roughcast, is little changed, though as I walked in its pleasant garden I found it difficult to imagine the famous preacher being bundled through a back window and over the garden wall pursued by a drunken rabble.

Wesley Cottage survives in Seend, Melksham, where he preached from its front steps. At Devizes he found the town in an uproar, fomented by an advertisement of "an obnubilative pantomime entertainment" referring to his visit. But of all the many places round here to which he came Bradford-on-Avon is the most interesting. Twelve months after his evangelical conversion he knocked on the door of Bradford vicarage at ten-thirty in the morning and asked the vicar's permission to preach in his church. The vicar replied that it was not usual to preach on week-days, but he would be glad of his assistance on a Sunday. Wesley then called on an old acquaintance who met him with arguments and said that at Oxford he (Wesley) was regarded as crackbrained. So Wesley preached at Bearfield and had lunch with "good Mrs. Bailward". A small income is still received from a Bailward legacy for the support of Methodism in Bradford.

For a time Wesley visited the town on alternate Tuesdays—fifty-two visits are recorded, after which his place was taken by his brother. In fifteen weeks they paid eleven visits. In the tiny chapel (or blindhouse—so called because of its lack of light) on the bridge, a Methodist preacher once spent a night guarded by soldiers. But what I particularly looked for was Wesley's old chapel hidden away in Market Street, formerly Pippett Street, opened in 1756, not much to look at and now belonging to the Bradford-on-Avon Club. Two billiard tables, almost lost on its wide floor space, have replaced its pews. It was empty and dreary as I sat under the gallery trying to recapture the scene when Wesley preached under the window where once the pulpit stood, and when, on one occasion, he declared he would no longer be cooped up in a room and, marching his congregation out of doors, took his stand by Bradford bridge. The friendly custodian brought me a tray of tea and said, "I don't think Wesley would have minded his old building being used for a game of snooker." His answer, I think, would depend on how far its present occupants support the fine-looking church up the hill which has replaced it. And a plaque on the wall of the old building would not be out of place. He opened another chapel later at the top of Coppice Hill (1790), but this has recently been closed, though its schoolroom is still used for worship.

At Corfe in Dorset he preached under the shadow of the Castle in the courtyard in front of Well Court which was formerly a school and, long afterwards, the studio of Mr. F. H. Newbery, who took great pains in preserving this picturesque property which is partly medieval, partly Georgian. It derives its name from the ancient well from which the Purbeck marble workers drew water for their work. The entrance is through an archway opposite the post office.

Wesley had close family connections with Dorset to which the Rev. E. V. Tanner of Weymouth recently devoted a series of articles in a parish magazine. Wesley's great-grandfather Bartholomew Westley, son of Sir Herbert Westley, was rector of Charmouth. The story goes that when Charles II, after his defeat at Worcester, was riding south in disguise he stayed overnight at the Queen's Arms waiting for a vessel to take him to France. The boat failed to arrive and the ostler at the inn, becoming suspicious, went with all speed to inform Parson Westley who was a strong Puritan. The parson, however, was at his devotions and as no one was allowed to disturb him, by the time he reached the inn the Royal party had fled. "I should have snapt him," he said, "if my prayers had been over earlier." Later he was ejected from the living and practised medicine.

His son John on leaving Oxford founded a small society in Radipole and afterwards became vicar of Winterbourne Whitechurch, but was also ejected in 1662. He was offered a house, rent free, at Preston, one of two thatched cottages on the right hand side of the road out of Weymouth, since converted into a single house. It was at one time the vicarage and is now known as Manor Cottage and occupied by Mrs. Venables Kyrke, J.P. This old thatched cottage was the early home of Wesley's father, though Wesley himself, contrary to popular belief, never knew it.

A memorial to this grandfather of Wesley was erected in Castle Street, Poole, in 1938, which read: "In the Guildhall prison which stood in the centre of the road near here, the Rev. John Wesley, M.A., first Independent Minister in Poole and Grandfather of the Founder of Methodism, suffered six months' imprisonment for conscience' sake in the reign of Charles II." His wife was a daughter of John White, the eminent divine, and a niece of the celebrated Dr. Thomas Fuller.

Persons of the name Westleigh, Westeley, and Westley, had long resided in this area. There was a nun—Isabel Westleigh—in the Nunnery in Shaftesbury in pre-Reformation days. Prebendary John Westley was vicar of Sturminster Newton in 1435, a John Westleigh was rector of Langton Matravers in 1481, and James Westley was bailiff of Bridport in 1691.

Wesley, however, paid little attention to the area. Tradition says he was urged to preach in Bridport, but replied that the Gospel was already preached there in the parish church, and his labours were needed elsewhere. But remembering these family associations, he wrote to his brother in 1768: "Such a thing has scarce been these thousand years before, as a son, father, grandfather, *atavus*, *tritavus*, preaching the Gospel, nay, and the genuine Gospel, in line. You know Mr. White, sometime Chairman of the Assembly of Divines, was my grandmother's father."

In this neighbourhood there is also Wesley House, Bourton, on the London-Exeter Road, which is reputed to be the former Goose Inn where Wesley lodged on his journeys. A house is still shown in Swanage where he stayed, and he preached in a meadow there near Manwell Lane. A tablet in the Methodist Church records an incident from the *Journal*, of a Mrs. Burt who walked from Swanage to Salisbury—forty miles—carrying her baby, and waited on Wesley after his sermon, inviting him to Swanage.

CHAPTER EIGHT

IN THE HEART OF ENGLAND—BIRMINGHAM—THE BLACK COUNTRY—HONEST MUNCHIN—AN UNPUBLISHED LETTER—FRANCIS ASBURY—COALBROOKDALE—A METHODIST PARISH—HILTON PARK—LEICESTER CASTLE—DONNINGTON PARK

DR. JOHNSON referred to "the boobies of Birmingham", and Wesley called it "a barren, dry uncomfortable place", but that was when Lichfield overshadowed it, and the city of today was but a modest place of call on Wesley's northern journeys. It was hard going for Methodism. A rugged Nonconformity born of the Five Mile Act already existed there, and Birmingham never became an outpost of the Revival. Charles Wesley was pelted with stones and turnips in the Bull Ring, and the bells of St. Martin's were rung to drown his voice. John Wesley and Whitefield followed, preaching in the Bull Ring, on Gosta Green, and in a garret in Steelhouse Lane. By 1750 a building marked "Methodist Meeting" appears on a local map, probably a lean-to shed at the corner of Steelhouse Lane and Whittall Street, which in 1751 had its pews and pulpit stolen and was burned by a mob. Later a derelict play-house was acquired in a dingy court off Moor Street.

It was a period of hard campaigning. Trade was bad, finances were small, the Circuit was poor. Items in old account books make quaint reading, such as: "Mrs. Glover, for washing Mr. Mather's shirts, 4d." The names and occupations of those who pioneered are of poor men and small tradesmen. It is a far cry from that dreary preaching house behind the alleys of Moor Street to the modern Central Hall and the thriving churches of the suburbs, and from a town of packhorses and cobbled streets to the crowded city of today. Yet give a thought sometimes to that untiring pilgrim riding up to the Bull Ring, stabling his horse at the Swan, rebuking a tramp in Erdington village, and see his shade haunting the dark courts and alleys on a summer's evening as if in the shadows a phantom congregation still awaits him. Many figures are there in the twilight; Brother

Bridgin, for instance, a steel toymaker of Steelhouse Lane, past eighty, who sometimes accompanied Charles Wesley on his tours and lived, we are told, to be 107, and even at that age could walk to the chapel.

Next comes Cherry Street, formerly Crooked Lane, where once the cherry orchards blossomed. In 1782 Wesley preached for the last time in the old playhouse and on the following day opened the new "House", which served for forty years until a new chapel replaced it. Here Wesley in his eighty-third year gave Communion to five hundred people. His last two visits are worth recording. In 1787 he reserved the whole of the coach between Manchester and Birmingham for himself and his party. They left Manchester at midnight, had two breakdowns, and after nineteen hours on the road reached Birmingham at seven o'clock the following evening. And in 1790, at the age of eighty-seven, he came by way of Stourport and Quinton, preaching here for the last time to an immense congregation, but only with difficulty because of failing sight.

Wind, rabble and fleas were Methodism's chief local trials; first the open street, then the mob, and the dilapidated playhouse. Nor must we overlook the Wednesbury riots. The Black Country opposition to the preachers was the most violent in the kingdom. The district was wild and undeveloped, an area of scattered collieries; its inhabitants rough and easily roused; its amusements, bull-baiting and cockfighting. This was forty years before the first mail coach ran through Wednesbury and when the roads were quagmires.

From Birmingham I took the Chester road, by Sutton Park with its lakes, over Barr Beacon, through Aldridge, bursting with building activity—no longer a village clustering round its ancient church—and down the hill into Walsall, crowded on market day, the town centre bright with roses and gay red litter baskets. The High Street curves up to the high Cross above the steep steps to the church with its wide view across the town to the Cannock Hills, and to Barr Beacon which stands out like a green island in the submerging tide of new estates. It was here that Wesley was more roughly handled than in any other place, thrown down the churchyard steps by an infuriated mob, beaten, and dragged by the hair down the long hill to the bridge over the stream (which now flows underground) at Digbeth.

Only the tower and chancel of the old church remain; the

rest was rebuilt in 1820. Walsall, now humming with prosperity, was a small community, mostly of miners. The streets he knew are gone or, like George Street, are dilapidated, and no trace remains of the upper room at the Castle Inn or over the stables at the Green Dragon where he held his first services. Bit by bit the old pattern is disintegrating. But I caught a glimpse of it as I looked down from the church wall upon the street below packed with market stalls and thronged with people. It was crowded in the spring sunshine, and its life and colour made it almost like a foreign scene.

The Horse Block in Wednesbury, from which Wesley preached at least thirty or forty times when it stood in the High Bullen, is in a neat enclosure in front of the premises of the Spring Head Mission, just off the main road. It originally formed the steps to the door of a malthouse against which carts were backed to load and unload. For many years after Wesley's death no special occasion was complete without a service at the Horse Block, which in 1891 was removed to its present site. It has six steps, mostly of brick and obviously restored, but the top ones are of the original stone, worn and blackened with age.

In the vestry of the Mission is the late Dr. Dingley's collection of Wesleyana which includes three items of local interest: a sugar bowl used when Wesley took tea in the cottage of Mrs. Griffiths at Hobbs Hole, the white bonnet she wore on that occasion, and the table from which he preached in her front garden. Her husband had placed it outside for the service, but when it became impossible to proceed, Wesley went into her cottage and had tea, and while he was there the crowd set fire to its thatched roof. These simple objects are mementoes of the stormiest scenes of Wesley's career. For six days there was rioting against him in this area and the persecution lasted for eight or nine months. Charles Wesley records that Wednesbury was as the mouth of Hell. Hobbs Hole is now lost in a building estate, so is Holloway Bank, and Francis Ward's house, No. 92 Bridge Street, where Wesley sheltered, has gone, its site occupied by Woden House.

Holloway Bank or the Hollow, barely a mile from the town, provided a natural amphitheatre and is said to have held five thousand people. It was near the bridge crossing the Teme, but only its name survives; when the new road was made, the Hollow was filled in. Overlooking it, opposite Hawkins Street, was John Sheldon's house, which also sheltered Wesley and

15. *Above*, Southfield Farm, Brean, Somerset, from which Thomas Hicks rode to Bristol, heard Wesley preach and so started Methodism in these parts. The Hicks family still occupy the property

Left, the house now called Wesley Café at Winchcombe, Gloucestershire, where Wesley stayed

16. Wesley had, on occasions, to escape from an angry crowd while visiting Port Isaac in North Cornwall. He is said to have preached from the window of Victoria House, *above*, and also from these steps on The Plat overlooking the harbour

where Methodism in this area was born. The first thing Sheldon did after his conversion was to sell off his gamecocks. His house, Crabb's Mill, overhung the Hollow.

Wesley attended worship in Wednesbury parish church and probably preached there after the riots had subsided. He often preached in the old Town Hall—a quaint building which stood on pillars above the Butter Market in the market-place opposite the Golden Cross Inn. It was removed in 1824. It was in his first chapel here, which no longer exists, in Lloyd Street, and in which Francis Asbury was converted, that Wesley in a crowded service suddenly put up his hand and stopped the singing, saying, "You are bleating like cows in that corner, and a man in the gallery has been singing on a false note."

The riots, provoked in part by local clergy and led on one occasion by an abusive and drunken vicar, were of the utmost severity. Charles Wesley was attacked on the steps of the Market House in Walsall, when his brother ran to his assistance. It was then that a mob from Walsall, Darlaston and Bilston fell upon him in Walsall churchyard and dragged him the length of the town, when windows were broken and the Riot Act was read. Later he made his way from the Horse Block in Wednesbury to Ward's home in Bridge Street, and the house was surrounded. As dark came on, through heavy rain, accompanied by two or three hundred of his followers, he walked the two miles to Bentley Hall to rouse the magistrate who was in bed and would not be disturbed. He went on to Justice Persehouse in Walsall and was refused admission. Then the mob came on him like a flood and dragged him to the mill dam. For five hours he was at their mercy, until their leader, a profligate collier and prizefighter named Munchin—a giant of a man—moved by Wesley's courage, rescued him, carrying him on his shoulders through the river and bringing him at midnight to Ward's door. Charles Wesley's hymn "Worship and thanks and blessing" is believed to have been composed to mark their deliverance and was sung to a tune called Wednesbury. "Thy Glory was our rearward, Thine hand our lives did cover . . . The world and Satan's malice Thou, Jesus, hast confounded." The next day Wesley rode into Nottingham, for he would allow no riots to deter him. "He came," says his brother, "like a soldier of Christ. His clothes were torn to tatters."

Every year for more than forty years Wesley came this way.

As for "honest Munchin", he became an ardent Methodist, lived to be eighty-five, and his cottage at Hollow Bank was still occupied in 1925 by his descendants. It stood by the Fountain Inn, but no longer exists. Sheldon was a tenant of the Earl of Dartmouth of Sandwell Hall who sometimes attended the Horse Block services. "When I come here," he said, "I am Brother Dartmouth." A grandfather clock from Sheldon's home, which had been wrecked by a mob, passed into the possession of Mr. J. B. Field of Birmingham. Sheldon lived to be 102 and his wife 99, and among their descendants are well-known Birmingham families. It is remarkable how many of the old names survive of those who helped Wesley in this area—the Aults, Bissekers and Partridges, the Sheldons, Hunts and Fields, the Marshalls, Botteleys and Beddoes—families with an unbroken and distinguished record of Methodist devotion continuing to this day.

Edward Hand's house at Blake Street was another property set on fire. West Bromwich Methodists also suffered. There was a preaching room in Paradise Street, opposite the present cinema, and No. 58 Paradise Street and the courtyard of Oak House, now a public museum, were among other scenes of Wesley's services. In Gad's Lane he preached under a sycamore tree, and he probably visited No. 64 High Street, the home of James Jones, one of his first recruits. He also preached at the Momble at the bottom of King Street, Dudley. Temple Street, Bilston, is named after Wesley's Chapel which once stood there, with a flourishing Sunday-school where John Etheridge, Bilston's philanthropist, taught, and the teachers were fined sixpence every time they were absent.

Cotterell's Farm, Toll End, Tipton, was another Methodist centre, and at Stourport the central portion of Wesley Church is part of the older chapel in which Wesley preached. In the pulpit of Wesley Church, Bloxwich, is a beautifully polished chair with club feet on which he stood in a street in Oldbury (Plate 22*c*). The Bible he used in Noah's Ark Chapel, Wolverhampton (since replaced by the Darlington Street Church), is in possession of Miss Hilda Horobin. Stourport has interesting connections with him, where he visited members of the Baldwin family and preached in the house of Mr. York, now occupied by a doctor, and still one of the fine houses in the town. Stamford House, in a lane in Amblecote, a mile and a half from Stourbridge, is still standing, where a trap-door, since removed, was made in the dining-room ceiling to enable those in the bedroom to hear him.

In New Street, Worcester, we find a small café bearing a plaque: "This building was opened by Rev. John Wesley, M.A., Fellow of Lincoln College, Oxford. The first Methodist Chapel in this city on Wednesday, March 11, 1772." But the building is undistinguished and its appearance gives no evidence of its former use. The notice in its window, though, would have pleased Wesley, which reads: "Cleanliness and quick service." I walked down Lowesmoor where Wesley often stayed at the White House with the Knapp family who were glovers in the city. One of his last letters was written to Susanna Knapp. He had hoped to visit her, but within a fortnight he had died and she went up to London for his funeral. Mrs. Agnes Cooke of Colwyn Bay has in her possession the following letter which has not, I think, hitherto been published:

To Mr. John Knapp
Mrs. Ann Knapp
in
Worcester
Cross Post.

Bristol
Aug. 22, 1781

My dear Sister,

I do not know where your letter stopped But I did not receive it till yesterday. I am glad to hear that your little one is better & that your Health is in a measure restored. If you can believe, all things are possible to her that believeth.

My intention was to have been with you at Worcester the Saturday after the Conference, and to have stopped on Sunday, but my being called away to London, deprived me of that pleasure.

Let Sister Farmer now watch and pray, and she need no more enter into temptation. Nay, her having turned a little out of the way for a time, may make her more wary as long as she lives.

In the contest wch was in the Salisbury Circuit, John Walker was far less to blame than his opponent. He is a good preacher and a good young man. He must be *near* yr Circuit because I have work for him to do *in* it. I am

My Dear Sister
Your ever affectionate Brother,
J. Wesley.

But to return to the Black Country. At a later day, we read in Mr. H. H. Prince's *Early Methodism in West Bromwich*, James

Botteley addressed the following lines to a girl in the choir who wore bright ribbons:

If good old Wesley now could view
And Whitefield take a squint or two
  At saints in this our day . . .

If they could view the pious maids,
In veils and lustres of all shades
  And tricks and top-knots gay . . .

If they could view the gay old dames
Lamb fashion-dressed in streets and lanes,
  Haying on Sabbath day,
To Chapel a new gown to show
With silk adorned or furbelow,
  My friends, what would they say?

Francis Asbury, pioneer of American Methodism, whose statue stands in Washington, was born in Handsworth in 1745. The house (Plate 22*a*) to which his parents removed and where he lived as a boy is in Newton Road, Great Barr, at the back of the Malt Shovel Inn. Services were held for over fifty years in its front room. It has recently been acquired by the County Borough of West Bromwich for preservation as a memorial to this Black Country boy who, when he died, had created in America the largest body of Methodists in the world. Methodism had travelled far since Wesley faced the stones and turnips of the mob and preached without a church in the wind and the rain.

Madeley in Coalbrookdale has almost a foreign look. The long reach of the Severn flows through the deep valley where terraced houses cling to the hillsides, and narrow alleys and worn brick steps climb steeply from the main street, and deserted warehouses and derelict buildings line the river. This was the scene of the first iron and china industries. Wesley records how he walked the length of the town to inspect the building of the Iron Bridge—one of the wonders of its day. John Fletcher, newly ordained, had refused the offer of a comfortable living, choosing rather to serve miners for the rest of his days in a wretched industrial parish. Few stories of the Revival are more extraordinary than that of this son of a Bernese nobleman who, after seven years' theological training in Geneva, had served as a soldier of fortune in Spain and the Netherlands, and who exercised in Madeley one of the most remarkable parochial ministries in the history of the English Church.

Madeley presented a model of Church unity. "Methodism was Church, and Church was Methodism." He introduced into his parish the entire Methodist process and organization, so that Methodism, far from supplanting or competing with the work of the parish church, fulfilled Wesley's original intention of supplementing it. Fletcher became his closest collaborator, and married Mary Bosanquet, a devoted Methodist and a great friend of Wesley.

His vicarage lies away from the town. Following the main road up the hill from the Bridge I came to the plain, though attractive, seventeenth-century house with its fine front of well-pointed brick, and its four rooms on each of its three floors, structurally little changed. For twenty-five years this was the home of Methodism's foremost saint, and during that period Wesley was a frequent visitor.

It was a moving experience to stand in Fletcher's bedroom and to pass from it into the tiny prayer chamber where we are told that up to 1951 "the breath-soiled patch on the wall opposite to his *prie-dieu* remained just as it was when he died".

The vicarage stands above the slag heaps of the valley in a setting still reminiscent of an older day, among medieval and Elizabethan buildings. But the church is not the same, and it is strange that so little has survived of the older sanctuary, which was crowded in his day. Only a small pulpit, a Jacobean Communion table, and the bells remain. A few mementoes of Fletcher are displayed, including his sword, and outside, in the churchyard, is his iron tomb. Wesley also preached in Madeley Woods, and in the same area, in Broseley Parish Church, in the Market House there, and in the Assembly Rooms.

It is no great distance from Madeley to Hilton Park, near Bloxwich, formerly the seat of the Vernons, where Wesley was the guest of Sir Philip Gibbes with whose family he was on close terms of friendship. Buried in the Record Office are ten or so unpublished letters in Wesley's hand addressed to Mary and Agnes Gibbes. Rain was dripping from the trees of the long avenue as I came to its main entrance. The house, built in 1700 and enlarged in 1830, stands with its windows opening upon the lake, and on the main lawn a sacred statue marks the present use of the property which was recently acquired by the Sisters of the Order of St. Joseph of Bordeaux. The good-natured Mother Superior with twinkling eyes told me the story of how she came to the great empty house when it was on the market, thinking it might serve as a school, and finding it unsuitable, but seeing its possibilities, she was able to secure it and transform it into an Old People's Home. And now where once the great preacher came, in these same rooms that welcomed him, the Sisters of St. Joseph carry out their good work. The former library is a dormitory, the entrance hall is a lounge, and all is sweetness and light in this home of mercy.

In Leicester we look in vain for the cottage in which both Bunyan and Wesley lodged, opposite St. Nicholas' Church. A picture of the old half-timbered structure appeared recently in *The Leicester Mercury*, and a tablet on the premises of Messrs. Dryad's furniture store marks its site. Round the corner, past Carey's Coffee Bar, is William Carey's cottage, in the old part of the city. Passing under the gatehouse by St. Mary de Castro Church, we come to the Castle where justice has been administered since the thirteenth century, though the building has been much altered and adapted, with a brick front dating from 1690, and its present appearance gives little idea of its former splendour. Here Wesley came to minister to condemned felons, and on the Castle Green is a metal plaque which reads: "On this Green prisoners from the Castle dungeons paid the last penalty on the executioner's block. On his first visit to Leicester John Wesley chose this spot to preach to the assembly."

He had a friend who was vicar of Markfield where he preached in the parish church and also at Ockbrook—a Moravian stronghold—and he stayed a number of times with the Countess of Huntingdon at Donnington Park. Between 1742 and 1748 his visits to the Park were frequent, but nothing remains of the mansion he knew. Of the thousands today who visit its race tracks, how many recall its former associations! The Park remains a fragment of English landscape as it was a thousand years ago, with its memories of John of Gaunt, Bolingbroke, and Chaucer, with its magnificent avenue of limes, its terraces and wooded glades overhanging the Trent. For generations it belonged to the Hastings family, where the widow of the ninth Earl dispensed lavish hospitality to the Methodists and Calvinists. The present Hall was built on the site of the old castle in 1795, and when the direct line died out the estates passed to a nephew, Lord Rawdon.

Derby has little to offer the Wesley pilgrim, though we must not overlook Sarah Crosby, who is depicted as Sarah Williams, the "blessed woman", in *Adam Bede*, chief friend of Dinah Morris, and was the first of Wesley's women preachers. And we must look for an old cobbled lane—St. Michael's Lane, by St. Michael's Church, below the Market, where among timbered and decaying cottages is the outline of an early chapel—a brick building with blocked-up windows, and a small shop front below. It was here that Wesley came after being prevented by rowdyism from preaching in the market-place on an earlier visit. Its lantern roof, formerly scheduled as of historic interest, was dismantled in 1956 after vain efforts to save it, and was replaced with corrugated iron. The building, in its decline, after being used by an organ builder, is now a dressmaking and corset factory. A tablet on its outside wall records: "In this building which was the first Methodist Preaching House in Derbyshire John Wesley preached on March 20, 1765." No record exists of its foundation, but it was in regular use until 1805. In its early days it had a tannery and knacker's yard adjoining, the stench of which was unbearable to its congregation on a warm Sunday.

Wesley also preached here on November 11, 1787 on behalf of the Nottingham General Hospital which he had recently visited and which had greatly impressed him. He had never seen one so well ordered, but, he wrote: "I am afraid there will not be much contributed by the poor congregation at Derby. However, I propose to do what I can in favour of so excellent a charity." A friend bore his expenses and the collection was five pounds.

It was on the road from Newport Pagnell to Northampton that Wesley overtook an abusive Calvinist and raced him neck and neck into the main street of the town. "He told me I was rotten at heart, and supposed I was one of John Wesley's followers. I told him, 'No, I am John Wesley himself.' "

What remains of Wesley's twenty-nine visits to the town? We can still see the building that was Dr. Doddridge's Academy, in Sheep Street, though altered and with the addition of another storey. This was once the town house of the Earl of Halifax, from whom Doddridge rented it. Here Wesley expounded to the students. No other local building exists in which he is known to have preached, though he may have used an old building still to be seen in Dickin's Court behind No. 109 Bridge Street.

Two of his meeting rooms, one on the Green near St. Peter's Church, the other in King's Head Lane, have disappeared. Captain Scott, of the Royal Horse Guards, an ardent Methodist, secured the use of the regimental riding school—a commodious building—in Fish Lane for Methodist services.

The site of Wesley's first chapel in Nottingham—the Octagon, near Milton Street—is now covered by the Victoria Railway Station. Before this he used the house of a Mr. James in Pelham Street, and another in Crossland Yard, Narrow Marsh, where the occupier, Matthew Bagshawe, cut a hole in the ceiling of his living-room so that the preacher stood in a raised position with his head at the level of the bedroom floor. In Newark, Wesley's Mill Gate Chapel is now a shop, still distinguishable by its architecture. He opened his Guildhall Street Chapel in 1787, travelling specially from London, and the Mayor asked for the service to be delayed in order that he and the aldermen might attend. As evensong at Coddington Church was held in the afternoon the vicar and his flock attended evening services in this chapel.

In Ashby-de-la-Zouch is the yard of the Bull's Head in Market Street where he preached, and he probably stayed at the inn. And Whittlebury Methodist Church, Towcester, preserves the pulpit he used there, and treasures a tradition that on the last day of the building of the original chapel he took off his coat and helped.

CHAPTER NINE

ASSIZE SERMON AT BEDFORD—LITTLE EASTON—NORFOLK—GAINSBOROUGH OLD HALL—A SHEFFIELD MEMORIAL—KINDER—UNDER THE CHEVIN—A TACTLESS LETTER—OLDEST HOUSE IN YORKSHIRE—THE OCTAGON AT HEPTONSTALL—HAWORTH BEFORE THE BRONTËS

BEDFORD had an Assize Sermon preached by Wesley, but he mistook the date, arrived the day before he was due and was none too pleased about it. "Had I known this in time I should never have thought of preaching it; having engaged to be at Epworth on Saturday." He stayed, however, and preached on the appointed day, March 10, 1758, in St. Paul's Church before the Assize Judge, Sir Edward Clive, and a large and attentive congregation, from the text: "We shall all stand before the judgement seat of Christ." After the service the Judge invited him to dinner, but Wesley, already delayed, was obliged to excuse himself, and rode on his way in a snowstorm. Luton Museum has a copy of the fourth printed edition of the sermon, *The Great Assize*. It was delivered from the magnificent stone pulpit, six hundred years old, with its fine traceried carving, from which on a similar occasion, years earlier, "an Assize Sermon had so offended Judge Jeffries, that he was only restrained by force from attacking the preacher." Wesley preached at other times on St. Peter's Green and in the upper room of a fifteenth-century building which formed part of the George Inn in High Street. "We had a pretty good congregation," he records, "but the stench from the swine under the room was scarce supportable. Was ever a preaching place over a hog-stye before? Surely they love the Gospel who come to hear it in such a place." Alderman Parker, a pioneer of Bedford Methodism, had a nephew, who, it was said, had the pigs fed during the hours of service to annoy his uncle.

Wesley complained more than once of drowsy congregations at Bedford and finally in desperation took as his text, "Awake thou that sleepest." "And never was more need," he says, "for a more sleepy audience I have not often seen." Once, after his friend Parker had died, he found himself homeless here. "I crossed over to Bedford, but where to lodge I did not know. But one met me in the street and said Mr. G. Livius desired I would go straight to his house. I did so, and found myself in a palace, the best house by far in the town." It stood in large grounds on the corner of Goldington Road.

Eleven miles from Bedford is Everton which had a famous Methodist vicar whose epitaph in the churchyard reads: "John Berridge, an itinerant servant of Jesus Christ". Wesley frequently stayed with him and preached in Everton Church, also in Wrestlingworth Church, near Potton, whose vicar, Mr. Hickes, was another close friend. In Luton Wesley was offered the use of the parish church, where he came on a snowy January day, and he tells us the glass had been removed from the windows on account of the severe frost, so he might just as well have preached out of doors! His first chapel in Luton was an oddly gabled building in Church Street. From Everton he evangelized many of the surrounding villages, and once in the depth of winter he preached at Harston, near Cambridge, by moonlight. He spent a night at Grantchester, preached at Melbourn, and had tea at the Bull, Royston. He seems rarely to have visited Cambridge and there is no record of his preaching there, though he spent a night there in 1731, supping at the Mitre and being entertained at St. John's College.

There is a local tradition in St. Neot's that he preached in what was formerly the Assembly Rooms, on the N.W. corner of the Cross. The room, now a warehouse, is on the first floor of the premises of the Co-operative Society. In Ely the house where he stayed survives (No. 31 High Street) along with the barn in which he preached.

Stony Stratford has an old pollard elm in its Market Square enclosed by a protecting rail with a notice saying that Wesley preached under it. He also used a barn which belonged to the Talbot Inn, which is now Nos. 81–83 High Street. The owner of the Inn, Richard Canham, was one of his leading supporters. Sir Frank Markham, M.P., in his history of Stony Stratford, refers to these sites and adds: "In 1778 the barn was leased to Thomas Allum for the use of the Rev. John Wesley for five hundred years, and the deed is now in possession of Mr. A. E. Higgs."

Wesley travelled to Colchester on the old Roman road from

Bishop's Stortford, off which, three miles from Dunmow, we come to Little Easton where Thomas Ken, the hymn-writer, was once rector. The following story is from a history of the parish, *Estaines Parva*, by R. L. Gwynne, a former rector, although there is no other record that Wesley ever preached there and he was not forty, but nearly sixty at the time. It is, however, a typical scene in the course of his journeys, and he often preached in this area.

> 1762. The following Sunday all the village gathered to the afternoon service to see and welcome the three Easton boys who had returned from the Wars. There was a gallery in the Tower, where sat the "singing men" and where also was an organ with a handle. Some seven tunes could be played on this wheezy instrument. The church was filled, everyone sitting according to his station; the males on the right, as you enter, the females on the left. When all were seated the Lord and Lady entered and took their seats in the chancel. After the service and three hymns, a very handsome man of about forty years of age entered the pulpit. He preached with an eloquence and a force which were irresistible. It was the Rev. John Wesley, Fellow of Lincoln College, Oxford, a friend of the Rector's. Mr. Wesley preached again in the churchyard and spoke of his visit to the plantations in America. The soldiers were much affected by his earnestness and one, George Raven, afterwards joined Mr. Wesley's Society, and became himself a preacher of the good news. George never forgot the text, "Fight the good fight . . . lay hold on life eternal."

The present rector tells me that there *was* a family called Raven living in the parish in the eighteenth century, also that the gallery has since been removed.

Two miles on, towards Thaxted, is the parish of Tilty where the church is the original gate chapel of the old Abbey. Near its altar is an interesting wooden chair upon which are carved the words: "My Lord and my God, John Wesley, 1776". It was acquired by the present vicar from an antique shop in Diss, but its history appears to be unknown (Plate 22*b*). Wesley stayed at the Red Lion, "the Great Inn", he called it, at Hockerill, now part of Bishop's Stortford—the dearest, he says, he was ever at; also with the Coles at the Manor House, Sundon, which Mrs. Cole had inherited from her uncle, Lord Sundon.

Wesley's first preaching place in Maldon was an old building, said to have Roman origins, known as the "Cats' Castle", because of an old lady who had previously lived there with twenty-one cats. Afterwards he opened a chapel the site of which is now occupied by Nos. 118–120 High Street, and later No. 74 High Street was used for preaching.

Colchester Town Council has marked the site of the first Methodist chapel in Essex with a plaque on the premises of Messrs. E. N. Mason & Sons, Ltd., in Maidenburgh Street. It was a twelve-sided building which Wesley visited at least thirty-two times. In front of it was the preacher's house, which at one time was occupied by Francis Asbury who became the first Methodist bishop in America. The entrance to this house is now the brewery offices next to Mason's, with gates at the side which formerly led to the chapel which had a vestry door at the rear opening into a passage to the Castle Bailey. Its pulpit is preserved at Culver Street Methodist Church along with an old Society book which has a page in Wesley's handwriting.

Further north is the parish church of Diss, with its square tower, and open arches through which at one time people danced on feast days. Wesley preached there in 1790. In Great Yarmouth one of the last remaining "rows" includes three cottages where he opened an upper room for his work. They run from the North Quay, Nos. 16–18, and bear a tablet marking the opening by Wesley of the first Methodist Mission in the town. And inland at Chubbocks Farm, Thurlton, near Loddon, an old building survives that he used. All that remains of the former preaching house in Lakenheath is a barnlike structure of 1756, scheduled as an ancient monument, which was licensed for preaching in August 1757, was visited by Wesley, and bequeathed by John Evans to the Methodists, but is no longer in their possession. It is said to be the first Methodist preaching house to be erected in Suffolk and is the last of its kind still standing.

The small village of Hempnall, nine miles from Norwich, in 1959 celebrated the bi-centenary of Wesley's visit with a service at the exact spot (and hour) where he stood at the junction of the three roads where the War Memorial stands. There was an oak tree there in his day, which was removed in 1919. Mr. C. G. Stammers gives an interesting account of Wesley's visit to a farmhouse in this area off the beaten track, occupied by John and Deborah Wheatacre. ("How did he find these remote places?" asks Mr. Stammers. "It has been said that even the man in the moon had to ask his way to Norwich.") Wesley arrived, soaked to the skin, having ridden through the flooded waters of St. Dunstan's which reached to his horse's belly, and through the swollen River Tass at Cupwade. But he made light of it. Dry clothes were produced and his vitality was irrepressible. No sooner was the table cleared than he preached, and the next morning after a bread and milk breakfast served by Peg the dairymaid, and family prayers, he was on his way.

A remarkable instance of Methodist longevity was given in *The Sleaford Gazette*, February 18, 1854, which advertised three sermons and a public lecture by the Venerable Mr. G. Fletcher of London who had been a contemporary of Wesley and was in his 108th year! Equally interesting is a pamphlet of 1840 consisting of seventy stanzas in verse "On the origin and erection of the New Wesleyan Chapel in Grantham".

> Wesley himself has stood
> In Grantham Street to preach;
> He here proclaimed the truths of God,
> And did poor sinners teach.

The chapel still exists, next to its predecessor which is now a garage.

> It stands in Finkin Street,
> The centre of the town;
> The Philosophic Institute
> Stands rather lower down.

A cottage, now used as an office, in the High Street of Winterton, bears an inscription that Wesley stayed there. It belonged to the Fowler family and Wesley preached from its front door. He preached in the parish churches of Haxey and Owston, and he declared that Newark was one of the most elegant towns in England. He took his stand in the market place of Chesterfield which was little more than a village, and occasionally he preached in a chapel in Bolsover, and also near its main street.

I had not far to look for Wesley in Gainsborough, for in its centre is the Old Hall in which he preached more than once, with its massive battlemented front of old brick and its two great Tudor wings. After a thousand years of history it was allowed to decay, but is now being splendidly restored. Near it is the old Church Lane Chapel, now occupied by the Trentside Electric Company, and which still has its original windows and door. In its office I was shown a picture of the building by a modern artist as it was when Wesley came there, with its rush roof, and when Church Lane had many fine houses, two of which adjoining the building are derelict. We must visit also the yard of the White Horse in which is a small store shed where he met his followers. He also preached in the Mart Yard and from the steps of Messrs. Swift's shop in the Market Place.

He climbed Boston Stump and preached in Raithby Church. And from Mrs. R. H. Tagg I learn of a well-established tradition that he preached in the drawing room of her Georgian house, Roydene Farm, Church End, Winthorpe. Raithby Hall, near Spilsby, was the home of Robert Carr Brackenbury, the beloved squire-preacher who at his own expense itinerated with Wesley, accompanied him to Holland, and pioneered his work in the Channel Islands. The chapel he built over his stables, although not Methodist property, is reserved in perpetuity for Methodist worship, failing the provision of an alternative. Apart from the pulpit it remains little changed. The entrance is through a stone recess in the stableyard with stone steps on either side leading to the chapel on the upper floor. The fine sounding board, two collecting boxes with handles a yard long, and the silver Communion cup survive, as well as the original box pews at the rear. After falling into disrepair the chapel was thoroughly renovated and reopened in 1936.

Wesley was in Sheffield eight days after preaching for the first time from his father's tomb and already a meeting house existed in Cheney Row, which two years later was demolished by a mob. It was probably near the main entrance of the present Town Hall. A second building at the end of Pinstone Lane fared no better, and by 1757 a factor's warehouse was used in Mulberry Lane, after which Norfolk Street became the mother chapel. Wesley visited the town forty-eight times.

He preached in Paradise Square on a site near the cathedral now in possession of Messrs. Greville and Stuart and suitably marked. A fine window in the chapter house of the cathedral depicts the scene and is full of symbolism. It shows the old church in the background, the glow of dawn, and among the crowd a man with a bandaged eye, and signifies Wesley's roots in the Mother Church, his early rising and preaching, and the persecution of his followers. In the cathedral, in the chapel of St. George which commemorates the Yorkshire and Lancashire Regiment, the oak desk which carries the Book of

Remembrance is reputed to have been used by Wesley. This box-like structure with sloping lid and pigeon holes was transferred to the cathedral when St. Paul's Church was demolished. Paradise Square, occupied today by barristers and solicitors, is well preserved, with its period houses, and paved and cobbled as of old.

As far back as 1733 Wesley had accompanied his father to Wentworth House, when the latter was consulting books in its library, and preached in Wentworth Parish Church with his father in the congregation.

Deep in the woods in the heart of Kinder is Alport Castles Farm where the old bridle track which Wesley used from Yorkshire into Lancashire runs through the farmyard. An annual love feast is held in its barn on the first Sunday in July which is unique in Methodism, having continued without a break for over two hundred years. Not far from here is the Snake Inn whose landlord in 1812 was a lay preacher. Once he walked fourteen miles to preach and found his congregation had gone to a public hanging. Not to be outdone, he went after them and preached to them under the gibbet.

Barley Hall Farm survives, at Thorpe Hesley, six miles north of Sheffield, and was the scene of stirring incidents (Plate 23*a*). Wesley stayed there on seventeen occasions, and his brother was once ambushed by a mob nearby. Wesley records that he preached under a shady tree there. Thorpe Hesley Methodism dates from 1738, and this tall, plain-fronted farmhouse takes us back well over two hundred years to Wesley's first associations with it.

The old Octagon Chapel in Rotherham has been replaced by Talbot Lane Church, but four miles east of the town at Bramley the village chapel still exists which Wesley visited. It is an attractive and well-preserved building, with a later extension, and it has the pulpit and footstool which he used, and in his own hand, in faded writing, the text from which he preached. Notice also the house opposite the chapel, which he visited, where Matthew Waterhouse, who gave the chapel, lived, and whose descendants still attend it. Half a mile away is Bramley Grange where on one occasion Wesley dined. Once, he says, when preaching in Rotherham, a donkey was one of his most attentive auditors.

He preached in the parish church of Wakefield, now the cathedral, and twenty-two years later opened a chapel in the town which is now occupied by the Society of Friends. The pulpit he used at Lee Moor is preserved at Stanley Methodist Church. An old deed at Rothwell Methodist Church, near Leeds, is of interest, dealing with the conveyance of a house, stable and yard in Butcher Lane for Methodist use, dated 1764. "For the sum of five shillings of lawful money of Great Britain," the Trustees to permit "John and Charles Wesley and whom they appoint their use for all time for ever after . . . provided also that they preach in the said house every Sunday in the afternoon and one evening besides in every week, and at five o'clock each morning, following. . . ." Wesley came here and also to Cown Chapel, Lepton. The former building was demolished and only the desk of its pulpit remains, forming part of the rostrum of the present chapel. He also visited in this neighbourhood the Moravian Settlement at Fulneck, then in course of erection.

Birstall had close associations with Wesley where he had a struggle with local trustees over the use of one of his chapels. The parish church registers contain the entry of a marriage he solemnized there. A memorial marks the spot in Ivegate, Bradford, where John Nelson, one of his preachers, was imprisoned in a cell three feet square, when his friends pushed food and candles to him through a hole in the door and remained outside all night singing. Nelson was born in Birstall. A tablet in the parish church pays a tribute to his memory, and his grave is in the churchyard. His study—a tiny building—is in the burial ground adjoining the chapel. In Thorne, Wesley borrowed a kitchen chair from Martha Meggitt to stand upon in the market-place, and whenever he came there she ironed his cuffs and ruffles. A member of the Meggitt family built a chapel in Muston, near Filey, and presented it with a chair used by Wesley, probably the above mentioned, reference to which is made in an old edition of Kelly's *Directory of East Yorkshire*.

Outside the porch of Ilkley Parish Church we find a gravestone with a reference to Wesley. It is that of George Hudson "justly celebrated for his superior skill and eminent success in surgical operations. He was intimately acquainted with the late Rev. John Wesley." At Pannal, in Hillfoot Lane, Dawcross, on the edge of Harrogate, a bronze tablet on a wall marks the site of a Wesleyan chapel "built in 1788 wherein John Wesley preached". No remains are visible from the road, but pulling

17. Digory Isbell's cottage at Trewint, near Altarnon, Cornwall. Wesley came here six times and two rooms were added to the cottage for the use of his preachers, one of which is shown *below*. Many interesting items of Wesleyana are exhibited in the upper room

18. Carines, North Cornwall, where there is a prophet's chamber. Wesley is said to have preached beneath the trees in the foreground. *Below*, the chapel at Cubert

aside the grass at the foot of the wall we find traces of its stone base.

He found that his chapel trustees could be as awkward at times as his preachers, as at Eccleshill, Bradford, where a legal deed was not drawn up to his liking. "I spent some hours," he says, "with the Trustees, but I might as well have talked to so many posts." Perhaps this explains the sentiments of one of the preachers who wrote:

> In Eccleshill they're stiff and proude,
> And few that dwell therein
> Do show they've any fear of God
> Or hatred unto sin.

Sixty years later the building was vacated, but we can still see it, though somewhat dilapidated, in Lands Lane, immediately behind the Victoria Hotel. It is used by Mr. W. N. Close, joiner and undertaker.

The large poster I saw outside Otley's ancient parish church would have warmed Wesley's heart. In bold letters it read: "This Church is for sinners only." He knew the church well and its registers contain his signature, for here he married Thomas Gill to Elizabeth Robinson. He visited the town about twenty times, mainly because the Ritchie family lived here with whom he was friendly. Dr. John Ritchie was a retired naval surgeon, his wife came from Bramhope, his son was a linen draper in the town, and his daughter Elizabeth became one of Wesley's most devoted adherents. For half a century their home, where the Otley Building Society offices stand, was open to Wesley and his preachers.

An interesting letter survives in which Miss Ritchie describes an early Methodist Conference:

> The preachers' dress has been largely debated, and what is converging towards worldly conformity is to be laid aside. We all lament dress as a growing evil among the Methodists, if the preachers are not patterns in this respect, how can they exhort the people? One morning, at breakfast, among a very few select friends, Mr. Wesley said he had some things to complain of, which he had better mention before half-a-dozen persons than before a hundred. Among other things, he spoke with disapprobation of the ruffles on Mr Dickinson's shirts.

Now the Rev. Peard Dickinson was both an Anglican clergyman and a Methodist preacher attached to one of Wesley's chapels, and this letter was tactlessly addressed to his wife. It ended: "My dear sister, let me beg of you, then, never to let Mr. Dickinson wear a ruffled shirt again. You both love our dear father too well to grieve him." We are not told what were Mrs. Dickinson's reactions!

Miss Ritchie, afterwards Mrs. Mortimer, was devoted to Wesley. He gave her his gold seal and other trinkets, and she was with him when he died, going specially to London to nurse him. When her own father lay dying Wesley had hastened to Otley, and preached his funeral sermon in the parish church.

At other times he preached in the open near the church, at the foot of the Chevin, the fine ridge on the south of the town, but the place most closely associated with him is the Drill Hall near the bus station—a plain and solid stone-faced building, with a typical chapel front and a cobbled yard at the side. This was the first Methodist chapel in the town and preserves much of its original appearance, although, within, all is bare and soldiers drill where Wesley preached to crowded pews.

In the pretty village of Bramhope the chapel to which he came has been converted into a pleasant private residence called St. Ronans. Inside all is modernized, but externally, especially at the rear, it shows its original form, while in front is the old chapel gate with its worn step. Bramhope Methodists now worship in a lovely church with memorial windows a little further up the road.

St. Peter's Parish Church, Rawdon, except for its tower, has been rebuilt since Wesley preached there. It stands above the road, with the vicarage close by, in a delightful setting and almost opposite the ancient and picturesque Layton Hall where Wesley is said to have stayed. I also visited Rawdon Hall, said to be the oldest house in Yorkshire, built in 1603 and surpassing even Layton Hall in beauty and antiquity. From the busy highway we turn by a lane into its quiet drive and can hardly realize we are only eight miles from the heart of Leeds. The house is quite unspoiled, with its gables, panelling and casements, its gracious rooms, and its coats of arms lining the walls of the oaken stairs. In its day it has lodged many famous visitors, and it is said that Wesley as an old man of eighty preached there. Colonel T. R. Nevin, its present occupant, would be glad of confirmation. In any case, Wesley preached for Lord Rawdon (afterwards the Earl of Moira) at his Irish seat and corresponded with him. The Earl had links with Methodism through his marriage to a daughter of Lady Huntingdon.

Kirkstall Forge, near Kirkstall Abbey, on the main road to Leeds, preserves a room where Wesley took refuge from a mob which had driven him out of Horsforth. Early proprietors of the iron foundry were among his supporters. He preached in Leeds Parish Church and in Yeadon, where he stayed with Jeremiah Marshall at Parkgate; also in Bingley Parish Church where on one occasion he paused in his sermon and rebuked a wealthy scoffer, fixing a keen eye on his interrupter and saying, "I heed your sneers no more than I heed the fluttering of a butterfly." His host in Bingley was Mr. J. A. Busfeild at Myrtle Grove—a Georgian mansion in the centre of the town, now adapted as Council offices. Wesley called it a little paradise. A fine beech avenue extends from the house to the river, and the grounds are now a public park.

Another of Wesley's original chapels is at Netherthong near Holmfirth, which was in regular use until recently, when it was sold to a local builder. Dry rot had attacked the roof and only after long deliberation was it disposed of, and its furnishings removed to Zion Chapel. It was twice visited by Wesley and was the sixth of his chapels to be built in England. Mr. W. Aubrook, Director of the Tolson Memorial Museum, gives the following details. When first built it was used alternately by Methodists and Independents. The parish church was hostile and an attempt was made to burn the chapel down, but Lord Dartmouth intervened by adding the land to his estate, charging the Methodists a nominal rent of four shillings and twopence (paid annually until recently), and thus established their security. The building, outwardly unchanged, has undergone interior alteration.

Mr. J. W. Hoyle, who attended it as a boy, describes it in his *Youthful Memories* as a "striking and not uncomely structure of grey gritstone, sturdily perched on the steep edge of a narrow glen and looking across toward the village crowning the nearby hill; with a plantation in the foreground, at the bottom of which murmured the clear waters of the brook and with a neighbouring pond and water wheel. . . . How many thousands of Methodist worshippers have descended the almost precipitous slope from the village, across the large stone flags that spanned the brook and then by an arduous climb to the long flight of 'catsteps' have reached the chapel!" There was no organ in those days, and an old bass player, "who could make his cello talk", led the choir. The story goes that on Wesley's departure his followers accompanied him through Hagg Wood singing the hymn: "Ye mountains and vales, in praises abound," and the silence of the night was broken by their exhilarating song:

> Break forth into singing, ye trees of the wood,
> For Jesus is bringing lost sinners to God.

Of Huddersfield he said, "a wilder people I never saw in England," but he was thrilled on later visits to find a gracious revival. He preached in the market-place and in the parish church, but a difficult point emerged, for its evangelical vicar, Henry Venn, who was an admirer of Wesley, desired him to withdraw his preachers on the ground that they were unnecessary in his parish, where he preached the same truths as Wesley. But the Huddersfield Methodists objected to being absorbed in the parish church. Venn paid a special visit to Bradford for a friendly argument with Wesley who confessed he was a little embarrassed and hardly knew how to act:

> It is a tender point. Where there is a gospel ministry already, we do not desire to preach; but whether we can leave off preaching is another question, especially when those who were awakened and convinced by us, beg and require the continuance of our assistance. I love peace, and follow it; but whether I am at liberty to purchase it at such a price, I really cannot tell.

He compromised by agreeing that his preachers should not visit Huddersfield more than once a month. He even went further and agreed to suspend Methodist preaching there for a year, but this vexed his preachers and they broke the agreement. Whereupon he wrote to his friend: "We both like to speak blunt and plain, without going a great way round about . . . I want you to understand me inside and out . . . I have laboured after union with all whom I believe to be united with Christ. I have sought it again and again; but in vain . . . I am sick of disputing." It was a candid and characteristic letter, closing with his famous appeal: "I desire to have a league, offensive and defensive, with every soldier of Christ." But it was not to be. Wesley was too far ahead of his followers in tolerance and understanding, and they, lacking his vision and always resisting him on this issue, widened the breach with the Mother Church.

Another strong supporter was the curate of Honley, who, after Wesley had preached in Honley Church, preserved the pulpit cushion which passed later into the hands of his successor, Charles Drawbridge, who highly prized it.

The stone steps from which he preached in the old White Bear Yard (now the Royal Hotel) in Barnsley have been re-erected in front of Pitt Street Methodist Church. Halifax Parish Church opened its pulpit to him, and he was often a guest at Smith House, Hipperholme, a mile or so out of Brighouse, which dates from 1672, where he preached from its galleried staircase. Heptonstall Chapel, an octagon, was erected in 1764 and Wesley preached in it before the roof was on (Plate 28*c*). He also preached in the old church at Heptonstall, now a ruin, and is reputed to have stayed at Lily Hall—a house on the steep road leading up from Hebden Bridge.

Heptonstall must be seen to be believed. Its exposed position above Hebden Bridge, the wildness of the surrounding moors, its narrow cobbled streets and closely huddled stone cottages, where every tree bends to the wind and the mist clings to the valleys, has a grey romantic beauty. Wesley came here regularly and No. 4 Northgate is still called "The Preachers' House", where the Society first met—a bright double-fronted cottage opening on to the street. The chapel in its sloping and crowded graveyard on the steep edge of the hillside is a good example of early Methodist architecture. I am not surprised that American Methodists include it in their coach itineraries, for it is well worth visiting. It was built by local craftsmen, assisted by members of the Society, but Wesley insisted on ordering the roof from Rotherham, which was brought over the moors on horse wagons, and local tradition says that when it came to the steep ascent out of Hebden Bridge scores of Methodists went to meet it, and when it was safely in the chapel yard they knelt around in thanksgiving.

The chapel was enlarged in 1802 when the gallery was extended right round it; its twelve pillars, two of which are now concealed by woodwork, are said to represent the twelve Apostles. It has a pulpit of fine mahogany and pews beautifully grained and shaped and of generous proportions. There is a remarkably good bust of Wesley, and in the vestry safe is the chalice he used. And, what is more, the chapel is well-attended and full of vigorous life. From the chapel I walked down the quaint street, which is little more than an alley with cobbles and a central runnel, to the ruined church of St. Thomas the Martyr where Wesley preached and where an annual Communion service is held in its roofless aisles.

The first Quarterly Meeting in Methodism met not far from here, at Todmorden Edge. The preaching place in Colne in Chapel Folly can be seen, with its front unchanged, but now occupied by a small engineering works. It was in this building on one of his visits that the gallery collapsed, so great was the crowd. He also visited a house, Southfields, in Nelson, which still exists.

Methodists should cherish a warm affection for Haworth, not only because of the Brontës, who came of Cornish Methodist stock on their mother's side, but also because of William Grimshaw, its one-time Methodist vicar. It was the centre of the famous "Haworth Round", and Grimshaw built a chapel there for what he called "the purer part of the congregation". Wesley (who came here fifteen times), his brother, Fletcher, Whitefield and John Newton all preached in the old church, and the Countess of Huntingdon paid two visits. The Brontës, sixty years later, must have found the village a thriving centre of Methodism. Grimshaw was an amazing character. The old church, since rebuilt (1879) except for its tower, was enlarged in 1755 to contain his crowded congregations. And when Wesley came a scaffold was erected for him to preach from on the east wall in the churchyard, behind the Black Bull, because of the multitude. I held in my hands the two enormous pewter flagons—the Grimshaw flagons, dated 1750—which were necessary for the thronged Communion services when as many as fifteen hundred at a time communicated. The top of the old three-decker pulpit is in use at the neighbouring church at Stanbury.

Haworth Church is within a stone's throw of the parsonage which is now the Brontë Museum. But the parsonage of Grimshaw's day, called Sowden's Farm, is some way from the church. I followed the path which winds out of the churchyard through the fields and came to the small moorland farmhouse with its open stone porch and massive heavily studded door, but this Tudor porch no longer serves as an entrance, and apart from these features the building is disappointing, and altered and modernized within. Wesley and his friends came here many times.

Grimshaw's old chapel, built in 1758 (opposite the Sun Hotel), has been demolished because of dry rot. Its fine mahogany pulpit, and Communion table and rail, along with a mural memorial, can be seen in the present chapel which was formerly a part of the Sunday-school adjoining the old building. And before we leave Haworth let us look in the Brontë Museum for Charlotte Brontë's copy of Wesley's edition of Thomas à Kempis, given to her by her aunt and inscribed "Charlotte Brontë—Her book".

CHAPTER TEN

YORK—PUMP YARD—THE "PRIEST" OF OSMOTHERLEY—ELIZABETH TYERMAN'S COTTAGE—YARM—THE DALES—WHITBY

WESLEY visited York no less than twenty-six times, each of which is carefully tabulated in a booklet by E. W. Dickinson. To trace his steps we must poke about the lanes and alleys of the city, and we must begin with Pump Court. It was Pump Yard in his day, and it lies off Newgate Street, near The Shambles, where an iron gate opens on to a courtyard hemmed in by offices. The only visible link with Wesley is the quaint projecting window of his first preaching house, on the ground floor of a firm of architects, Messrs. Stansfield and Burton (Plate 24*a*).

His first sermon in York was in College Street, Bedern, in a chapel of the Countess of Huntingdon. He was forty-nine at the time and his wife and step-daughter were with him. On the previous day he had been pelted with stones in Hull and had been obliged to drive off in a borrowed coach, packed with nine people, in which, he says, he was well screened by a large lady who sat in his lap.

On the following day he fared little better at Pocklington, where it rained and a fair was in progress, with little hope of a congregation, and he preached in a barn. Afterwards he rode into York through Walngate Bar and found the city plastered with posters denouncing him as a papist.

A year later he reached the city from Robin Hood's Bay and preached in Pump Yard. "Hot as an oven," he said; it was hot weather and the room was crowded, but this small, often crowded, room served the Methodists of York for five more years. It was not a poor and humble group which met there. "Many of the rich and honourable crowded in among us," he records, and describes it as the richest Methodist Society in the kingdom, comparable only to that of Cork, and expressed the fear that his preachers might become enervated by such affluence. "Capua corrupted Hannibal," he said, using one of his favourite quotations. Another time he declared that his York congregation was by far the genteelest since he had been in Edinburgh.

But the oven, as he called it, proved too small and stifling, and in 1757 during a heat-wave he marched his Pump Yard congregation into Blake Street, now a main shopping centre, where he preached under the shadow of the Minster. The next day he set about finding more convenient accommodation and went round the city soliciting gifts. Dr. Cockburn, an old schoolfellow, gave him a hundred pounds. Two years later Wesley preached in Pump Yard for the last time, then transferred his flock to their newly-built Peasholme Green Chapel in Aldwark, which is now a warehouse occupied by a firm of ironmongers, Messrs. Hardy and Holgate, and has little evidence of its former use. The gateway and passage remain, though not the original gate, and the preacher's house adjoins. A tablet on the outside wall reads:

> This building erected in 1759 was the first and for forty-six years the only Wesleyan Chapel in York. John Wesley conducted the opening Service on Sunday, July 15, 1759 and preached here on many subsequent occasions. Its use as a Wesleyan Chapel was discontinued in the year 1805.

This unpretentious building has been the scene of many exciting occasions. Wesley presided here more than once over the York Circuit Quarterly Meeting. Here he dispensed Communion to hundreds at a time. Here in 1780 he was angry on learning that morning worship had been discontinued, and demanded an explanation. Here he publicly censured a York printer, who was a lay preacher, for issuing a hymn-book without his authority, though he breakfasted with him at 3 a.m. the following day at his host's in Lady Plackett's Yard, and all was harmony when he entered his coach to leave the city as the clock was striking four.

In this same building he was welcomed by eager and crowded congregations. When it proved too small, the benches were removed to accommodate the crowd, and later two side galleries were added at a cost of £75. Here, when he was eighty, at a memorable service, many were in tears and a fire seemed to run through the congregation as he preached. And here he came for the last time, at the age of eighty-seven, preaching on the Saturday evening and twice on the Sunday—"a prodigy of the age," wrote the editor of the *York Courant.* Wesley's host was Joseph Agar, who was later a sheriff, and who gave large sums to Methodist funds. There is a tradition that on that same Sunday Wesley also preached at All Saints. His diary records the visit, but it may have been only to worship in that lovely Norman church which has one of the finest lantern towers in the country.

On a Sunday morning, twenty-six years earlier, after preaching at eight o'clock in his own chapel, he attended morning service at St. Saviourgate. The rector, to whom he was unknown at the time, seeing him present in canonical dress, sent the sexton to inform him that the pulpit was at his service, and Wesley preached to "an elegant congregation". After the service the sexton said to the rector, "Sir, he is the vagabond Wesley you warned us of!" To which the rector replied: "Ay, we have had a good sermon." Wesley preached there many times afterwards and had close links with it. The church survives, though dreary and deserted, and is used as a store by the Castle Museum.

He also preached in St. Mary's, Castlegate; St. Michael and All Angels in Spurriergate; St. Maurice's (since demolished) and St. Margaret's in Walngate. There is a nice story about the latter. Among Wesley's supporters was its churchwarden, Samuel Wormald, Joseph Agar's friend, who asked if Wesley might be allowed to preach in St. Margaret's. The vicar sent this gracious reply: "The Vicar presents his respectful compliments to Mr. Wormald, and assures him that Mr. Wesley is very welcome to St. Margaret's pulpit tomorrow."

At Poppleton Wesley preached in the main street and the churchwardens called out the bellringers to drown his voice. He travelled fourteen miles on to a lonely house in Foggathorpe, and Mr. E. E. Townsley of Vancouver recalls that the Manor House at Foggathorpe (which formerly belonged to his uncle) had two window-panes (since removed) inscribed with a text and Wesley's name. At Howden Wesley stayed at Portarlington Hall with his friends, Henry and Mary Bell. He was always happy at Swinefleet, where he preached in the parish church and under the elms outside it. He loved these villages of the Wolds where the "lantern saints" came down the lanes in the dark to his services.

Forty miles north of York is the moorland village of

Osmotherley where a terraced road winds round the hillside to its wide and quiet street. Originally it was a strong Roman Catholic settlement with a Franciscan Friary, and within a mile are the extensive ruins of Mount Grace, a fourteenth-century Carthusian Priory, but the village is also full of memories of Wesley. His first acquaintance with it was under curious circumstances. A priest, or former priest, Father Watson Adams, had called upon him in Newcastle, saying he had heard so much about the Methodists that he could not rest until he had come to find out more about them. "I told him," said Wesley, "he was welcome to stay as long as he pleased, if he could live on our Lenten fare." Adams stayed for a week and returned home well satisfied with his journey.

A week or two later Wesley preached at the Buck Inn at Northallerton when Adams was in his congregation along with a Quakeress from Osmotherley, Elizabeth Tyerman. Adams invited him to preach in his house at Osmotherley and, though it was late and he had already travelled over fifty miles that day and preached three times, Wesley immediately rode the seven miles of hilly road to the village, where the inhabitants were mostly in bed. Adams, however, roused them and soon had collected a congregation in his Franciscan chapel. It was midnight when Wesley got to bed, but he was up and preaching again at five the next morning, and some of the congregation had waited up all night for fear of not waking in time to hear him. His hearers, made up mostly of Roman Catholics, were deeply moved, and Elizabeth Tyerman asked for baptism and Wesley baptized her in her own cottage.

Adams, it seems, had been a Franciscan priest who had married his housekeeper, and continued, for some reason, to live in the Presbytery. This plain stone double-fronted house in the main street is now a private residence, with an upper room reached by an outside staircase still in use as a Roman Catholic chapel. More than once Wesley stayed in this house and after more than twenty years came for the last time when Adams lay dying to pay his respects to his old friend. He also preached in the parish church, in the churchyard, and from the Market Cross where he used the ancient five-pillared barter table.

The small stone-built sanctuary which, a stone's throw from the Cross, hides itself up a quaint cobbled path next door to Elizabeth Tyerman's cottage, is one of the oldest Methodist chapels in the world. Think of Wesley as you tread that path and of his "popish" friend and of the Quakeress, and of how often they came that way together—a strange trio united by the grace which transcends all barriers! What a story could be written of those more than twenty years of Wesley's Osmotherley associations! Yet today the chapel is not used except as a Sunday-school! Luke Tyerman, who was converted there, in his *Life and Times of Wesley*, deprecated its discontinuance as a place of worship. "The local Methodists forsook it for a more pretentious building, not a whit more adapted to their needs and destitute of the unequalled memories belonging to the ugly but venerable pile, now left, we fear, to rats and ruin." It is not, however, an ugly building—its very quaintness makes it picturesque, and it has not been left to decay, but it calls for a worthy renovation as a unique memorial of Wesley in these parts.

The Society book of the old chapel is in the possession of the Misses Dobson who live opposite Adams's house. Its survival is providential, for many years ago it was thrown accidentally on the fire and only narrowly escaped destruction, since when it has been insured, although no insurance can replace this faded quarto volume of thirty-four closely written pages dating from 1750 (Plate 25*a*). Entries recording those who "preach'd hear" include: "1752, April 27, 28. Laid out for Mr. John Wesley, Wife, Daughter, Wm. Shent, John Haime, 5s. 2d. . . . June 18, 1772 Ye Reverend and Pious Jon Wesley preached here. Ex." —the "Ex" presumably meaning excellent. Miss Dobson also showed me the pulpit stool, four or five inches high on four wooden pegs, used by Wesley on his visits.

In Northallerton he preached in the dining-room of a house which is now the Golden Lion. Yarm also has strong Methodist associations, where George Merryweather fitted up his hayloft for services. An old inhabitant of a century ago never tired of describing Wesley's visits which she remembered as a child—his cassock, black silk stockings, large silver buckles, and lumbering old carriage with a bookcase inside it. She remembered how he had asked her to help him on with his cassock and she had to stand on a form to do so and he had thanked her and said a short prayer. Once with a playmate she accidentally ran the pole of his carriage through Mr. Merryweather's parlour window! She recalled also that a maid, on entering Wesley's bedroom, found his coachman rolling himself vigorously up and down the feather bed, and wondered what on earth he was up to. He explained it was because his master would not sleep in it until it was made as hard as possible. The house still stands in the High Street and is little changed since Wesley stayed there, though the quotations from Young's *Night Thoughts* scratched on the window-panes of the front bedroom he occupied and of a downstairs room can hardly be attributed to him. The hayloft, which was at the rear of the house, has been demolished.

Yarm has the oldest Methodist octagon chapel in the world (Plate 28*b*). It dates from 1763 and is the second oldest chapel to be in continuous use for Methodist worship. You will find it tucked away in an alley behind the High Street. The original building, of small red brick known as Old Flemish, has had its walls heightened and a gallery and organ added along with outer vestries, and its pulpit has been replaced. But the erection in 1873 of a large entrance porch of white brick, with two staircases to give better access to the gallery, is out of harmony and obscures the older part of the building.

Turning to the Dales we find that Wesley frequented them all, often in rain and blizzard, along rutted tracks and bridleways. In Swaledale, some miles beyond Reeth, is the small village of Low Row by the tumbling waters of the river with an overgrown Methodist graveyard behind the Institute. If we climb to the north of the village we reach the green plateau known locally as "The Blades" which is ringed round with five old cottages. Here, with his back to Prospect Cottage (now replaced by a modern cowshed) and facing the wide moorland stretch towards Reeth, Wesley preached when he came that way. We may well wonder how in such a place he secured a congregation, but there were lead mines in the neighbourhood. The high grass land extends further up the ridge towards Gunnerside and along its smooth stretch, known as "The Barf", the miners used to race their ponies. Wesley too would come that way from the Dales beyond. Now the old cottages have been modernized and are used as week-end retreats.

In Teesdale, at Newbiggin, is the oldest existing Methodist chapel in continuous use since Wesley's day, but we had difficulty in finding it. The rain was teeming down and the beauty of the hills was lost in the downpour. At Middleton we stopped by the cattle market and inquired for Mr. Philip

Beadle, who was pointed out to us among the cattle pens. It was a fortunate encounter, and with much useful information he soon put us in the right direction.

The chapel, erected in 1760 and enlarged in 1860, stands above the Alston Road which runs up the Dale, and on the old road to the lead mines. It is a sturdy stone building in excellent external condition, with its neat walled yard facing a meadow and with a line of white cottages in the lane behind strung along the hillside. It made a bright picture in the clear rain-washed light (Plate 23*b*). But the interior is disappointing. There is a stepped floor with a dozen varnished pews, an enormous long-funnelled coke stove, and two cane-bottomed chairs by the plain Communion table. Its homely pulpit, used by Wesley, with an old Bible box and a folding ledge for kneeling, was brought from Field Head, the hillside farm where Methodism in Newbiggin began.

For two hundred years this chapel has borne an unbroken witness. Such chapels were built frugally, often out of the pockets of the poor. This was erected for about sixty pounds and when it was built it had fifty-seven members. Today Newbiggin is little more than a hamlet; in those days the Dales were prosperous with lead mining and were more thickly populated. The London Lead Company, which was controlled largely by Quakers, built dormitory accommodation near the mines, and the combined Quaker and Methodist influence resulted in strongly supported religious enterprise. We also visited Low Houses where, after Field Head, the Teesdale Methodists met for ten years and were visited by Wesley—a small white-walled farmhouse up a lane just off the main road below the chapel.

He preached also in Middleton Parish Church, a mile from Pickering, which has Saxon origins and a Norman arcade with massive pillars and arches leading to the north aisle and a sounding board above its pulpit beautifully engraved with a star. The division of the village of Hawnby into an upper and lower part is a direct result of Methodism, because an unsympathetic landlord turned the Methodists out of their homes. There were forty of them who, when driven from the upper village, built little houses round their chapel down by the river. Wesley, who came here, refers to this in his *Journal*.

John Leland in his nine-volume *Itinerary* describes Whitby as "a great Fisher Toune", with a new "key, rokkes and a cliffy shore". But not only fishermen lived in its crooked streets. Wesley a century or so later found it full of weavers, sailmakers, shipbuilders, and workers in the alum mines. An affectionate and modest people, he called them—"not a ruffle nor a fashionable cap among them". He preached on the hill with its 199 steps (191 in Wesley's day); under the cliff to those who could not climb the hill; on the green above the church, where the bells were rung to disturb him; and in the market-place.

His octagon chapel, Ebenezer, in Henrietta Street, which "ill-contained the congregation", suffered through subsidence, was rebuilt seven stories high on piers, lasted fifteen years, and collapsed (providentially, says Wesley) through a landslide. Wesley Chapel replaced it—a curious and depressing building, recently demolished, which had a lofty front and forty steps up to its entrance. Whitby people must be good climbers.

When Wesley arrived to open it, the building was unfinished; there was no front to the gallery and to prevent accidents a row of stout Yorkshiremen sat on the edge with their feet dangling over the heads of the congregation below. Because the stairs were not yet in place people entered the gallery by a ladder through the windows, and so great was the crowd that Wesley had to be hauled in through a window near the pulpit. But all this was meat and drink to him. He was back in the pulpit at five the next morning and his services continued at night and on the following Sunday, with an extra one thrown in for the sake of the country people. It was a golden summer for his Whitby followers.

Among them was Daniel Duck, vicar of Danby, who always went over to hear Wesley, and a copy of whose diary survives. On Wesley's first visit his members were meeting in houses near Boulby Bank at the top of Capleman's Yard, and at the New Way. He stayed sometimes with a builder, William Ripley, who helped to establish the Whitby cause. There is still a Ripley's Yard in the old town.

At Robin Hood's Bay Wesley's old chapel, perched precariously on a crumbling cliff, is tumbling into the sea. Its south wall has the date, 1779, with a sun-dial. I remember preaching there on holiday visits and the thrill of standing in Wesley's old pulpit. The property was sold about thirty-six years ago, when the Manor House was bought and adapted for Methodist worship. There was a quay in the Bay in Wesley's day, and he preached both there and in the Square. He visited the town eleven times.

There are few places in this area that he left unvisited. At Guisborough a table was provided for him to stand upon in the market-place, but there was so strong a smell of fish that he was almost suffocated. It is said that he stayed a night at Hunmanby Hall. The Rev. J. L. Webber, who lived in Hunmanby sixty years ago, says that Lady Mitford who then occupied the Hall showed him the bedroom in which Wesley is supposed to have slept. There is no record of the visit, though Mr. Webber in seeking confirmation found it supported by a very strong tradition in the Mitford family which no one had ever questioned. In 1784 Mrs. Osbaldiston lived at the Hall and is mentioned in Wesley's *Journal*. "We stopped in a little town where Mr. Osbaldiston lately lived, a gentleman of large fortune, whose lady was as gay and fashionable as any." The little town is almost certainly Hunmanby, and the old Hall is now a well-known Methodist school for girls.

He preached in the yard of the White Horse Inn, in Hengate, Beverley, and in Hilton Yard. "Not a rude word," he says, "as we rode from one end of the town to the other." He slept in a tiny room, described as a powder cupboard, at No. 47 North Bar Street Within (probably the shoemaker's house mentioned in his *Journal*). Mr. Victor Mallet, who formerly occupied the house, tells me that his bedroom opened upon this small room with its wasp-waisted iron fire-place.

In the vestry of Bishop Burton Parish Church, near Beverley, is a fine bust of Wesley, carved from the trunk of a giant elm under which he once preached on the Green. When the tree fell in a storm about 1825 the Squire, Mr. Richard Watt, had the bust carved and presented it to the local Wesleyan chapel, but so little was it regarded by the Methodists that years afterwards it was sold in a sale of work to raise funds. The vicar, the Rev. W. A. Pearman, bought it for £2, and twitted the Methodists for selling their master for forty pieces of silver! He found, however, that the bust was in poor condition and badly worm-eaten and sent it to a firm of wood carvers to be treated and received it back as good as new and placed it in the vestry. The foreman, who soaked it in paraffin and reconditioned it, was evidently a wag for he entered the following item on his time-sheet: "To re-baptizing John Wesley, and curing him of worms, 25s."

19. Gwennap Pit, Cornwall, the scene of famous gatherings of Methodists from Wesley's time to the present day

Left, at Methrose Manor Farm Wesley held Quarterly Meetings and baptized children in this font in the little courtyard. Direct descendants of those who entertained Wesley still live here

20. The third prophet's chamber in Cornwall—Alice Daniel's cottage at Rosemergy which, it is hoped, will be restored, for it is worthy of Methodist pilgrimage

Left, the pulpit at Hea Moor Wesley Rock Chapel near Penzance which is built over a stone from which Wesley preached in a nearby field

Below, Wesley's telescope, now in St. Ives Museum

In Bridlington the bells were rung to disturb Wesley's service in the priory churchyard, and he moved on to the market-place where he doubled his congregation. He also gave a sermon at Bridlington Quay "to a stupid and ill-mannered congregation". The house and yard where he lodged are in the High Street of the old town.

At Selby, he stayed always at Barlby Hall, two miles from the town. Selby gave him a warm welcome. So great was the crowd on his first visit that he was obliged to preach in a garden, which is now the entrance to the Park, near the present chapel. Christopher Oboe's house in Andus Street, Gowthorpe, since rebuilt, was a "pilgrims' inn" for the preachers. The first meeting-house was in the Leeds Arms yard in Wade Street, since removed by slum clearance, but the old chapel in Micklegate has survived as a marine and rag dealer's warehouse and is the building to which Wesley came. At the age of eighty-five he broke all records, beginning with a sermon in the main street and visiting within four days Hull, Hotham, Market Weighton, Pocklington, Thirsk, Ripon, Thorne and York, preaching in each place and twice in York.

The quay in Hull was thronged when he arrived from Barton. He preached in Holy Trinity and in a field near Great Thornton Street. The first meeting place was in the Ropery where on one occasion, following an attack, the congregation was imprisoned all night. The Methodists then acquired Henry the Eighth's Tower—a relic of the old Suffolk Palace—and met there, later pulling it down and building the Manor Alley Chapel on the site. Until recently a tree at the corner of Beverley Road and Clough Road was known as "Wesley's Tree". When George Yard Chapel was opened, Joseph Benson, one of his preachers, wrote to him eulogizing it, to which Wesley replied: "If it be at all equal to the new chapel in London I will engage to eat it." However, he was delighted with it on his next visit, when he again preached in Holy Trinity and dined with the vicar. When he came two years later forty of his supporters set out from Hull in chaises and on horseback and met him in Beverley, but he was now a tired and aged man and while they were at their meal in the inn he slipped away unnoticed.

CHAPTER ELEVEN

NORTHUMBRIA—A CITY MEMORIAL—THE ORPHAN HOUSE—GATESHEAD FELL—A RUNAWAY COACH—THE CAMBO THORN TREE—LOST VILLAGE OF PLESSEY—ALLENDALE—A SHATTERED ROMANCE—BLANCHLAND

FROM London to Bristol—the largest city of the West—then diagonally across England to Newcastle in the warm-hearted north, Wesley spread his lines of communication. And in Newcastle-on-Tyne a granite obelisk and drinking trough provided by the city honours his memory. It is in Sandgate down by the harbour where at seven o'clock on a Sunday morning he first took his stand with one of his preachers and, with hardly a soul in sight, began to sing the Old Hundredth. In the afternoon a crowd listened to him on the hill by the Keelman's Hospital. Eight months later we find him taking his Newcastle followers to Communion at All Hallows Church, and holding services in a room in a narrow lane which is now Lisle Street. Then he bought a piece of land outside the Pilgrim Street Gate, though he had but twenty-six shillings towards a building scheme of seven hundred pounds.

Here he erected his famous Orphan House—a complete misnomer, for it was never an orphanage, but, like his London and Bristol headquarters, a community centre including a school and bookshop and used mainly as a hostel and for preaching. It was a clumsy ponderous pile with a wooden shanty on the roof for his study, a courtyard in front, a small garden and stable behind, but it housed one of the first Sunday-schools in the country, with an attendance of a thousand scholars, also a Bible Society—fifty or more years before the British and Foreign Bible Society existed. It had, in course of time, one of the finest choirs in the north, which included two brothers afterwards famous, Lord Eldon and Lord Stowell, and its musical tradition is continued to this day by the choir of Brunswick Chapel.

On a cold March day, only three months after the stonelaying, Wesley preached at its opening. It mattered little to him that it had neither roof, doors, nor windows, and that he had no funds. He stood among the scaffolding and preached on the parable of the Rich Man and Lazarus, and that night among the bare walls by lantern and moonlight he held a midnight service.

Here he came year after year, met his preachers, held his Conferences, and was nursed in an illness by Grace Murray. It was here that Alexander Kilham was ordained. It was near the Pilgrim Gate outside the walls, among fields and farms where the cobbled street ran out to the Town Moor.

This building served for a hundred years and was replaced by a Wesleyan day school. In 1957 I watched its demolition—a dreary scene of broken walls and piles of rubble. Outside its boarded front in Northumberland Street the shopping crowds passed by oblivious of its two centuries of history obliterated in the dust. In the changing pattern of the modern city nothing remains of the original building except its keystone and a stone head of Wesley from over the entrance preserved in Brunswick Chapel. In the street behind, in a narrow and congested corner among the yards and warehouses, I found a small stone shed which seemed to be the only structural survival and where possibly Wesley stabled his horse, but this too has now disappeared. A large shoe store now occupies the site, No. 51 Northumberland Street, with a plaque on its wall referring to its former history.

Brunswick Chapel, opened nine years after Wesley's death, lies round the corner, and with one of the largest congregations in the north preserves to a remarkable degree the tradition of the Orphan House. It has also a collection of precious Wesley relics, though it is strange that a room is not set apart for their better preservation and display, Mr. Fox, who looks after the premises, produced them from the vestry cupboards! In the safe is the original deed of the Orphan House conveying the property to Trustees for "charitable uses", dated March 15, 1745, with Wesley's seal and signature. (A letter exists in which Wesley calls John Stephenson, a prominent citizen, to heel for not dealing with the matter more promptly. "Three months are passed, and that article is not fulfilled. And now you say you can't conceive what I mean by troubling you. I mean to have that article fulfilled. I think my meaning is very plain.")

Of particular interest is the Communion plate from the Orphan House—three pewter cups, one of them damaged as if by fire or burial, and two love-feast cups; also Wesley's pulpit drinking glass on a pewter stand; and his own faded copy of his *Primitive Physic*. More general items consist of the trustees' minute book of the Orphan House, old class tickets, and a collection of early Methodist literature including a fascinating volume of portraits of the first three generations of preachers (1730–1812). Among framed engravings on the premises is one of the Orphan House, and a good one in colour of Wesley preaching in Hospital Square which deserves to be reproduced. It shows him, after speaking from the stone steps leading to the upper storey of the Guildhall, being protected from a hostile crowd by a fishwife, Mrs. Bailes. A muckle woman, as one called her, she protected him by throwing her arms around him and saying in local dialect: "If ony yen o'ye lifts another hand to touch ma canny man, a'll floor ye direckly," and she ran by his horse's side down to Sandgate, saying, "Noo touch the little man, if ye dare!"

St Andrew's was the parish church used by the Methodists: "our own Church," says Wesley. In its churchyard is the tombstone of Wesley's step-daughter and son-in-law, Jane and William Smith, with a reference on it to Wesley and to Mrs. Wesley's burial in Camberwell. It was in this church that Grace Murray married John Bennet, with Charles Wesley present.

Dr. K. Shallcross Dickinson of Linby has in his possession a wooden "easy chair" given to him by a descendant of Andrew Marshall. It has a brass plate on its arched back which reads: "In this chair sat John Wesley, M.A. for rest and refreshment, the honoured guest of Andrew Marshall, in his house in Pandon Dene, Newcastle-on-Tyne. 1742–1784."

In his eighty-seventh year Wesley visited the city for the last time, when his sight was so feeble that he could not see to give out the hymns, but his voice was still strong and his spirit remarkably lively. He preached to the children in words of not more than two syllables. He then left for a three weeks' tour in Scotland, travelling as far as Aberdeen, and on the return journey covered the distance from Glasgow to Dumfries, about seventy miles, in a single day. But his strength was almost exhausted and when he attempted to preach few could hear him, but from there to Carlisle and Hexham and back to Newcastle came the tireless traveller, facing crowded congregations.

He was invited to preach in Lamesley Church on Gateshead

Fell, but the vicar changed his mind and he preached instead in the Methodist Chapel ("hot as a stove," he says). Sir Henry and Lady Riddell of Ravensworth Castle with many of their household were present. Wesley spent two days in administration—transcribing the stations of his preachers and drawing up a plain deed for the settlement of his chapels, saying, "I will no more encourage that villainous tautology of lawyers which is the scandal of our nation." He then left for the last time the city he loved and recorded this tribute: "I know no place in Great Britain comparable to it for pleasantness. A lovely place and people."

And then, as if all that were not enough for so aged a veteran, instead of driving homewards, his carriage took the road to the hills—Weardale, Stanhope, Durham, back to Sunderland, through Hartlepool, Stockton and York, down the Yorkshire coast to the fishermen at Whitby and Robin Hood's Bay, inland to Pickering and Malton, and on to Scarborough, Bridlington and Hull.

He often crossed Gateshead Fell which in winter, he says, was "a great pathless waste of white". Low Fell Wesley Memorial Church has several interesting mementoes, including a pane of glass, bearing a text and his name, which is one of the original window panes of two rooms called Wesley's Rooms which adjoined the original building, the site of which is now occupied by the manse. A mahogany table and wall cupboard from them are preserved, also a large stone on which he stood under a tree on rising ground a few yards from the old chapel and preached to the crowd which could not be accommodated within. Low Fell is now a thickly populated suburb of Gateshead. He paid thirty visits to the town. Ravensworth Castle, scene of the Northern Tattoo in recent years, was rebuilt in 1808. Lamesley Church can be seen from the train, on the left, going north approaching Low Fell station. Wesley once arrived there without his preaching robes and waited until a woman on horseback fetched his black gown from the Orphan House—if he had preached without robes it might have been said that he had left the Anglican Church, a notion which at all costs he was anxious to suppress.

An old man of these parts within living memory described Wesley as "a bonny little man, with such a canny nice face", wearing "knee breaches, black stockings, and buckles on his shoes, wiv his bonny white hair hanging on his black gown, and a clean white thing like two sark necks, hinging down on his breast".

Old memories of Low Fell are preserved in a memorial tablet to William and Jane Bell:

> They builded better than they knew,
> The conscious stone to beauty grew.

He was a baker, and he and his wife when they died left their house to Methodism. Thomas Wilson in a north country book called *Pitman's Pay* (1826) wrote: "During their lives they entertained gratuitously all the preachers sent hither on duty, both itinerant and local. . . . An excellent Sunday-school which was established in January 1789, is attached to this chapel. . . . Above 100 children are taught here by the hard-working industrious men connected with the chapel. Their labours for many years have been unremitting, and productive of much good to the population of this neighbourhood." And Samuel Barnes, the village schoolmaster, wrote this epitaph:

> Here lies the corpse of William Bell,
> The great good man of Gateshead Fell.

Wesley visited the Fell on Whit Sunday, 1784, soon after they had both died, and was obliged to "preach abroad", because of the multitude moved by their death.

Modern Gateshead is so full of churches it is difficult to realize that with the exception of St. Mary's, and St. Andrew's, Lamesley, the old chapel was for a long time the only place of worship in a wide area. The population of the town was seven thousand, and the main road north from Birtley ran, not as now through Low Fell, but through Wrekenton and down Sheriff Hill; and in Gateshead through traffic was by way of Bottle Bank, a steep and narrow street, before ever Church Street existed.

The rector of Sunderland, John Hampson, was an ex-Methodist preacher. He had formerly been curate of St. John's Church, near the docks, where we find among the handsome brass pillars forming an extension of the altar screen an inscription recording that Wesley preached from its pulpit, and in its old collection journals are entries of two charity sermons which he preached there. He was described at the time by an eye witness as "the venerable man, moving down the aisle, with tremulous step, leaning on the arm of Mr. Hampson, the clergyman". It is also of interest that the first extended biography of Wesley was written by Hampson and published in Sunderland.

On the north bank of the Wear is the ancient church of St. Peter's, Monkwearmouth, parts of which, including its Saxon porch, date from 674 and existed in the days of Bede. Wesley preached there a number of times, the vicar being a friend of his, and in 1944 a united service was held there commemorating Wesley's evangelical conversion. Years afterwards C. F. Andrews, before his ordination, served there as a lay reader.

At Whickham, outside Newcastle, is the old Swalwell Presbyterian Church just above the market-place, now used as a schoolroom. Wesley, when preaching in the market, was invited by its minister to come in out of the rain and use his church, and he, wet from head to foot, thankfully accepted.

Charters Haugh Chapel, one of the oldest buildings in the Fatfield area between Sunderland and Durham, was converted from a disused engine house which once served Charters Haugh pit and Wesley preached from its pulpit. Prudhoe, nearer Newcastle, has a stone in the wall of its Council Offices marking yet another of his preaching sites.

Among the few remaining eighteenth-century buildings in the picturesque village of Horsley, on the main road between Newcastle and Corbridge, is a house in which Wesley stayed and preached and where Charles Wesley lived for ten weeks when he evangelized the area. For a hundred and thirteen years it served as a meeting-house, and Whitefield as well as the two Wesleys preached from its doorstep. The house, which was formerly thatched, lies at the west end of the village and is now the home of an artist, Mr. George Muris, and has a petrol filling station attached to it. Wesley's initials—J.W.—which he is said to have carved, are in the stonework beside the door. Jonathan Simpson occupied the house in those days, a maker and repairer of farm implements, who made a reading desk for the preachers' use—a homely affair, now at Wesley's Chapel, London, where until recently it was used for luncheon hour services in the forecourt. It is an interesting relic—tall, slender, with a kneeling ledge and a wooden candlestick.

John Downes, one of his best preachers and something of a genius, came from this village. Of his mother, Wesley said: "A splendid woman, and not sixpence in their home!" The Horsley painting of Wesley was taken from a carved engraving made by Downes with a pointed stick which he whittled for the purpose. And a clock he made out of bits and pieces is in Carville Chapel, Wallsend, and still goes after two hundred years. A mile and a half from Horsley is Nafferton Farm, near the Roman wall, where Wesley also came, now occupied by the Agricultural Department of King's College, Newcastle.

Once when travelling from Newcastle to Horsley, Wesley's horses bolted and his coachman fell off the box. It happened at Benwell Hill and Wesley had with him his step-daughter and her two little girls. "The horses," he says, "flew down the hill, like an arrow out of a bow." It was an alarming experience. They careered over the narrow bridge across Denton Burn, turned into the Chapel House farmyard, then through a gate "as if it had been a cobweb", and ended up in a cornfield on the edge of Walbottle Quarry.

A letter from Mrs. Katharine Trevelyan led me to Saugh House, near Cambo, twelve miles from Rothbury, where a service is held each June under a thorn tree in memory of Wesley. The house lies back from the main road as it runs northward from Cambo. Through a gate at its side leading into a field we find a small copse enclosed with iron railings, and a stone, recording: "John Wesley preached here on his 79th birthday, June 17, 1782." The enclosure is part of the Wallington estate presented to the National Trust by Sir Charles Trevelyan. Wesley stood under a thorn tree, and the present tree was planted by the late Sir George Trevelyan to replace the original. It is known as Wesley's Thorn and is included in the volume published by Country Life, *Historic Thorn Trees in the British Isles*.

The Cambo Women's Institute Book—an interesting local production—also gives details. Cambo was a mining neighbourhood with a colliery in the Pit Field and another at Saugh House. Pack-horse roads and the main coach route ran through the village. The Chevy Chase coach passed that way, and Capability Brown, the landscape architect, was educated at Cambo School. The *History of Northumberland* quotes an old inhabitant: "I've seen 5 or 6 carriers' carts loused (loosed) up yonder. They came up from Redesdale and sometimes stopped the night at the Old Highlander or somewhere and went on to Newcastle. The railway put a stop to all that." The Old Highlander is still there near Wallington House—an unlicensed inn, for Sir Walter Trevelyan was a temperance reformer who allowed no public houses on his estate. When Wesley travelled there the village was a lively community, with spinning, stocking making, as well as mining, also cockfighting and smuggling, and with the heads of the country folk stuffed with fears and fancies of warlocks, witches and boggles.

A story of Wesley's Thorn Tree has passed into local folklore. In those days the farmer at Saugh House, called Cook, was a noted fiddler, popular at every barn dance and harvest supper. But on the day that Wesley came he was so impressed by the sermon that that same night he buried his violin under the thorn tree and never played again.

Further north we find Wesley preaching in the market-places of Morpeth, Alnwick, Wooller and Berwick, and in the lovely village of Felton he spent a night at the Old Angle Inn, now a private house.

We searched for the lost village of Plessey, or Placey, as Wesley calls it, and we should have by-passed it but for Lady Ridley of Blagdon. Details of it are given in her *History of Stannington Church*, including the following interesting reminiscence.

> An old man called Mr. A. W. Richardson, aged ninety in 1956, wrote to me when I was compiling material for the village history and said: "My grandparents often talked of their early days at Plessey and I remember Grandfather telling of what old residents told him when he and Grandma first settled in Plessey in 1836 about John Wesley coming to Plessey every time he was going his rounds. It appeared from what the old people said that John Wesley didn't always have a cordial reception. For some reason or other half the villagers were against him and so bitter was the feeling that it amounted to regular rows and fighting."

This whetted our curiosity, and we searched among the stubble fields with their grassgrown humps and hollows of buried walls and outcrop coal. At South Sholton Farm Mrs. Nicholas Ridley put us on our way, past the level crossing and a row of cottages with an odd-looking tower in a field, to Plessey Hall, former home of the Earls of Plessis, where the Earl of Derwentwater is supposed to have hidden during the Jacobite rising, and on to Plessey Mill Farm, which is pure seventeenth century in a lovely setting, with its ancient mill by the river. But Plessey village still evaded us until, at the cross roads, we found Mr. Burman who has lived there for seventy years, and under his guidance the buried village came alive.

Only two of its cottages survive. The former toll gate, the Three Shires Inn, the smithy in the quarry—all have gone, but behind the cottages is the ancient wagon way along which the coal was carried to the coast. There were seven coal shafts by the river, before the colliery was closed in 1815, when its three hundred miners were moved elsewhere and the village was pulled down.

A few hundred yards back along the road by which we had come, past the six-acre field called Plessey Checks where the houses once stood, is an iron gate on the right hand side of the road, beyond which a terraced path with wide views overlooks an extensive and overgrown quarry, deep and wide and ablaze with gorse. Wesley knew a good preaching site and nowhere in Britain could he have found a better. Here in this wooded and sheltered spot he preached to the miners of Plessey.

Interesting letters survive which he wrote to Lord Ridley's ancestor, Sir Matthew Ridley, Bart, M.P., who was Mayor of Newcastle at the time. In one he said: "I have no fortune in Newcastle. I have only the bread I eat, and the use of a little room for a few months in the year." In another he offered to preach daily to the soldiers—fifteen thousand of them—then encamped on Newcastle Town Moor, concerned for their welfare, "and I desire no pay at all for doing this."

Allendale in those days, with its lead mines and smelt mills, had a larger population, and the spacious Square of Allendale Town was crowded for the Friday markets and half-yearly pay days when Wesley sometimes preached. They were rough cock-fighting crowds. Jacob Rowell, a notorious cockfighter, was converted, and became one of his preachers. On one occasion Wesley was driven from the churchyard and stoned outside the Golden Lion. He then took refuge in the woods across the ravine by the church, where he preached in a circle of beech trees which can still be seen in the grounds of the Deneholme Hotel.

"Follow the path," said Mrs. Simpson of the hotel, "keep to the hedge and you'll come to it." So I took the path to the right of the hotel by the deep and wooded ravine, past a field of cabbages to a seat commanding a wide view with the church tower showing above the tree tops, and followed to where the path dipped steeply into the depths of the wood where the trees, shutting out the sky, were like ghosts in the twilight. Suddenly the beech circle lay below me, unmistakable, like a fairy ring, with a small rock, a foot high, at one end, offering a natural stand for a speaker and commanding the full length of the glade. It was like Nature's own cathedral with its tree-lined slopes and its long aisles of beeches reaching into the darkness.

Keenley Chapel, a few miles from the town, though greatly altered, is the oldest Methodist chapel in the north of England. Its trust deeds go back to 1750 and are among the oldest in Methodism, specifying that the Trustees "shall from time to time and at all times for ever hereafter take care that a Preacher or Preachers appointed at the yearly Conference of the Methodist Preachers . . . preach and expound God's Holy Word in the said house at convenient times" according to Wesley's doctrines.

The chapel, with a runic cross on each of its two gable ends, stands on high ground with magnificent views. Two wicket gates lead into a triangular graveyard where Wesley preached under a sycamore, and behind the chapel is a fine avenue of beeches and the entrance to Forest Hall, where only a single cottage remains of the farm buildings which Wesley knew.

The most romantic survival of Wesley's visits to these parts is Hindley Hill, the scene of his final parting from Grace Murray, but only a barn and broken walls remain of the original buildings (Plate 26*a*). This isolated farm, two miles from the chapel, reached by a long steep lane from the main road, was occupied by James and Hannah Broadwood—a branch of the family which produced the Broadwood piano. A later farmhouse now faces the ruins of the older one across the farmyard where chickens roost among the rotted beams and crumbling walls, with part of it used as a barn stacked with farmgear and sacks of meal. Its walls are stout enough for a fortress, there is a gaping window in the rear, the stone casements are decayed by frost. Above are the dilapidated remains of "the Long Room" where Christopher Hopper, who lodged there, kept a school, and which was used for Methodist worship. Poking among the nettles and rubble I found the stone entrance step, worn down by age, with holes at each side which held the door posts—a good souvenir for a local church or museum, for Wesley preached from it on three occasions. And two old fireplaces remain, one hidden behind piled up sacks of grain.

Grace Murray, Wesley's Newcastle housekeeper, had just nursed him through an illness, and Wesley, susceptible to those who nursed him, had resolved to marry her. "She nursed the preachers," says Elsie Harrison, "and broke their hearts," and drove the women mad with jealousy. But no romance was ever less romantic. Sliding into it, he knew not how, he had said, "If ever I marry I think you will be the person," and had actually entered in his diary: "My marriage would bring little expense if I married one I maintain now, who would afterwards desire nothing more than she had before." But Charles Wesley was horrified when he heard of it, and Grace had another suitor—John Bennet, one of the younger preachers and with a private income.

Such was the situation when Wesley reached Hindley Hill with Grace Murray and two of his preachers. In his own mind the matter was settled, but her feelings were confused. She was naturally surprised and flattered; to have two such strings to her bow could hardly have been disagreeable to an attractive widow. At all events, she arrived at Hindley Hill as Wesley's prospective bride, and the affair was the talk of Methodism.

But not for a moment would Wesley allow feelings of the heart to interrupt his work and within the hour he was off to Whitehaven, with Grace Murray watching him mount his horse and ride on his way. He had intended returning for her within a few days, but then came Charles Wesley's swift intervention. He rode post-haste from Bristol to Newcastle and on to Whitehaven, and after a stormy interview with his brother, crossed the fells to Hindley Hill and burst in upon Grace Murray. What he said we hardly know, but two hours later he had her riding pillion behind him to Newcastle and within the week saw her safely married to Bennet in St. Andrew's Church.

In 1947, at the Circuit bi-centenary, a pilgrimage was organized to Hindley Hill, led by Dr. Leslie Newman who impersonated Wesley. With others in eighteenth-century costume he rode on horseback to the farm and a film was made of the proceedings.

At High House, in the same neighbourhood, is another chapel, built in 1760 and visited by Wesley. It stands forty yards from a patch of land known as Wesley Garth where a thorn tree under which he preached is carefully preserved by the Weardale Rural District Council, and is throwing out new shoots.

Over the hill in Weardale is the enchanting village of Blanchland where he preached in the churchyard, by the Cross on the left hand side, when a row of children sat through his sermon as quiet as mice under the churchyard wall. He had travelled from Newcastle and the moors were white with snow; and here in the lovely valley of the Derwent he had come upon the Abbey ruins which stand across the market square and had been impressed by their splendour. He probably held a service in a room of the Crewe Arms, an ancient hostelry with a unique interior, originally the Abbot's house. In one of the old houses of the village, formerly the monks' warming-house, Mrs. Gowland gave me details of Bay Bridge where Wesley preached under a tree which some years ago fell in a gale, and where the Methodists were obliged to build their chapel outside the village, because land was refused to them in Blanchland.

Returning to the north of the county, we find Wesley in 1764 riding over the sands to Holy Island, which he describes as "once the famous seat of a bishop: now the residence of a few poor families who live chiefly by fishing." He preached to the inhabitants in what was once the market-place, "and distributed some little books among them, for which they were exceeding thankful."

He seemed fond of islands. When in Scotland he visited the Bass Rock, off North Berwick, formerly a state prison. After a rough crossing he landed with difficulty, climbing on hands and knees, and found the Castle inaccessible. He was an accurate observer, and naturalists find interest in his reference to the Solan geese (or gannets) which breed by thousands on the sides of the rock, and lay but one egg "which they do not sit upon at all, but keep it under one foot (as we saw with our eyes) till it is hatched."

CHAPTER TWELVE

FROM SEVERN TO SOLWAY—SHREWSBURY—CHESHIRE—"PEAR TREE PREACHERS"—THE OLD PORT OF PARKGATE—BISHOP RYLE—NEW MILLS—BUXTON

It was August and Shrewsbury sweltered in the sun; only the river was cool, stippled with gold as it caught the sunlight. In this cheerful town, with its handsome castellated railway station and profusion of antiquities, I made for Fish Street for it was here at No. 1 that Wesley preached on his first visit, having travelled up from Wednesbury, with a sore throat, a pain in his side, and on a miserable beast. The narrow street of Tudor inns and cottages was crowded with sightseers, curious to see his arrival. "When I came in," he says, "my head ached, as well as my side. I found the door of the place where I was to preach surrounded by a numerous mob. But they seemed met only to stare." His next visit was in a snowstorm, after being battered by hail and storm, when one of his horses collapsed on the way at Church Stretton.

The small double-fronted house still stands, in excellent order, with its bright paint and hanging baskets of geraniums. The ground floor—the scene of the preaching—consists of two panelled rooms, with movable screens dividing them, and a smaller chamber, now a bedroom, where the preacher stood in full view of the congregation in both rooms.

A romantic background lies behind this plain-fronted house which opens directly on to the street and faces St. Alkmund's Church. A poor woman who earned her living mending stockings had been converted in London. Back in Shrewsbury, as she visited from house to house in the course of her work, she built up a small Methodist group, and so successfully that the Presbyterian minister, the Rev. Job Orton, declared that "this poor stocking-mending Methodist" had converted more sinners than he had by all his preaching.

Next we meet with John Appleton, a prosperous currier, Warden of his Guild and a Freeman of the city, who had been shocked, when on a visit to Bristol, by clerical opposition to the Methodists and on his return took a house, fitted up a room for preaching and became a lay preacher. Later he rented the Shearman's Hall, now demolished, at the top of the High Street—a fine building in its day, but which, with the decline of the clothing trade, had deteriorated and after ninety years' use as a playhouse was adapted for Methodist worship. After this a commodious chapel was built by Appleton in Hill's Lane at his own expense, but this also has disappeared. So high was Wesley's regard for this devoted currier that when he died he turned out of his way to preach his funeral sermon.

There are others who come into the picture—and a fascinating picture it is: the Loxdales, the Hattons, the Hills of Hawkestone, the Lees of Langley, the Powises of Berwick House (where Wesley also preached), Captain Scott, the ill-fated Lady Glenorchy, John Fletcher—then a young Swiss tutor at Tern Hall and not yet ordained—and the hospitable Mrs. Bridget Glynne. What a tale could be told if only we could recover the colour and quality of that lost age, with its solid social and family background and closely integrated life! "I preached," Wesley records, "at Shrewsbury to a large congregation among whom were several men of fortune."

Mrs. Glynne usually entertained Wesley as her guest in her comfortable home in Dog Pole. When he made the long journey from the Black Country—and he made it many times—fifty miles at a stretch on a winter's day, he would come past Weeping Cross, through the Abbey Foregate, up Wyle Cop into Dog Pole which was then the opulent area of the town, thankful no doubt to reach her welcoming home. Fine period houses still stand in Dog Pole, but Mrs. Glynne's is unidentified.

Here, then, was the pattern—aristocratic, evangelical, and well-flavoured with a humbler element; the saintly Fletcher, the warm-hearted currier, the poor stocking-mender; and the room with the folding walls in the narrow, dingy and ill-paved street, where Wesley, having changed and eaten, stepping down Bear Steps from Dog Pole, preached to the eager company which awaited him. In the bright sunlight it was not easy to recall those murky nights, with the oil lamplight sending its fitful gleam through the shadows or those cold dark dawns, with the sprightly preacher stepping out of the gloom, but history and devotion are written in every part of that cobbled street. And Fish Street retains its shape and atmosphere. The old inns are there, the tumble-down buildings, Grope Lane and Butcher's Row, with the magnificent Abbot's House round the corner—all as in his day, the street still cobbled, with paved wheel ruts for the passage of a single cart.

On the London Road, four miles out, on the banks of the Tern, a white mansion marks the site of Tern Hall, a family seat of the Hills, ancestors of Lord Berwick, to which Fletcher came as a tutor and where he preached his first sermon, close by, in Atcham church. It was on the river bank that he met "a pious domestic", and as a result, along with an excise officer, formed a Methodist group. In later years Wesley desired him more than any as his successor, but he declined the prophet's mantle and in the end pre-deceased him.

Berwick House lies on the other side of the town, on the Baschurch Road. Wesley preached in the chapel in its grounds—the only Anglican pulpit save those of Madeley and Broseley opened to him in the whole of Shropshire.

Chester Methodism began in the Tarporley area, at Alpraham, near Beeston Castle, where as far back as 1744 a religious group met for prayer and Bible study in the vestry of Bunbury Church. It had the approval of the Bishop of Chester who presented it with a copy of Burkitt's *Notes on the New Testament*—a hefty volume, afterwards chained to the wall of the church where we can still see it. Later, however, the group met with some opposition and was transferred to the house of the parish clerk and schoolmaster—a black and white cottage still standing below the church. Afterwards, it removed to the Moat House Farm in the next village of Alpraham, the home of Richard Crawley, whose pious enthusiasm is reflected in the rules which he drew up and sold at a cost of a penny for display in his home and those of his friends. The fifth rule reads: "We neither receive nor pay visits on the Lord's Day, for we and our House desire particularly on that Day to serve the Lord."

To this farm, in due course, Wesley came by invitation. It happened through an Alpraham girl, Ann Smith, in service in London who had heard Wesley preach and had been converted, and who afterwards became the wife of Dr. Whitehead, Wesley's physician and biographer. Through this girl and her mother news reached Crawley of Wesley's next visit to the north, and he invited him to Moat House Farm and informed him that

21. The chapel at Winchelsea where Wesley preached in 1789. *Below*, Wesley House, Rolvenden, Kent

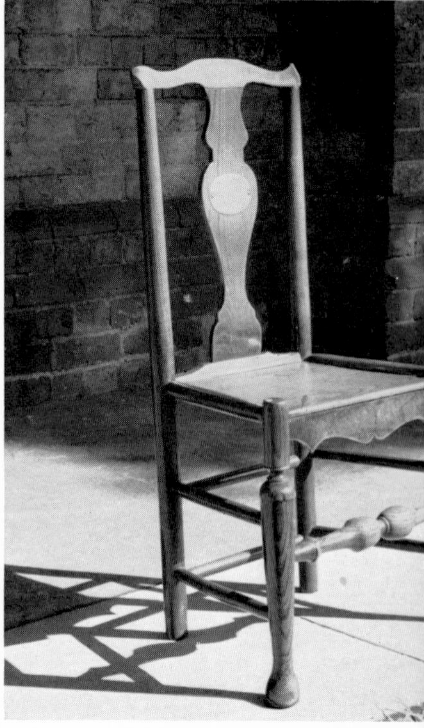

22. The home of Francis Asbury—pioneer of American Methodism—in Great Barr, Staffs. *Below*, a chair at Tilty Parish Church, Essex, which is carved with the words "John Wesley 1776", and, *right*, a chair now at Bloxwich, Staffs, on which Wesley stood to preach to a crowd in Oldbury in 1773

the vicar of Acton would allow him to preach in Acton Church. The vicar, however, later withdrew his permission.

This was the first of a number of visits Wesley made to Alpraham, and the farm is still there in Whetnall Lane (Plate 26*b*)—a picturesque, brick-built, ivy-clad farmhouse with lattice windows, and an immaculate lawn overlooking the remains of its ancient moat. It was rebuilt about 1840, but in appearance is little changed. It was an open house to the early preachers, and Mr. Arthur Cheers, the present occupier and a good Methodist, preserves its tradition.

He showed me the orchard where Wesley preached at five o'clock in the morning, before the villagers went to work. It was under a pear tree, where the preachers took their stand Sunday after Sunday and because of it they were called "Pear Tree Preachers". When, a hundred years later, the tree fell in a gale, it was replaced by the Tollemache family of Peckforten Castle who owned the estate. Squire Tollemache wrote to the Methodist minister:

> Until I received your letter I knew nothing whatever of the interesting associations connected with a farm of mine, called the Moat House, in Alpraham. Had I been aware that John Wesley once preached under a particular pear tree on my estate, I should have taken the greatest care of that Tree, and provided against its being blown down. I cannot say how sorry and annoyed I am to hear of the disaster that has befallen this tree. I quite approve of another being planted in the same spot, and when I hear it is planted, I will have it surrounded and protected by a good fence.

So there today is the new pear tree, though now itself showing signs of age, and with a stone inscription recording Wesley's visit and commemorating the introduction of Methodism into Cheshire.

But even in this quiet spot rioters, well supplied with liquor, found their way and were dispersed by Mr. Davenport of Calveley Hall. Davenport, who had heard Wesley preach in Bath, invited him to the Hall and on his departure asked him to promise to visit him on his deathbed. The Hall was demolished five years ago.

After calling on Mrs. Ada Jackson, a descendant of two well-known families of Wesley's era—the Hichens and the Jacksons—I made my way back to Bunbury church which is dedicated to St. Boniface. The vicar, the Rev. Maurice Ridgeway, is well-informed and deeply interested in local Methodist associations.

He showed me the church vestry where the first group had met, out of which came later the Alpraham and Chester Societies. Methodists today should cherish a warm affection for this magnificent church, the proportions of which are almost those of an abbey. Its earliest foundation was a wooden church in the eighth century, followed by a collegiate church in the fourteenth century, much of which remains, though a landmine, dropped during the war, caused serious damage and also destroyed the forge opposite, where Wesley stood to preach on Good Friday, 1751, before going into the church.

Chester was a frequent calling place on his way to Ireland, and in the course of fifty years he visited it no less than thirty times. It became the head of a flourishing circuit which included Manchester, and even Madeley in the Black Country. And he had many personal friends there—the Crawleys, the Wallers, the Gilberts and the Briscoes—solid citizen families. On his first visit he brought his bride—the banker's widow. And from Chester he addressed the solemn appeal to his preachers, to be opened and read after his death, exhorting them to stand together.

The Chester of today, with its narrow streets blocked with cars and its week-end crawl of coastal traffic, is a noisy nightmare compared with its quiet atmosphere when his horse clattered over its cobbles. But the pattern is unchanged: the walls on which he walked still encircle the inner city; the Rows which he admired remain, also the Roodee, where he preached. He had a high opinion of Chester. "The greatest convenience here," he records, "is what they call The Rows; that is, covered galleries which run through the main streets on each side, from east to west, and from north to south; by which means we may walk both clean and dry in any weather, from one end of the city to the other."

George Catton of Huntington Hall was the first to open his home to the preachers, followed by Richard Jones, a tobacco pipe manufacturer, who lent his house in Love Lane (now Love Street), after which a barn was fitted up—a large and lofty structure with a gallery—on the north side of the old Square, opposite the church of St. Martin's of the Ash. The Square was much larger than now, and buildings cover most of its site. Here, in the oldest part of the city, where to this day ancient names like White Friars, Black Friars and Grey Friars survive, Wesley preached on his first visit after an open air service near St. John's Church. A tablet on the wall of St. John Street Methodist Church suitably records the occasion.

On this visit Wesley was suddenly recalled to Bristol and on returning to Chester nine days later found that a mob had damaged the preaching house. "Were there no magistrates in the city?" he asked. That night in a further riot the house was destroyed. But, undaunted, he preached near its ruins and afterwards attended service at St. Martin's Church where the vicar in his sermon denounced the outrage. His followers resumed their meetings in Love Lane and with great energy rebuilt their preaching house in the Square.

A letter in my possession, written by Wesley to one of his preachers at about this date, shows that his work in Chester was well established and mentions Sister Barlow of Manchester who "has both a searching and healing spirit", whom he hopes will remove to Chester.

There were signs of disturbance on his third visit, when he acquainted the mayor, who called out the town crier to proclaim throughout the city that any further trouble would be severely dealt with and threatening the Riot Act. The mayor was probably Thomas Broster, and among disturbers who were brought before him and castigated was a brother of Sir Richard Perrins.

Meanwhile the cause prospered and a new site was secured on the Boughton side of the city, now in the City Road area, where in 1764 an octagon chapel was built. There was no City Road in those days and, of course, no railway station; the area has entirely changed and the chapel has disappeared. It stood on or near the site now occupied by the City Road Presbyterian Church, which has an interesting old print of it hanging on its vestry wall. The approach to it was by an avenue lined with small houses and gardens leading out of Foregate, between the present City Road and Seller Street. A manse adjoined it with a large and pleasant garden. Chester was one of the first circuits to provide comfortable quarters for its ministers.

In those days there was a stout postern gate called The Bars, a little below Love Street, dividing Foregate from Boughton, "not far from which," reads a 1789 Directory, "stands the Octagon, a chapel where a numerous and respectable body of Methodists regularly assemble." The chapel was built on Wesley's recommendation in the form of an octagon. Six years later a Conference direction was issued: "Build all preaching houses, if the ground will admit, in the Octagon form. It is best for the voice, and on many accounts more commodious than any other."

It was decided to provide a belfry, but a bell could only be used by permission of the bishop. The bishop agreed on condition that he preached the first sermon in the new building, but this was too much for the Chester Methodists, who smelt a rat, suspecting an episcopal consecration. Their descendants today would give a different answer.

Among the many stained glass figures in the cloisters of the cathedral is one of Wesley, the work of the late Archibald E. Nicholson, taken from a portrait and showing Lincoln College in the background. A brief biography beneath it mentions Wesley's power as a preacher and refers to him in generous terms as "undoubtedly the greatest religious influence in eighteenth-century England". Anglicans, it adds, must bear a considerable part of the blame that his followers became separated from the Church and "reunion must be the object of the prayers and aspirations of all".

Parkgate, a thriving port in those days, was often used by Wesley on his Irish journeys. Now sands and salt marshes cover the wide estuary where the tide once carried a busy ocean-going traffic, when boats anchored in Shotwick Creek and waves lapped the churchyard wall. For centuries the river, even as far up as Chester, carried army convoys and the ships of traders. But by the mid-eighteenth century the New Quay at Neston had been abandoned and Parkgate became the port of the river, with a regular service of packet boats to Ireland, and with ferries across the Dee to Flint and Bagilt, which was the shortest route from Liverpool to Wales. A steam packet, *The Ancient Briton*, made three journeys on every tide. And three times a week a mail coach ran between Parkgate and London.

It also developed as a holiday resort, with a theatre and Assembly Rooms. "You can't think how soult the water is," wrote Mrs. Emma Hart, afterwards famous as Lady Hamilton, "and there is many laidys bathing here." But she complained that it cost her a shilling a day for a bath horse. "It is great expense and it frets me when I think of it." We can still see the house where she stayed, facing the Chester Arms, and, across the fields, the cottage where she was born—the daughter of a blacksmith.

This was the Parkgate Wesley knew, mentioned repeatedly in his *Journal*. Its sea front today wears a sad and deserted air. The sea has receded and the salt marshes, covered with samphire and sea pinks, stretch as far as the eye can see. Only the stables remain of the former Pengwern Arms, now the Boat House Tea Rooms. The watch house faces one of the old slipways. The Assembly Rooms with their ornamental iron balcony are a private house. The old customs house is next to the Chester Arms. And Mostyn House School—the main building facing the estuary—has replaced the George Hotel where in all likelihood Wesley stayed, as well as Handel and other notabilities.

Half a mile up the lane to Neston, on the right-hand side and opposite some charming Georgian houses, we find a tablet on a wall which reads: "John Wesley preached near this site in the small house, 1762." This refers to a chapel which once existed there. Three years later he was obliged to wait two days in Parkgate and visited Liverpool. When delayed on another occasion he preached "to most of the gentry of the town", and morning and evening the following day. In 1787, finding no boat, he booked a place on the Holyhead coach, but when roused by the porter at 2 a.m. he was told that the coach was full. Wesley says that his fare was refunded and he took a post-chaise which overtook the mail coach at Conway and he arrived in Holyhead an hour ahead of it. His last visit to Parkgate was in 1789 when he disembarked with his carriage in which he had sat during most of the voyage from Ireland.

Turning to the Potteries, he was often in Burslem, and in Newcastle-under-Lyme he lodged with the mayor and called it one of the prettiest towns in England. He preached in its market-place, and its museum has a weatherworn stone head of a preacher in bands (probably Wesley) removed from the Ring O' Roses inn, now the site of a car-park. Nearby we can see his old chapel with its gallery stairs, but otherwise changed out of all recognition and used as a workshop.

From Stoke to Macclesfield we pass Mow Cop—mecca of radical Methodists, a grim and stony Zion rising from the foothills. And in Macclesfield there is Roe House, a Georgian residence (now divided into two—Nos. 65a and 67 Roe Street) where Wesley was a welcome guest. At No. 65a I found Mr. and Mrs. Gunby well aware of its history, and their two boys told me that when a door in the house bangs mysteriously they laugh and say, "There goes Wesley's ghost!"

No. 67, which takes in the larger part of the original house, has the Adam fireplaces, gracious drawing-room and vaulted landing ceiling of his day, and the handsome sweep of stairs up which more than once he carried his bedtime candle. It has a plain exterior, its door opening direct from the pavement, but inside we walk straight into the eighteenth century, and its well-preserved interior, in contrast, almost takes our breath. Here Hester Anne Roe, an interesting figure in early Methodism, lived as a girl with her uncle who was mayor of Macclesfield and its leading manufacturer. This goes back to the days of water power, when Macclesfield with its silk mills was an early and a thriving, though small, industrial community. Her father had been vicar of St. Michael's, Macclesfield's parish church, which with its chained copy of Foxe's *Book of Martyrs* had once known a Presbyterian in its pulpit.

His brother, Charles Roe, was a button and twist manufacturer, shrewd, self-made and the town's wealthiest citizen. But, though evangelical, he was antagonistic at times to the Methodist tendencies of his family, his proud heart torn between the claims of piety and worldly prudence, and strange stories are told of his harsh treatment of his sons. This old house has known its hours of tragedy and drama. Hester Roe pleaded at one time to be allowed to remain as a servant rather than be cast adrift on account of her Methodism. And there was a tragic night when a great coach drawn by six horses lumbered up to the door, having travelled from Bath, carrying two of his sons, and a bed on which lay the lifeless form of their brother who had been ill and had died on the way.

In Christchurch, the clock tower of which can be seen at the end of the street, we read the glowing eulogy on the monument erected by Charles Roe's widow and ten children lamenting "a most indulgent husband, a tender father, and a general loss" and recording that "he provided at his own expense the elegant structure which encloses this monument . . . Reader, when thou hast performed the duties which brought thee hither THINK OF THE FOUNDER OF THIS BEAUTIFUL EDIFICE And aspire after the Virtues which enabled him to raise it."

He built the church for the ministry of David Simpson, curate of the parish church, one of Wesley's younger friends, and a pioneer of Sunday-schools, and under whose fervent evangelism Hester Roe had been converted. But his preaching proved too evangelical for St. Michael's and led to his suspension. This provoked protests and Charles Roe built Christchurch for his use—but also, it was said, with a business eye on its potential pew rents, graveyard fees, and building plots in the pasture land attached to it.

In this spacious galleried church with its high pulpit (not the old three-decker Wesley used, nor the same Communion table), its box pews and wide central aisle, Wesley preached to crowded congregations. He described the church as by far the most elegant in the kingdom—a flattering over-statement—and also remarked on its fine organ, which, though he may not have known, once belonged to Handel. Little Sarah Maclardie, the organist's daughter, twenty-two years later became the wife of Dr. Jabez Bunting who was four times President of the Methodist Conference.

On Good Friday 1782 Wesley preached twice in this church and gave Communion to thirteen hundred people, and on the following Sunday he again preached twice, with eight hundred communicants. The same evening he went on to preach in the Methodist chapel and afterwards held a love feast. He was approaching his eightieth year. David Simpson, the vicar, regularly attended the Methodist services and love feasts, and Christchurch still maintains its vigorous evangelical witness. As for Hester Roe, she married James Rogers who was minister of City Road Chapel, London, at the time of Wesley's last illness, and both were among those at his bedside when he died.

In the centre of Macclesfield is Water's Green, below the parish church—a fine open square, from which, beyond the railway station, we see the Derbyshire hills. Here Wesley often preached, on one occasion, he says, to "thousands and thousands"—but, though exact in so many ways, he was apt to exaggerate, great as they were, the numbers who thronged to hear him.

A stable was the first Methodist meeting-place, beyond Temple Bar, after which a small preaching house was rented by two of his followers, George Pearson and Elizabeth Clulow, but with grave misgiving. "Ah, George," Mrs. Clulow had said with a sigh, "we shall never be able to fill it. Why, it will hold forty people!" But within a month it was so crowded that a hole had to be cut in the floor to enable those in the room below to share in the services, and as a result John Ryle, grandfather of Bishop Ryle, gave land and material to build a chapel on condition that Mrs. Clulow paid the workmen's wages, which she did, and the chapel was opened four years after Christchurch. Thus Christchurch and Wesley's Chapel in Macclesfield grew up together and in close and fruitful association.

It lies in Sunderland Street, near the bus station—a typical square box of a chapel with a high slated roof and its plain brick wall flanking the pavement. At either side is a covered gateway, each with a side entrance into the building, and beyond each is a narrow yard where, on one side, the preacher stabled his horse, while the other led to the manse, now occupied by the chapelkeeper. A bold sign on the outside wall reads: "Wesley's Chapel", along with the dates of its foundation and enlargement.

But if the outside is dull, the interior is gracious. Slender pillars carry a wide gallery, and each neat polished pew has its old-fashioned door. Fortunate are those who worship here, for every inch is holy ground. The vestry from which Wesley emerged in full preaching robes to face a thronged congregation, though no doubt reconstructed, is of graceful proportions. And on the rear wall of the chapel is a memorial to its benefactor, John Ryle of Park House, who gave a thousand pounds to its erection, with a second inscription below it which reads: "This tablet was cleaned and renovated in the year 1880 by John Charles Ryle, D.D. 1st Bishop of Liverpool, in token of his deep respect for the memory of his grandfather, John Ryle, Esq., and for the memory of his grandfather's friend, the Rev. John Wesley, M.A." How that would have warmed Wesley's ecumenical heart!

Such a building, so full of history, so charged with memories, is irreplaceable, and should never lightly be discarded. Atmosphere matters more than bricks and mortar, and here is a glory and tradition reaching back to Wesley himself. The outside, however, calls for the attention of a first-class architect. Those iron gates, those porticoes, the brick walls and woodwork—all might be restored as in Wesley's day to the very colour of the paint; the result would be a building (and a shrine) of which both Macclesfield and Methodism would be proud.

Old Mrs. Ryle heard her first Methodist sermon, sitting on a "bake-stone", and when her son John became mayor, Wesley was in the mayoral procession to St. Michael's. It was Easter Sunday, 1774. The new mayor had just been elected. He was a Methodist who regularly attended the Sunderland Street Chapel which he had so handsomely benefacted. Wesley on the preceding Wednesday was at Congleton where letters reached him requiring his return to Bristol on urgent business. He took a post-chaise, covered the one hundred and forty miles, spent two hours in Bristol, and returned immediately to Macclesfield. He had not arrived when the civic procession was due to start, but at the last moment he appeared and took his place with the mayor and corporation as they entered the church.

One of Mrs. Clulow's sons became town clerk of Macclesfield, the other, William, practised as a solicitor in London, drafted Wesley's Poll Deed of 1784, and drew up his will, which can be seen at Somerset House. It consists of two and a half double sheets, closely and neatly written, edge to edge and on both sides, with Wesley's signature given three times, his seal in black wax, and his monogram: "Believe, Love, Obey." A codicil, not in his hand, deals with his manuscripts.

From Macclesfield over the hills to New Mills—the road almost impassable in those days—we make for a hamlet with the odd name of Bongs (meaning the Banks), on the slopes of Cobden Edge, between New Mills and Mellor. Wesley preached here from the angled doorway (Plate 25*b*) of a group of stone-built cottages, now a farm, and his high-backed preaching chair is preserved at Mellor by Miss Margaret Sigley. He stayed with William Moult whose descendants still own the estate. Paradise Farm, higher up the hill, is said to be so named because Wesley, charmed by its situation, likened it to paradise.

But it was a steep climb up to Bongs and it was not long before a chapel was built in New Mills. This was in 1766 when the new mill by the river had only just been opened, and where in place of the present streets were open fields. It was built where the Sunday-school now stands; its date stone is still above the door, its pulpit is in Whitfield Chapel, and its property deed remains, full of quaint detail, referring to

> . . . the erection of a neat and commodious Meetinghouse or Chapell for the service and worship of Almighty God, by and with the assistance and connivance of many pious and charitable Christians in the neighbourhood who have contributed largely in

order to promote and carry on, so usefull, necessary, and laudable a work . . . In pursuit of so salutory and pious an undertaking . . .

the Trustees in case of the failure of the Conference to appoint a minister "shall and may choose a Minister orthodox in doctrine and circumspect in his morals".

The list of seatholders also survives. "On the north side, the road to the pulpit John Beard 2". "Thomas Beard, the whole of the gallery with the usual road belonging thereto". The pews were the property of their occupiers, and when a new chapel replaced the old building in 1808 they were conveyed by legal deed to the trustees. The document reads:

> Whereas the said Chapel from the increased populosity of New Mill and its neighbourhood is become too small to contain the devout inhabitants desirous of assembling to hear Divine worship there, and on account of the situation cannot be conveniently and sufficiently enlarged, and whereas the parties hereto have proposed to erect and build another Chapel at New Mill in lieue and stead of the present Chapel,

the signatories being owners or proprietors of seats, forms or pews agree to sell the same for the sum named in the deed to the trustees. The signatures and seals of about fifty seat-holders follow, who received amounts ranging from 5d. to £2 12s. 6d., the total being £34 12s. 9d.

The old account books show numerous payments for "ringing the bell", generous contributions to Stockport Dispensary and Manchester Infirmary, and such items as "a Colection for Doctor Cox Mishnares" and "a colleckshan for the Missionares". Teetotalism was unknown and George Barrowclough of the Bull's Head benefited to the tune of £10 for "ale for the workmen" when the 1808 chapel was built, every sitting in the gallery of which was let before the building was completed. It cost £3 a year to light with candles. The chapelkeeper's clogs disturbed the congregation and the trustees invested 3s. in a pair of light shoes; 3s. 6d. was paid towards a bassoon and later £7 12s. was expended in a double bass.

Old minute books of the local preachers' meetings also survive from which we learn that the administration of the Sacrament was imperative at every meeting. Brother Goddard was accused of dropping some very unguarded expressions in a sermon at New Mills. It was unanimously agreed that Mr. Dawes shall speak to Brother E. pointedly respecting his want of ability and inform him that he is required to confine himself to half an hour in his sermons, and also to keep to the subject he proposes to speak upon, and if there is no amendment during the next quarter he must be left off the plan. At a meeting at Compstall those present included Sister Shaw, who having made tea for the members, took her seat by the stove and occasionally intervened with advice.

A minister stationed there thirty years after Wesley's death seems to have had a bad time, for he left behind him this note written at half-past four in the morning on the day of his departure: "Fare thee well, New Mills. I pray God that *no other preacher* may *ever* pass thro' what I have passed through during my one year sojourning in thee. Amen and Amen, *1000* times Amen."

Four thousand bodies lie buried in the chapel graveyard, which includes a cholera grave, a public grave, a town grave for castaways, and the remains of a man who was hanged for a crime he never committed. And there are quaint epitaphs, such as:

> My sledge and hammer lie reclined.
> My bellows, too, are out of wind,
> My fire's extinct, my forge decayed,
> And in the dust my vice is laid.
> My anvil's broke, my iron's gone,
> My nails are drawn, my work is done.

Grace Murray, who by Charles Wesley's swift intervention was snatched from Wesley's attachment and swept into the arms of John Bennet, has local associations. Bennet came from Chinley and one of his descendants, Mr. J. M. Bennett, gives interesting information about Wesley's visits to the homes of his ancestors; at Ashen Clough where services were held in the outbuildings, and at Chinley End where Wesley enjoyed "a pinch of tea". Grace Bennet long outlived her husband, residing with her five sons at Chapel-en-le-Frith, dying at the age of ninety. Her grave is in the burial ground of Chinley Independent Chapel.

Wesley preached at Leek several times, once in a silk shed at Sleighs at the bottom of Edward Street, and on Easter Sunday, 1788, he gave Communion to fifteen hundred communicants in St. Edward's Church. He preached also in a cottage in Bakewell, now boarded up and overgrown, in a lane behind the church. Chinley Chapel, Milton, founded in 1662, is closely associated with him. It is now affiliated to the Congregational Union. And there is a barn in the Alport Valley in which he sheltered from a storm, where an annual service is held in his memory.

At Hayfield he stayed in what is now the Royal Hotel, but which was then the vicarage. On the day before his visit the vicar's two-year-old daughter had died. Wesley went on to Manchester and returned twice the following week, on the Thursday to conduct the burial and on the Sunday to preach in Hayfield parish church.

Among other places which heard him in the Peak were Chapel-en-le-Frith, Bradwell, near Eyam, probably Grindleford, also Chelmorton and Buxton. At the latter in 1783 he conducted a wedding in St. Anne's Church, travelling from Derby in a post-chaise at three o'clock on a May morning, and bringing the bride with him. At 9 a.m. a passer-by saw the old man—he was in his eightieth year—cross the road to the church, white-haired, in a white surplice. At 11 a.m. he was on his way to Nottingham, where he arrived at seven-thirty—an hour late for his service there.

On another occasion he spoke from a rear window of Hawthorn Farm, Fairfield Road, on the opposite side to St. Peter's Church which was also crowded to hear him. The house is still occupied by the Smith family whose ancestors entertained him there. Tradition says that on his first visit to the town he rested in a whitewashed cottage at the top of Bath Road.

The little town of Crich (or Creitch, as Wesley called it) has one of the oldest Methodist chapels—a typical preaching house with its plain front, gallery and high pulpit, founded in 1765. Unfortunately no records survive, but Wesley visited it and stayed with a Mr. Smith in a house still standing on Crich Common. Before the erection of the chapel he preached from an outcrop of rock on the ridge known as the Tors above the lower end of the town. It was in this chapel that on one occasion when a preacher failed to arrive, a steward went to a neighbouring house and returned with a book of sermons which he proceeded hurriedly to turn over, remarking: "I have several sermons here and will read one of them, but I don't know which to read." A voice came from the gallery: "Read the shortest, Henry."

Wesley's first visit to Knutsford reminds us that he was a

devoted evangelist before his heart-warming experience in Aldersgate Street, for outside Princess Street Methodist Church is the short flight of three steps from which he preached on March 20, 1738. The steps stood then in King Street, outside a building now replaced by Messrs. Bradley's shop. When the premises were altered, the firm presented the steps to the church. On his next visit he preached in a thatched cottage near the Cross Keys Inn.

CHAPTER THIRTEEN

SEVERN TO SOLWAY CONTINUED—STAYLEY HALL—MANCHESTER—THE OLD DOG INN—A HOUSE OF FRIENDSHIP—LANCASHIRE TALES—OLD KENDAL PLAYHOUSE—AMBLESIDE—CROSSING THE ESTUARIES

FROM New Mills Wesley made his way to Stockport—the first of twenty-four visits. He preached, he says, "at poor, dull, dead, Stockport, and not without hope that God would raise the dead." This was on the Carr Green opposite Petty Car Hall, the home of Mrs. Smallwood, and the first centre here of his work. But though progress was slow he soon revised his opinion of Stockport. A simple chapel was built in Hillgate, without galleries or pews, the pulpit for which was obtained from a parish church in Altrincham, and was carried the whole way (nine miles) by James Chadwick on his shoulders. This chapel, rebuilt in 1784, passed out of Methodist hands and is now the Central Hall.

Wesley stayed with Mr. Matthew Mayer at Portwood Hall, a farmhouse in pleasant surroundings, formerly the town house of the Dukinfields, with a deer park and orchards. But the area now is beyond recognition in the old part of the town, and the building, much altered, is the Liberal Club. A chair of plain oak with a low seat and a sloping desk on its high back, used there by Wesley, is preserved at Didsbury College, Bristol. Matthew Mayer was a pioneer of Stockport's famous Sunday-school.

Stayley Hall, where Wesley stayed and preached, in Millbrook, Stalybridge, is now almost derelict, with hens pecking among its rotting floors, though its front and roof remain. It is a fourteenth-century manor, with mullion windows, and holes in its gables for owls who were believed to keep buildings free from vermin. An old diary refers to "a township belonging to the Lordship of Staley, wherein Sir George Booth, Knight and Baronet, hath a fine old Mannour House called Stealey Hall, and goodly lands and great possessions." It came to him through his wife, a descendant of the Stayley family. A tablet referring to Wesley's first visit was placed on its wall in 1946. The tenant in his day was probably Robert Lees. Dr. John Whitehead, Wesley's physician, executor, and biographer, was a schoolboy living in the town at the time.

St. Anne's Church in the heart of Manchester has a bronze plaque on its churchyard wall recording, among other items, that Wesley preached there. But how different was its setting in those days when St. Anne's Square (formerly Acres Fields) was lined with trees and private houses! Wesley visited Manchester as early as 1733 to consult his friend, John Clayton, an Oxford Methodist who was curate of Trinity Church, Salford, as to whether he should succeed his father at Epworth or go to Georgia, and he preached in Trinity Church. On his return from Georgia he revisited Clayton, after which their paths diverged, and it was nine years before he came again. In 1747 he preached at Salford Cross, near Greengate, at the corner of Gravel Lane, where an engine was brought out to obstruct him and he was obliged to move into a yard.

Messrs. W. H. Smith and Sons' premises, near Blackfriars Bridge, stand on the site of a three-storied building in the garret of which the first Manchester Methodists met. It overhung the Irwell, in a large yard behind the Rose and Crown which looked into Deansgate. They were humble and congested quarters; the ground floor was a joiner's shop, the second floor was in private occupation, and the garret itself was a combined living-room, bedroom and work-room, with a spinning wheel and a bed. Getting up to it was a neck-breaking business, and its cracked beams and crowded meetings made it dangerous. The old Coldhouse Baptist Chapel was used next, in Withy Grove, until the erection of the first meeting house in Birchin Lane, off Church Street, which served for thirty years. A bronze tablet on the wall of the premises of Messrs. F. Lloyd Rees, Ltd. on the corner of Cannon Street, states:

> The first Methodist preaching house in Manchester was built in Birchin Lane at the rear of this building. Here John Wesley preached on Easter Day, 1751, A.D. This was the cradle of Methodism in Manchester for thirty years until Wesley opened the first Oldham Street Chapel in 1781.

Then follow Wesley's seal and monogram picked out in red,

and the inscription continues: "John Wesley's seal and monogram. 'I look upon all the world as my parish.'"

If we walk up Birchin Lane, between the warehouses, to Stationers' Court which retains its original gas lamps and traces of older buildings, we find that the private parking area through iron gates at the rear is still called Chapel Yard. Nothing remains but old names recalling a vanished age. Wesley and Whitefield often came down this narrow street, the Conference met in the chapel that stood here, and once a guard was set at its door to protect it from an angry mob.

The blackened walls of the cathedral, facing Exchange station—the Old Church, as Wesley calls it—more than once welcomed him to its pulpit, when Clayton was its chaplain, and the first Methodist sermons in Manchester were preached here. Whitefield came to it six times. With its five broad aisles it is the widest church in England, magnificent with its richly carved stalls, light and graceful clerestories, chancel screen and choir, still preserving the pattern of a medieval collegiate church. And the austerity of its altar should satisfy the most radical Dissenter. Wesley also visited the ancient Chetham Hospital and Library (opposite the cathedral).

He preached in a Moravian chapel at Audenshaw, and on the other side of the city at Millington, near Sale, is a building with a plaque recording his visit. A cottage has replaced Boothbank Farm near Timperley, an important early centre of Methodism in these parts and where for many years after his coming an annual Good Friday pilgrimage was made.

In Altrincham his chapel in which he preached in 1790 is now the Mission Church (All Saints) of St. Margaret's parish, where on the occasion of its 150th anniversary Methodists joined with Anglicans in a united service. At Styal, off Styal Road, a Cross marks another scene of his preaching.

Wesley paid the last of his twenty visits to Warrington at the age of eighty-seven and an eyewitness has left this description: "He stood in the wide pulpit, and on each side of him stood a friend, and the two held him up, having their arms under his armpits . . . His feeble voice was barely audible, but his revered countenance, especially his long white locks, formed a picture never to be forgotten." He left the chapel by the side door leaning on his two helpers, and the stone stairway down which he walked remains, where he moved towards his carriage to go on to Liverpool. The chapel was in Bank Street. He

23. Barley Hall Farm, Thorpe Hesley near Sheffield, where Wesley stayed on seventeen occasions. *Below*, Newbiggin Chapel in Teesdale, said to be the oldest Methodist chapel in continuous use since Wesley's day.

24. The window in Pump Court, York, which is all that survives of Wesley's first preaching house in the city

Below, a barn in Grassington, Yorks, in which Wesley is said to have preached

preached also in a chapel in Balham Lane, and he stayed with John Gandy in the Cornmarket where on one occasion the congregation followed him and, as they lingered, he came to the door and from its steps preached another sermon.

The *St. Helen's Reporter* recently referred to a maroon-upholstered dining room chair which had belonged to him, now in the proud possession of Nutgrove Methodist Church. On Wesley's death it had passed with other furniture to one of his nieces, Mrs. de Rock Jones of Prescot.

Only two chapels were erected in Liverpool in his lifetime: Pitt Street and Mount Pleasant. Pitt Street, the Mother Church, was then in a good residential district on the edge of the town which only numbered twenty thousand inhabitants. Mount Pleasant, never so popular, was more central. Both were closed in 1905. Pitt Street, a stone's throw from the present Central Hall, is now covered with tenements, and Mount Pleasant is a billiards hall. Wesley is depicted in a window of the cathedral.

Southport was little more than a village where a few farm-houses brought him to a halt and he preached from a "cop" at the junction of two lanes, almost opposite the site of the present Southbank Road Methodist Church. In "wicked Wigan", as he called it though he really had little to complain of there, the Methodists worshipped for seventy years in their own building behind the parish church in the yard of the Buck i' th' Vine inn. Wesley preached there before the roof was on, as well as after its completion. When the Standishgate church was built the old chapel was bought by the railway.

The first Methodist meeting place in Preston was an upper room of the Old Dog Inn, which still stands, thirty yards below the parish church. Martha Thompson, a nineteen-year-old girl of Preston, became a domestic servant in London where she heard Wesley in Moorfields and was so deeply moved that she forgot the errand on which her employer had sent her and returned late. She was warned never to consort with the Methodists again, but she heard Wesley a second time and was converted. Her employer then had her put away as mad. A note reached Wesley telling him of her plight, investigation followed and he not only secured her release, but took her the greater part of her journey back to Preston on his pillion. She sought out the nearest Methodist Society, at Brimicroft, six miles from Preston, and walked there every Sunday and for a time was a member of a class at Cockshott House, a farmhouse a few miles out. She opened in business as a milliner in Church Street, where her neighbour, Mrs. Walmsley, kept the Old Dog Inn. Mrs. Walmsley joined her in going to Brimicroft, and a Methodist fellowship met upstairs in her inn. Later a room was hired in St. John Street, and the first chapel was built in 1787 in Back Lane.

Wesley's four visits to the town were great occasions. Crowds lined the pavements of Fishergate to see him pass and more than once he preached from the steps of the obelisk in the market-place. Among the earliest Methodists in the neighbourhood was Mrs. Nuttal, a lady of independent means living at Walton-le-Dale, to whom Wesley wrote: "Do not imagine that all in the Society are angels." When he heard that she was dying he paid her the last office of friendship. "Hearing that one of our Society, near Preston, was at the point of death, I turned a little out of my way to spend half an hour with her."

Six miles from Preston, on the Lancaster Road, we come to Brock House, Brock, the home of Alderman Mrs. Ann Rainford, J.P., who, despite her busy life, finds time to welcome visitors and opens her grounds for an annual Methodist garden party and other fêtes. It is known as the House of Friendship. On an April night in 1765 Wesley, frustrated by a sudden change of plan, rode out of Preston towards Kendal and as dark came on turned his horse over a small stone bridge and found a welcome in the home of a friend, James Edmondson, at Brock House (Plate 27). The picturesque bridge, green with moss, over a clear stream, just off the main highway, and the gracious house beyond with its eight windows and black-columned porch, are little changed—a patch of old-world beauty, restful to the eye and in welcome contrast to the encroaching spread of roadside garages and bungalows. And all is equally gracious within, with period furniture and the pleasant dining room where Wesley preached. Wesley called it "the house of a friend", and since he came there its friendly tradition has been preserved and not least by Mrs. Rainford who for thirty-six years has lived there and treasured its memories.

Near here in the Ribble valley is the pretty village of Chipping which in those days had an evangelical vicar, J. Milner, who was a friend of Wesley and accompanied him on his journeys in these parts. Wesley stayed more than once in his vicarage and preached in Chipping Parish Church. On two occasions attempts were made by a small noisy element to hinder him. On one of them he was forcibly prevented from entering the pulpit and obliged to abandon his sermon and hand over the service to Milner. The latter got into trouble with his bishop for allowing Wesley the use of his pulpit, but Milner told his Lordship of the Bolton barber, who, when Wesley went into his shop to be shaved, said as he lathered him, "Sir, I praise God on your behalf. When you were at Bolton last, I was one of the greatest drunkards in the town; but I came to listen at the window, God struck me to the heart, and I was converted." The bishop replied by talking about order, but Milner said he had nowhere seen so little order as in the bishop's own cathedral, and that he knew not a single clergyman in the whole of Lancashire "that could give the Church's definition of faith, and stand to it".

Elsewhere in Lancashire, there is Kebb's Cottage, Darwen, in excellent preservation and still occupied, on the lower slopes of the moors to the south-west of the town. It stands on an ancient highway, the Limersgate, formerly a packhorse road, and was an isolated house when Wesley preached there. In Bolton, on a corner off Hotel Street, near the Town Hall, a large plaque informs us that we are near the site of Wesley's first Bolton Chapel, and he also preached at the Market Cross. Mrs. E. W. Lord has the chair he used when he preached in her ancestor's cottage at Lord's Fold on the outskirts of the town. The Clayton Street Chapel, which he opened, was rebuilt in 1816. At Trinity Methodist Church, in Church Street, Westhoughton, there is a large basalt boulder with a flat surface, suitably inscribed, which came from Barnabas Farm at Wingates where it served Wesley as a pulpit in the farmyard. In Old Chapel Street, Blackburn, his chapel is now used as a builder's store and is likely to be removed shortly to make way for a new market.

In this area we must not miss Bagslate, near Rochdale, with its memories of the "Round Preachers": of Owd Ab o' Slenders (Abraham Lord) in James Ashworth's *Lancashire Tales*, a rugged weaver and revivalist who sat in the gallery over the clock and enlivened the services with loud and disconcerting ejaculations. At one prayer meeting he said: "I'll buy a pound of candles for every soul that's saved." There were thirteen converts, and thirteen pounds of candles were added to the chapel store. Also of John Ashworth—a "bread and cheese preacher", that is one who had only two or three sermons—who once on entering the pulpit said: "Th' owd text again, and if ony of you can mend this owd stick, you can come up here and thry." All this was in Wesley's day, and later came fiddles, clarionets, flutes, horns and "serpents". The old chapel has gone and a new and imposing one has replaced it, but Bankhouse remains, a large farmhouse, beautifully situated on the high slopes of The Nabs, near Woodhouse Lane, with wide views from Blackstone Edge to Rooley and Ashworth Moors. There was a barn here—Blomley's Barn, at the lower end of the buildings, where the Society met and a bridge was built over Naden Brook for the convenience of the congregation, known as Methody Bridge.

Wesley came here at least twice, when Samuel Healey, later of Liverpool, was his host. It is a substantial stone-built seventeenth-century farmhouse with a large stone mantelpiece in its sitting-room, curiously engraved with quaint devices. But its most interesting feature is the handsome pair of oak dog-gates at the foot of the staircase, richly carved with twisted pillars, surmounted by the figures of two large wooden dogs. They separate a landing from the living-room, and Wesley used this landing as his pulpit. Tradition says that Whitefield also came here.

Further north, at Skipton, is a bronze tablet on the wall of a cottage at the foot of Chapel Hill which marks the site of what was known as "John Wesley's Forum" and records that Wesley preached there. That was in 1764, but nearly forty years earlier Wesley, before his ordination, had been offered a post in a Skipton school, and had written to his mother:

> A good salary is annexed to it . . . But what has made me wish for it most is the frightful description, as they call it, some gentlemen who know the place gave of it yesterday. The town lies in a little vale, so pent up between two hills that it is scarce accessible on any side, so that you can expect little company from without, and within there is none at all.

Wesley, however, declined the offer or it may have been withdrawn.

Mr. Jack O'Connor was my guide in Kendal who has interesting scrapbooks of local history, and old sample books of patterns carried by Kendal traders in the days of packhorses.

We visited the house where Romney, the painter, was apprenticed in Redman's Yard, and the market place into which formerly two narrow streets ran where now there is only one, by the old town hall, the clock turret of which remains above a shop on the corner. At the end of the market-place is the former town playhouse, now a furniture store, where both Wesley and Whitefield preached. There is the outside staircase, with its gallery and window from which they addressed the crowd below, but no memorial marks the building and few who pass it are aware of its history. It is said that Wesley, preaching outside in the rain, suggested they should rent it; it had already been used by Lady Huntingdon's preachers. Stephen Brunskill, the earliest lay preacher here, describes it in the story of his life.

> Being told that the proprietor was a very civil man, two of us waited upon him to ask the favour of being permitted to preach in it, which he readily consented to, and gave us the key. But still we wanted a congregation. However, the playhouse being situated in a very convenient part of the town, in the centre of the market place, and having stairs on the outside leading to the gallery, we determined, the day being fine, to preach at the door, standing on the stairs. We agreed to have preaching at one o'clock, and again at four, and cast lots whether of us should preach first, and it fell upon my friend. We went to the place at the time appointed, and before we had done singing the first hymn, a few persons had collected together, and before our brother had done preaching, there might be some hundreds.

The services roused great curiosity, crowds gathered, clergymen listened at the windows on the opposite side of the Square, and "the people were as still as in a church".

As a result the playhouse was rented for six guineas a year. Brunskill next determined to form a Society and asked any who wished to join to remain after the congregation had been dismissed.

> At first it appeared as if a great many were going to stay; but they began to look one at another, and at length they went away, one by one, till none were left with me but Mr. and Mrs. Barlow, and a man who assisted us in singing, but who had no desire to join us.

Just as they were leaving, however, eight young women who

had taken courage returned, and ten more were added in the next fortnight.

Some miles out of Kendal is Strickley Farm, near Hutton, once famous for Methodist services, where Wesley may have preached, and beyond it is Huttongate where he stayed at the Punchbowl Inn, probably the building now occupied by Mr. Dixon's grocery store. One of its closed rooms is said still to smell of beer! And behind the modernized shop we find in its low ceilings, crooked stairs and arrangement of rooms, clear indications of its former use. But it is when viewed from outside that we discern its original pattern, and see how the long grey stone building with its yard and stabling can hardly be other than the village inn to which Wesley came, and at its side we traced the line of the overgrown packhorse road, straight as an arrow, down which he rode from the moors.

There is a well-founded tradition in Ambleside that he stayed on his visits there at the Salutation Inn and sometimes took the direct mountain route over Wrynose and Hardknott to Whitehaven. Wesley records, on one occasion, that he prayed with the landlord before leaving, and, on another, that he called there for tea at seven o'clock in the morning. Once he made the long journey here from Haworth and rode on to Keswick, and it was his half-way house between Bolton and Keswick. On his sixth visit, when he was eighty-one, he was just sitting down to supper when he was told that a congregation was awaiting him. A local history refers to a tradition that he preached in a large room at this well-known inn and also from its steps, which is likely enough, for it stands immediately above the market-place.

If we approach Penrith from Hartside we are still in the steps of Wesley, but we must forget the modern highway and think of the road as he describes it: "The storm was exceeding high, and drove full in my face, so that it was not without difficulty I could sit my horse; particularly as I rode over the broad, bare backs of those enormous mountains which lay in my way. However, I kept on as I could, till I came to the brow of Hartside. So thick a fog then fell, that I was quickly out of all road, and knew not which way to turn." Two days before, he had been lost on Penruddock Moor, and on Alston Moor had missed his way. This terrible journey from Hindley Hill, near Allendale, was across one of the highest and most exposed roads in the country, crossing the Pennines between Black and Cross Fells before descending to the Eden valley. We can still see the old road down which he came, which joins the new road at Gamblesby where he preached in the school-house and on elevated ground, still indicated, outside Hill Top Farm.

In Penrith he used a preaching room up Crown Terrace Yard, off King Street, now a warehouse. As an old man he arrived once very tired at the Old Crown Inn and asked how long it was to service time. "Ten minutes," was the answer, whereupon he leaned back in his chair and fell asleep, awaking refreshed in time for the service, and the crowd was so great that he preached in the courtyard.

Whitehaven was his destination when he came this way, where he preached in Michael Street Chapel and St. Nicholas Church (both rebuilt) and in the market-place, and stayed with a bootmaker in Duke Street, where, in the words of Benjamin Briscoe, one of his leaders, "He had a bed something like unto Joseph's sepulchre, whereon never man lay but Mr. Wesley, which—after his death—induced my wife to buy it at any price, and she got it." A chair he used in this house is now in the Whitehaven manse. The Society also met in the Assembly Room in Howgill Street, its site now occupied by Messrs. Matthew Brown and Company.

Whitehaven was the scene of his stormy interview with his brother when the latter, primed with gossip, and angry and incredulous, burst in upon him and expostulated with him on the subject of Grace Murray. It was also the scene of the ministry of John Peacock, who was a great wrestler and had so large a family and arrived with so many cases of household goods that the circuit steward was aghast at the cost of the removal. Seeing them unloaded and the house full of children, he groaned: "What can be done with such a brood as this?" Whereupon the athletic parson extended his strong right arm supported by the other and exclaimed: "As the Lord liveth, if I hear any more of this, I'll break you every man." Houses in Carmichael Street have replaced the old manse which was next to the chapel.

Wesley preached at Hensingham and at The Ginns, at Drigg, and at Seaton, where "the poor people had placed a cushion to kneel upon of the greenest turf in the county". He also went through the Furness district from Hest Bank, crossing the sands of Morecambe Bay, the Leven and Duddon estuaries, and at Ravensglass—a slow and hazardous journey which saved him ten miles, but "there are four sands to pass, so far from each other that it is scarce possible to pass them all in one day, especially as you have all the way to do with a generation of liars, who detain all strangers as long as they can, either for their own gain or their neighbour's. I can advise no one to go this way. He may go round by Kendal and Keswick often in less time, always with less expense, and far less trial of patience." Traces of this perilous route are found at Kent's Bank where the remains of Abbot's Hall remind us that once the monks of Cartmel were responsible for appointing the guide over the sands. Holiday makers there can think of Wesley riding up the lane from the shore making for Flookburgh, where he slept, and the Leven estuary.

He found Ulverston disappointing. A convenient room had been prepared, but few people gathered, so, he records, "I went back quietly to my inn." He was many times in Cockermouth, where he preached in the Castle Yard.

At Grassington, which is the largest village in Wharfedale where originally a regular and thriving market was held, is an old barn in which Wesley preached (Plate 24*b*). It can be found on the left-hand side of Garrs Lane, which leads off the cobbled Square with its village pump, and itself forms one side of a rough square facing old houses with out-buildings on the two sides.

The sycamore under which he is said to have preached in Appleby is still to be seen, and Nenthead, near Alston, has a cornerstone near its chapel, with a semi-circular step, the scene of another sermon, as well as a barn a little further along on the right hand side of the Alston Road.

Alston reminds us of "Lowes' Balsam". Among the cock-fighting leadminers converted in Allendale was Matthew Lowes, who became one of Wesley's preachers, but through frail health and with a family of eleven children he found it difficult to make ends meet, and to supplement his income he prepared and sold a balsam which became popular. Other preachers acted as his agents, which led to Wesley's Conference order against "the buying or selling or making and vending pills, drops, balsams, or medicines of any kind". Chronic rheumatism compelled Lowes to retire from circuit work, but he continued to sell his balsam which on his death was taken over by an

Alston chemist, Mr. George Thompson, who sold it wholesale and retail as "Lowes' veterinary Oil". Later it was transferred to a William Laws and became "Laws' Oil", and passed eventually to a firm of Carlisle chemists who still sell it.

CHAPTER FOURTEEN

OVER THE BORDER—HARD TIMES IN INVERNESS—THE OLD TOTUM KIRKIE—FREEDOM OF TWO TOWNS—LADY MAXWELL—MANXLAND—THE CONFERENCE COACH BREAKS DOWN—A ROUGH CROSSING—THE CHANNEL ISLANDS

WESLEY declared that he would never preach in Scotland, and he went there against the advice of his friends. Whitefield told him bluntly: "If you spoke like an angel none would hear you." But curiosity and love of travel carried him over the Border and Scotland won his heart, though he never won the heart of Scotland.

He was received with coolness and reserve. Its stern Calvinism was alien to his warm nature, he was more at home in the Episcopal churches, and his insistence on an itinerant ministry was unpopular. Scotland preferred its own settled ways, and, if the rest of Britain were starved of theology, Scotland was full of it. So he came, on the whole, to a serious and pious countryside and to a psalm-loving people who refused to be swept off their feet by Methodist fervour.

Wesley, straining to avoid controversy, was stung by their sheer stolidity. "They know everything and feel nothing," he complained. He spoke so plainly that he wondered how they could bear it. They were as unresponsive as the seats they sat upon. But he acknowledged that they were good listeners. "The Scots," he declared, "were the best hearers in Europe."

His preachers too had a hard time in Scotland. There was one appointed to Inverness who, on arrival, found a colleague dying of fever in a lousy bed and another dead and buried, and who wrote to Wesley: "No man is fit for the Inverness Circuit, unless his flesh be brass, his bones iron, and his heart harder than a stone's." To which Wesley replied (with a gift of five guineas), "When I had only blackberries to eat in Cornwall, still God gave me strength sufficient for my work."

But though he found little enthusiasm he was received on the whole with respect and only once did he encounter violence.

That was at Aberdeen. He twice attended the General Assembly, comparing it unfavourably with his own Conference—shocking, he called it—"If any preacher behaved so at our Conference, he would have had no more place among us." He had also distinguished supporters, and two Scottish towns made him a Freeman.

During his twenty visits he covered most of the main towns, travelling up the east coast from Dunbar to Inverness, penetrating the Highlands through Dunkeld to Blair Atholl and Dalwhinnie—where he found the dearest inn in North Britain—journeying through Galloway and up the coast road from Stranraer to Glasgow.

On one breathless journey, when he could find no boat in Bristol to take him to Ireland, he travelled the 400 miles to Portpatrick in ten days, his horse, through no fault of his, jaded and worn to skin and bones—he had left it to rest for six winter months when some unscrupulous person had worked it hard. He had called at Liverpool and found no boat and had pushed on through wind and snow. "At Solway-firth the guides were so deeply engaged in a cockfight, that none could be procured to show us over." There was more sea than he expected; he was wet to the knees, and the waves as his mare plunged through them made him dizzy. He slept in a noisy inn at Gatehouse-of-Fleet, and visitors to the pleasant resort of Portpatrick can think of him on two occasions riding down its main street to the small harbour below the Castle, but from which the boat no longer sails to Donaghadee.

His only remaining octagon chapel in Scotland is the old "Totum Kirkie" (so-called because of its resemblance to a "teetotum" or spinning top) in Arbroath which he opened in 1772 (Plate 28*a*). Situated in the Ponderlaw, with a small paved forecourt, apart from the addition in 1882 of a high Gothic porch and, later, of a small hall, and a memorial window and oak panelling, it preserves its original form. The rafters and ceiling were renewed in 1958. Many make pilgrimage to this little church, and its minister and members take great pride in its care and preservation.

Before opening it Wesley preached in the Abbey 'Pend'—the rectangular gateway leading to the Abbey—and on the following day he was made a Freeman of the Royal Burgh of Arbroath. He records: "The Magistrates here also did me the honour of presenting me with the freedom of their corporation.

I value it as a token of their respect, though I shall hardly make any farther use of it."

Perth had honoured him when in the previous week he had preached there in the Guildhall and been the guest of the Provost. "I preached," he says, "once more at Perth to a large and serious congregation. Afterwards they did me an honour I never thought of—presented me with the freedom of the city," and he quotes from the Latin Parchment which in English reads:

> The illustrious order of Magistrates, and honourable Court of Aldermen, of the famous city of Perth, as a proof of their well-merited esteem and affection for John Wesley, have invested him by a solemn oath with the immunities of the above-mentioned city, and with the privileges of the fellowship and brotherhood of a Burgess: this 28th. day of April, in the year of our salvation, 1772.

"I question," says Wesley, "whether any diploma from the city of London be more pompous, or expressed in better Latin." What did Wesley do with these parchments, for they seem to have disappeared?

The oldest Methodist chapel in Scotland is at Dunbar where a tablet gives its date as 1764, but Mr. Wesley Swift thinks 1770 is probably more correct, which is the year when Wesley first preached in it, and called it "the cheerfullest house in the kingdom". It was then a small building of whitewashed walls and plain interior. Among its thirty members were two young men, afterwards famous, who carried with them the influence of this humble sanctuary into devoted and distinguished careers. One was Thomas Rankin, a pioneer of American Methodism. The other was Dr. James Hamilton, F.R.C.P., a young Dunbar physician who rose to great eminence in his profession in Edinburgh, Leeds and London, and died in Finsbury Square at the age of eighty-seven, having been a lay preacher for nearly sixty years. He was perhaps the only layman who has ever preached the official Conference Sermon. When Wesley developed a hydrocele, following a riding accident, it was Hamilton who attended him professionally, and insisted on his consulting a surgeon and having it removed.

Two other chapels of Wesley's day survive: Dalkeith, near Edinburgh (1789), still Methodist property, though used for other purposes; and Dumfries (1786–89), now business premises. The early chapels built in Aberdeen (which was the first), Edinburgh, Dundee, Glasgow, Dumfries, Inverness and elsewhere, all of them opened or visited by Wesley, have disappeared. The one in Aberdeen was in Queen Street; that in Edinburgh was at the head of Leith Wynd, its site now covered by Waverley Station; Inverurie had a thatched chapel with open roof and unplastered walls. We can see the house where he stayed in Banff—"Wesley House" at the bottom of the Strait Path. It is still occupied, the lower part as a shop, the upper storey reached by a stair which opens from a fend or close.

The pulpit chair in Aberdeen Methodist Church was given to him by a lady who lived near Banff. He politely accepted it and put it into his carriage, but on reaching Aberdeen, probably finding it an encumbrance, he presented it to the Society there. And in the vestry of this church is a framed Minute describing the financial arrangements for the Aberdeen preachers, countersigned: "I entirely approve of this, John Wesley."

He often passed through Dumfries, which he called a clean, well-built town, but he found the barn which was rented for preaching a trial, having no proper windows and needing candles even at midday. He preached twice in this improvised building and was thankful when a chapel was built in Queen Street.

Lady Maxwell and her friend, Lady Glenorchy, supported his work in Edinburgh and were among his correspondents. The former lived in Chalmers Close and afterwards at Saughton Hall and Coates Hall, at each of which Wesley made his home when in that area. She was left a widow at the age of nineteen and joined the Methodists, although she remained a communicant member of the Established (Presbyterian) Church. She was a great benefactress and extremely kind to Wesley's preachers. Mr. Wesley Swift gives such instances as:

> Lady Maxwell takes the liberty of asking Mr. Dall's acceptance of the enclosed for the purpose of procuring a few Bottles of good red Port of which some glasses should be taken every day." And in a case of illness: "If Mr. Dall is at a loss for a Professional Gentleman, he will be very welcome to send in Lady Maxwell's name to her surgeon . . . If Mr. Wood is employed Lady Maxwell desires no Money may be given.

Wilhelmina, Viscountess Glenorchy, equally pious, rented

an empty Roman Catholic chapel in Niddry's Wynd for Protestant worship, providing Episcopal services, and also permitting its use by Presbyterians and Methodists. Her plan, however, broke down. Wesley tried in vain to persuade her to become a Methodist, for she attended his services, and at her request he found a schoolmaster for a school she organized, and a clergyman for her chapel. But these were not enough for her pious Ladyship who employed, in addition, one of the Countess of Huntingdon's preachers. The upshot was unfortunate; she was influenced in the direction of Calvinism, severed her connection with Wesley, and closed her chapel to his preachers, which dashed his high hopes in Edinburgh and proved a serious setback there to his work.

As I climbed the steep ascent to Edinburgh Castle I thought of Wesley preaching on the Castle Green. He walked up Arthur's seat and several times visited Holyrood Palace—the stately rooms, he says, dirty as stables, the colours of the tapestry faded, pictures cut and defaced, the chapel roof fallen. In Glasgow he had a good friend in Dr. John Gillies who welcomed him to the old College Kirk. He preached also in the College Kirk and in the Town Hall in Aberdeen, but a service he attended at the English Church there provoked his criticism. The preacher's inadequate voice made a burlesque of the service. "Is there no man of spirit belonging to this congregation? Would it not be far better to pay this gentleman for doing nothing, than for doing mischief; for bringing a scandal upon religion?"

A story survives which throws light on those days. A poor old woman in a Glasgow street met the minister of the kirk she had been accustomed to attend, who asked: "Oh, Janet, where have you been, woman? I have no seen ye at the kirk for long." "I go," replied Janet, "among the Methodists." "Among the Methodists," quoth the minister, "why what gude get ye there, woman?" "Glory to God!" she said, "I do get gude, for God has forgiven me aw my sins!" "Ah, Janet," said the minister, "be not high-minded; the devil is a cunning adversary." To which she answered: "I dunna care a button for the deevil. I've gotten him under my feet. I ken the deevil can do muckle deal, but there is ane thing he canna do. He canna shed abroad the love of God in my heart; and I'm sure I've got it there." "Weel, weel," replied the minister, "if ye have got it there, Janet, hold it fast and never let it go."

Wesley formed numerous Societies, reaching from the Border to the Moray Firth, many of which have disappeared, but not without here and there yielding a rich harvest. There was, for example, the pleasant fishing village of Cullen on the Banffshire coast where a young fisherman, George Findlay, and a fisher girl, Ann McGillanders, were converted and married. They began a Society and later built a little chapel. And from that remote and lovely spot and early Methodist romance there came three generations of ministers bearing a familiar and honoured name surviving to this day.

Manxland, inseparable from the saga of its saints, teasing the tourist with a bewildering variety of runic crosses and Methodist chapels, sings:

> Our fathers have told how saints came of old
> Proclaiming the Gospel of peace.

Wesley followed in the steps of Maughold and Brendan, and when he died the Isle of Man, numerically, was second only to London in the list of his circuits, greater than Manchester or Leeds. Today there are no less than eighty Methodist chapels on the island.

In his two visits he covered its whole area and was loud in its praise. Never, he says, had he met a more loving and simple-hearted people! No Papists, Dissenters, Calvinists or disputers! Never had he seen such a body of stout well-looking preachers —twenty-two of them! And never had he heard such singing! Through the long June days the island was full of bird song; at Peel the Islanders had admirable voices and sang with good judgement. He was agreeably surprised: "Who would have expected this in the Isle of Man?"

Mr. David Crane, a leading authority on Manx history, told me that Wesley once breakfasted with his great-great-grandfather, the Rev. Daniel Gelling, rector of Ballaugh, so I sought out the old rectory. It lies on the road to the sea at some distance from the village, adjoining the old church of St. Mary de Ballaugh, and is a small plain but pleasant house with white walls, a slated porch and with green gates opening from the road on to a trim lawn and borders of roses. Wesley records the occasion; the friendly rector had brought his family to Wesley's service the previous evening—possibly in the disused chapel which lies in a hollow nearer the sea, though there is a tradition that he preached in what is now the front portion of Ballaugh Methodist Sunday-school. The rector invited him to breakfast the following morning, and after family prayers and "spending a little time very agreeably" Wesley went on to Kirk-Andrew.

At Lonan, eight miles from Douglas, is an old chapel, now used as a Sunday-school, with an inscription that Wesley preached there in 1781. But this neat pebble-dashed chapel, built into the side of the hill above the main road, with grass-grown flags outside its door and overlooking Bulgham Bay, was then much smaller, with walls of puddled clay and a thatched roof. Inside is the pulpit from which he preached, yellow varnished, with two brass candle holders, and beside it is the plain oak chair which he used.

The War Memorial at Lezare, on the road from Ramsey to Peel, opposite the entrance to the Ballakalingan estate, has replaced the tree under which he stood and preached. It is a pity, however, that this fine stone Cross which so appropriately marks the site, though for another purpose, includes no record of his visit.

Visitors to Castle Rushen in Castletown should look for Wesley's chair which is preserved in its museum along with an old Wesley print. The chair, which is of faded oak with a square back, was used by him on two preaching occasions outside the Castle in 1777. He lodged in a house in Arbury Street. Castletown, he said, reminded him of Galway.

In Peel a brick building, a few feet square, at the corner of Mount Morrison is said to be the spot where he addressed a crowd gathered on the hillside below. This structure stands in the grounds of "Jacky's House" which was built by two brothers who carried up every stone of it from the shore for its construction. The vicar of Peel would have invited Wesley to his pulpit, but was forbidden by the bishop. So Wesley preached on the sea-shore, also in a large malthouse in the market-place, and in the churchyard where today the old red sandstone church is in ruins. And there is a small preaching house he used on the Shore Road, which was the first Methodist chapel on the island and is now occupied by the Rechabites and the Salvation Army.

The Peel Guardian in 1942 reported that a travelling pulpit belonging to Wesley had been presented to the Athol Street

[illegible] Robert Swann Preach'd here —— X
October ye 10 Thomas Carlill preach'd here X.
Octo: 20 David Simpson 1771 Preach'd in our Church here & afternoon wonderfull
Octo. 23 Thomas Hanson Preach'd here
Octo. 25 Joseph Thompson Preach'd here
Novr 1 James Odie Preach'd here
Novr 4 Thomas Hanson Preach'd here
[illegible] Jno Heslop Preach'd here Sunday—
Novr 18 Robert Swann Preach'd here
Novr 29 Jas Odie Preach'd here
Feb. 7. 1772 Thos Carlill Preach'd here: 1 Sam. 20. 3: but a Step betwixt [illegible]
Feb. 12 Thos Carlill Preach'd here —Ex
Feb. 26 Thos Hanson Preach'd here—
March 11 Robert Swann Preach'd here—
March 16 Jas Odie Preach'd here—
March 25 Thos Carlill Preach'd here Ex:
April 7 Thos Hanson Preach'd here
22 Robert Swann Preach'd here
May 6 Thos Carlill Preach'd here —Ex.
May 20 Tho Hanson Preach'd here X
June 3. Robert Swan Preach'd here
June 7 White Sunday John Richardson Preach'd here many to here
June 18·1772 ye Reverent & pious Jno Wesley Preach'd here EX
[illegible] Isah 66: 2. 9: EX:

25. *Above*, an extract, mentioning a visit by "The Reverend and pious John Wesley", from an old Society Book of 1750 at Osmotherley. *Below*, stone cottages (now a farm) at the Bongs, Mellor, where Wesley preached from the angled doorway

26. The remains of the old farmhouse at Hindley Hill, now smothered in nettles, which was the scene of a famous romance in Wesley's life. *Below*, Moat House Farm, Alpraham, where Wesley preached and where early Methodist preachers were welcomed

Methodist Church and described it of light but substantial wood, easily lifted with one hand, bearing a scratched inscription, "John Wesley H." The pulpit was formerly in the possession of a family called Harley, and Wesley preached in the village of Harby, Leicestershire, either of which may account for the letter H. This inscription, however, seems to have disappeared or is obscured by a bronze plaque which reads: "A pulpit of John Wesley." It was originally used by Wesley in the Leicester area.

The Old Square in Ramsey lies at the end of Church Street, where in former days the main streets of the town converged. A drab-looking hall here occupies the site of a former residence in front of which Wesley stood on a June evening and preached to "well nigh all the town", and again at five the next morning, but the Cross which then stood in the Square has disappeared.

In Douglas he preached in the market place, in a building at the rear of Victoria Street Church, and outside the old St. Matthew's Church, since demolished, the site of which is now covered by the market hall beyond the bus-station near the harbour. He also preached in Braddan churchyard, and in the open at South Barewle and Kirk-Andrew.

Unfortunately, apart from Mr. J. L. West's presidential lecture to the local Antiquarian Society, which is of general but not detailed interest, there is no modern history of Manx Methodism. A little local enterprise could well gather up old memories and traditions, which are fairly plentiful, before they are forgotten, and a plaque here and there to mark Wesley's visits would be of value.

The island is full of legends, but I could find no basis for the story told me by Mrs. E. Quayle that her ancestor, Thomas Corlett of Keilthustag, once hid Wesley there in a bin of oats after he had been chased out of Andreas, that he remained undiscovered and was smuggled out at midnight in a farm cart. Wesley would hardly have omitted such a lively incident from his *Journal*, and the story more likely concerns one of his preachers.

While on the island he visited the grave of Bishop Wilson at Kirkmichael and passed by Bishopscourt "where good Bishop Wilson resided near threescore years". He described it as venerable though not magnificent. He also walked through the grounds of the Nunnery in Douglas which are still to be seen.

So to his summing up—"Having now visited the island round, east, south, north, and west, I was thoroughly convinced that we have no such circuit as this, either in England, Scotland or Ireland." And a verse of one of his preachers is worth recalling:

The *Cumberland* hills and the mountains of *Wales*,
He frequently crossed in his way;
And bleak *Caledonia*'s high rocks and deep vales,
And swift running torrent of *Spey*.
Hibernia too felt his fostering care,
As round it and round it he ran,
Each city, each village, each town had its share,
Nor did he forget little *Man*.

Today we can breakfast in Manchester and reach Jersey (by air) in time for lunch. The same journey (by road and sailing-ship) took Wesley over twelve days! He was in his eighty-sixth year when he went direct from the Conference in Manchester to Southampton—which took him five days—and embarked.

For the first stage, from Manchester to Birmingham, he chartered a special coach, bringing preachers back with him from the Conference. They set out at midnight and were due in Birmingham at five o'clock the next morning. But the load of fourteen preachers was too much for the coach, which broke down outside Congleton and was abandoned for another. Within an hour this too had broken down, and they arrived in Birmingham at 7 p.m., after nineteen hours on the way. Wesley stepped straight from the coach into the chapel and preached to a waiting congregation, and at 5 a.m. was on his way in a post-chaise. He rested for an hour in Worcester, changed horses at Tewkesbury and reached Gloucester at 5 p.m. where he preached—the hottest night, he says, he had ever known in Europe. He was off at 2 a.m. the next day, reaching Salisbury at half-past four in the afternoon, after his post-chaise had failed at Malmesbury and he had sent to Bristol for another. He preached in Salisbury, left at four the following morning, and gave three sermons in Southampton before sailing.

On the sea crossing he fared no better, for his boat was driven by gales, first into Yarmouth (Isle of Wight), where he preached twice in the Market House, then into Swanage where he held a service in the Presbyterian Chapel, and, after narrowly escaping being wrecked, landed off its course at Alderney. Here he slept in a five-bedded room in the Divers' Inn, which was gutted during the German Occupation and rebuilt in 1950. The following morning he preached on the shore before the boat took him on to Guernsey, where the first things he noticed were the narrow streets and tall houses of St. Peter Port—still the same; and the abundant variety of fine fresh fruit.

He stayed five days with Henri de Jersey at Mon Plaisir, St. Jacques, on the outskirts of the town. A riding block by the road-side has a plaque on the wall behind it recording that he preached there as well as in the house on his two visits to this island. Before going on to Jersey he walked on the Pier, and with his companion, Dr. Coke, dined with the Governor. Things had changed for the better since the first preachers were drummed out of their pulpits, blown out with gunpowder in Guernsey, and pelted with peas and rotten eggs in Jersey.

Jersey Methodism owed much to Robert Carr Brackenbury, the Lincolnshire squire, who, because he had a smattering of French, was sent by Wesley to evangelize the island. He was the first Free Church minister there, and for seven years with princely generosity maintained the work at his own expense. Wesley urged him to preach in French. "Surely you need not be careful about accuracy. Trust God, and speak as well as you can."

Brackenbury's house, where Wesley stayed and preached, is still standing—No. 15, Old Street, St. Helier—a typical double-fronted terrace house of the period opening directly on to the street. When I first knew it, from its front door one could look right through to the garden where Dr. Adam Clarke once picked a bunch of grapes which weighed twenty pounds, but now only part of the front remains, the house has been much altered, and the back is a workshop. Brackenbury had prepared a large hall in the house for Methodist services.

Wesley attended service at the parish church and rode out to St. Mary's where he preached in the parlour of a house called Le Marais, now a stable. Then, as bad weather prevented him from re-embarking, he continued to preach in St. Helier, in the Assembly Rooms—"The Long Room", as it was then called, of the present United Club situated over the Hall-à-blé on Corn Market. He preached twelve times during the eight days he was in Jersey. "Here we are," he says, "shut up in Jersey;

for how long we cannot tell." When he finally set sail the weather was again unkind, and after further delay in Guernsey, instead of travelling to Southampton, he was landed at Penzance!

CHAPTER FIFTEEN

WALES—FONTIGARY—FONMON CASTLE—WENVOE—PEMBROKESHIRE—LLANELLY—THE GOWER—TYDDYN HALL—SALLY GWYNNE—ROUND CADER IDRIS—ANGLESEY

WITH a clean wind sweeping the coast road from Barry and the sea shimmering in the April sun I came to Fontigary Farm. Bungalows here are springing up like mushrooms and Rhoose has its holiday camp, but there are still the paths that go down to the sea and the lanes running into the hills. Opposite the bus stop on the main road is a country club with a car park and built-out annexe. Do not be put off by its recent conversion, for this is the former Fontigary Farm, the old stone-built farmhouse abutting directly on the roadside, facing the fields and the sea, to which Wesley came, though within, all is transformed, with a modern lounge and cocktail bar.

Mrs. Robert Jones of Fonmon Castle lived here after her husband's death, the house forming part of her estate, and here Wesley, who had often been her guest, calling on his way from Neath to Cardiff, found her dying of cancer with her children round her. That night in a room in this house he preached from the sombre text, "It is appointed unto men once to die." He had intended to go on to Cowbridge the next day, but "being much importuned to give one more day to a dying friend, I yielded and desired another Preacher to go and supply my place". He preached again, then, changing his mind, went to Cowbridge after all, where he spoke in the Market Hall, and returned to Fontigary to take his last leave of his friend.

By the side of the farmhouse is the lane with its signpost to Fonmon and a lovely lane it is, by a babbling brook, over a bridge by a weed-covered pond and a blacksmith's forge whose fire has been long extinct, past a thatched cottage to where, through a gate, lay the long green drive under the shade of elms leading to the stone-walled Castle and where I walked ankle-deep on a carpet of violets. Formerly a gravelled drive ran to the front of the Castle, where now stretch wide, undulating and gracious lawns (Plate 29*a*).

The Castle, with its eleventh-century tower and memories of the Civil Wars, belonged to Robert Jones, a young squire converted under Howell Harris. He was a man, we are told, "truly inclined to piety, and very loving to assist those who come together to keep Religious Societies thereabouts; an example of godliness in his house and neighbourhood."

Harris often stayed at the Castle, but the squire, reluctant to accept Calvinism, invited Charles Wesley as his guest, and as a result, a Society—the second in Wales—was formed in his home. The Castle lay on Wesley's annual route from Bristol to Holyhead, "so that once a year," he wrote, for he was on close terms with the family, "as long as my life is prolonged, I hope to have the pleasure of seeing you at Fonmon." The visits continued after the squire's untimely death. He stayed here on his way to his brother's wedding at Garth. Mrs. Robert Jones consulted him about her children's education, and he discussed with her the advisability of sending her son to his new school at Kingswood. "If your son comes there, you will probably hear complaints; for the discipline will be exact; it being our view not so much to teach Greek and Latin as to train up soldiers for Jesus Christ." But her son, as Wesley anticipated, proved a difficult pupil and he later advised his withdrawal.

Descendants of Robert Jones still occupy the Castle, which in the hands of Sir Hugo Boothby is well-preserved and its fine collection of pictures includes a portrait of Robert Jones by Reynolds and a delightful group of the family in Wesley's day by Hogarth. Its long drawing room with its windows overlooking the wide parkland was much admired by the late Queen Mary. Wesley preached in the dining room, which at one time was fitted up as a chapel, and also in the courtyard.

From Fonmon it is no great distance to Porthkerry church with its low-roofed lych-gate, its renovated tower standing high above the sea, its leper's window and linenfold screen. In this small church Wesley preached one of his most famous sermons: "By grace are ye saved through faith." He had preached at Wenvoe in the morning and a large congregation welcomed him at the Castle at night. On the following day he preached again at Porthkerry. On a Sunday four years later he preached four times in these places, beginning at 7 a.m. in the Castle, going on to Wenvoe and Porthkerry, and ending with an evening service at Fonmon. It is a pity that Porthkerry Church bears no outward sign or record of its close links with early Methodism, which include also a visit by Charles Wesley.

But from where did the people come? Porthkerry village can hardly have changed since then—a quiet spot with but a handful of houses flanking a village green, with a seat for the wayfarer, and ducks on a pond. Mr. Bert Bowen, who has lived next to the church all his life, pointed out to me the outline of a doorway on the wall of Glebe Farm, from which Wesley is said to have preached to a crowd on the Green below, and the farmer, Mr. Ewart Davies, confirmed the story before setting me on my way through the woods to Glan-y-Môr.

Wenvoe I knew only as the site of the Cardiff television mast, but the real Wenvoe is of historical interest. The thirteenth-century church of St. Mary with its squat clock-faced tower and ancient yew tree lies just off the main road from Cardiff to Barry, but it has been much renovated and provided with a new pulpit and pews since Wesley preached in it. Six fine yews flank the short path to the Old Rectory—a square stone-built house faced with roughcast, but it is doubtful if it was the house that Wesley knew. Professor Atkinson, its present owner, thinks it may have replaced an older building in the latter part of the eighteenth century. Wesley's last visit there was earlier, in 1762.

For fifty-six years John Hodges, an Oxford friend of the Wesleys, was rector of Wenvoe, and his rectory was a regular place of call. More than once he accompanied Wesley as he journeyed north and he was a member of his first Conferences. But later Wesley found him less enthusiastic. "I preached once more in Wenvoe Church," he records, "but it was hard work. Mr. H. read the prayers (not as he once did, with such fervour and solemnity as struck almost every hearer, but) like one reading an old song, in a cold, dry, careless manner; and there was no singing at all. O! what a life was here once! But now there is not one spark left."

Hodges, however, has his place in early Methodism, and Wenvoe played its part. For long his grave was overgrown, its whereabouts in the churchyard unknown, until the present rector, the Rev. W. J. Christopher, found it, uncovering it with his own hands, and had the old lettering restored which marks "the remains of the Pious and Reverend John Hodges".

Wesley's first sermon on Welsh soil was on the village green of Devauden, near Chepstow. One of his hearers, a poor woman, followed him on foot all the way from Chepstow to Abergavenny and on to Pontypool and Cardiff, where he preached in the Shire Hall and she was converted. But the next day, he records, he faced in Newport the most insensible, ill-behaved people he had ever seen in Wales, one old man during most of the service cursing and swearing incessantly and threatening him with a large stone. At Newport on another occasion he describes his hearers as wooden as the benches they sat upon.

In St. Michael's churchyard, Lower Machen, a stone and yew tree are pointed out as the site of one of his services, and in the same neighbourhood he preached by the Rhymer river and at Pant Glas Farm, Bedwas. The National Museum of Wales preserves the preaching desk he used at Pant Glas.

In Pembrokeshire he was on ancestral ground, for his mother came, on her mother's side, from a well-known local family—the Whites of Henllan. Griffith White was High Sheriff in 1676, his brother John became Member of Parliament for Southwark, whose daughter married Dr. Annesley and was Wesley's grandmother. But Wesley in his travels paid little heed to his ancestry and apart from Epworth his *Journal* is curiously bare of references to local family associations.

He paid fourteen visits to this area, preaching at the Cross in Tenby and near the Castle in Haverfordwest, riding up its steep and stony mountains and nearly engulfed in the quick-sands from Llansteffan Ferry to Gower. Of the latter he said: "I wonder that any man of commonsense, who has once made the experiment, should ever ride from Pembroke to Swansea any other way, than by Carmarthen."

At Pembroke he was invited by the vicar to preach in St. Mary's, but was forbidden by the mayor—a curious intervention, for the mayor had no authority in the matter. The room used on his Pembroke visits, behind the York Tavern where he stayed, is now a store-room. Miss M. Jenkins who kept the Tavern for thirty-six years tells me that her father had it for sixty years before her, and he had told her that Wesley had a large room above the brewhouse behind the inn, with stone steps and a handrail leading up to it, with a side entrance to the street. It was known as the Meeting Hall and Wesley held fortnightly services, arriving from Narberth on a white pony. He also preached in the main street, the Town Hall (probably the present Market Hall), the existing Monktown Church, and

St. Daniel's—a small church still standing, but no longer in use.

It may have been due to his family connection that he made so many good friends in the area—the Greens, the Vaughans of Trecwn, the Bowens of Llwyn-y-Gwair, the Phillips, the Warrens, the Wogans of Wiston. He speaks of elegant and genteel congregations and describes the Haverfordwest Circuit as the most important in Wales.

He was the guest of the sheriff, Mr. Green, at No. 24 Bridge Street, now occupied by Messrs. Hopson and Sons, tobacconists. Descendants of the Green family are still associated with the Haverfordwest Chapel and possess a chair and table used on his visits. The chapel, still in use, was known as Wesley's Room and is reached through Chapel Lane which was formerly part of St. Martin's churchyard. The room was supplementary to St. Martin's, where Wesley often preached and baptized.

A bronze tablet on the wall of the Grammar School, at the junction of Tower Hill and Dear Street, marks his last visit to Wales. He was in his eighty-eighth year when he preached from a horse-block outside the Blue Boar, which stood near the Fish Market on ground now absorbed by the school. He used the broad shoulders of John Green as a desk on which to rest his Bible, and a direct descendant of John Green in the person of the mayor of Haverfordwest, Major John Green, T.D., unveiled the tablet in 1956.

In the neighbourhood, in a wooded and mountainous valley, is Trecwm House, near Letterston, where Admiral Vaughan ran his household like a ship, mustering the family for morning and evening prayers. "The good old Admiral," Wesley calls him. He had four maiden sisters, the youngest of whom was over seventy. They attended the Haverfordwest Chapel, and five times Wesley visited their house, in the grounds of which a plaque marks the oak under which he preached. Llwyn-y-Gwair, near Cardigan, now an hotel, was until three years ago still occupied by the Bowen family whose ancestors often entertained Wesley there.

To this remote area Wesley gave a generous portion of his time. His voice was heard in Newport Parish Church, in St. Brynach's, Nevern, where his chapel has only recently been closed, in Cardigan, Howton and Jeffreston, in St. Thomas's Church and Queen Square, Haverfordwest, on the village green of Spittal, in Narberth market-place, and in the parish church of Little Newcastle. He rode to St. Davids and was disappointed—lovely country, but the town a melancholy spectacle, with but one tolerable good house, and the cathedral deteriorating. Tenby was no better. He called it the Kilmallock of Britain, referring to a town in Ireland.

Llanelly House in Llanelly in Sir Thomas Stepney's day was alive with Methodism. In the servants' hall the butler, Wilfrid Colley, led one of the earliest groups in Wales, and Sir Thomas, "the father of the poor", was no less devoted. The house is across the road from the parish church, in which Wesley preached, as well as in the house and churchyard. After Sir Thomas's death and the removal of the family, Wesley with sad feelings revisited the empty and desolate mansion. Eight times altogether he was in Llanelly and a tablet on the wall of the Public Library marks the site of one of his services. On his last visit, hearing that his followers were about to build a chapel, he blessed the project and gave the first guinea towards it.

On the Gower peninsula, in a lane at Oxwich, is a thatched and old-world cottage where Wesley slept as the guest of John Clarke, and at Great Pitton Farm, Rhossili, a heavy oak chair and book rest are preserved which stood in front of the window seat in the kitchen when he preached there. The farm, now occupied by Mrs. Beynon, has been altered, but basically is unchanged. Nor must we forget Trevecca with its memories of Howell Harris, where Lady Huntingdon established a theological college, visited by Wesley on its first anniversary. The building (Trevecca Isaf) is still occupied and is now known as College Farm, and is not to be confused with the Calvinistic Methodist College nearby that replaced Howell Harris's settlement which was also visited by Wesley. Lady Huntingdon's College was later transferred to Cheshunt and thence to Cambridge.

Trecastle, Llandefeiliog, Swansea and Llandaff were among other places he visited. His chapel at Watton in Brecon (where he also preached in the Town Hall and market-place) has been converted into private houses. His friend, Walter Churchey, a solicitor, lived in Brecon, and it is the birthplace of Dr. Coke, the founder of the Methodist Missionary Society. In Carmarthen Wesley held services on the Castle Green, in the market, and in Peter Williams's Calvinistic Chapel.

In central Wales it is in the Builth area that we trace his steps.

Llanidloes was the centre of a flourishing wool industry and on three occasions he preached outside its fine timber-framed Market Hall. The stone on which he stood has been removed to the back wall of the market and bears an appropriate inscription. The Bowen family entertained him at Tydden Hall, a farmhouse at Oakley Park, two miles from the town, still occupied by their descendants, who proudly preserve the bed on which he slept.

Maesmynis Church, near Builth, also has Methodist associations, for Wesley often preached there and in the neighbourhood. Its rector, Edward Phillips, sometimes accompanied him on his journeys, once as far as Caernarvon, and translated his sermons, as he preached, into Welsh. Charles Wesley's marriage, however, impaired their friendship, for the rector had also sought the hand of Sally Gwynne. Llansantffraid and Builth are among other churches Wesley visited; at the latter he spoke from a tomb at the east end of the churchyard.

It was on an April day in 1749 that he came riding up the road from Aberdare to Garth to officiate at his brother's wedding. He travelled up from the growing industrial towns of South Wales and he was making for Ireland via Holyhead. But first there was this pleasant family duty. His brother had chosen a Welsh bride, Sally, a daughter of Marmaduke Gwynne, the Squire of Garth, a local magistrate and landowner.

The romantic setting remains—the small church on the hillside with its path from the road winding up to it across the field, the river Dulas below, and, on the opposite bank, the eighteenth-century Garth Hall, from which the bridal party walked on foot. This house, which we see among the trees, was a home of generous hospitality, where Charles Wesley had been nursed during an illness by Sally Gwynne, and romance had followed. It was a large household including nine children, twenty servants, and often as many as ten guests. It is said that it was here that Charles Wesley composed his best-known hymn: "Jesu, lover of my soul," during a storm when a robin flew in at the window.

The marriage, which proved a singularly happy one, took place in Llanlleonfel Church (Plate 29*b*) which, though restored, preserves a picturesque and primitive simplicity. Charles Wesley's *Journal* describes the scene: " 'Sweet day! so cool, so calm, so bright!' Not a cloud from morning till night.

I rose at four, spent three and a half hours in prayer—singing with my brother, with Sally, with Beck. At eight I led my Sally to Church." Wesley married them and the marriage register contains this simple entry: "Charles Wesley and Sarah Gwynne were lawfully married, April 8, 1749."

Though Wesley knew Wales so well, by mutual agreement he left its evangelization mainly to his friend, Howell Harris. He loved its scenery and often described its beauty. But sometimes he met with rough conditions, in winter travelling through the snowy wastes of the Black Mountains, reaching Dolgelley (or Dalle-y-galle, as he calls it) in driving rain, soaked to the skin, and kept awake all night by a noisy company of drunken sea captains. At which of the two inns there he stayed is uncertain, so the slate tablet relating to his visits has been placed on the front of Ebenezer Chapel. We find him thrown from his horse on the icy road round Cader Idris—"the great mountain". If we travel the same road today and are caught in a storm we can still barely imagine what discomfort he suffered as he faced those endless desolate miles on horseback, wet and weary, often lost in the dark.

His objective was Traeth Mawr (the large estuary) at the mouth of the Glaslyn, where the treacherous marshes could only be crossed at low tide. (The present road was non-existent.) While waiting here on one occasion he sat down in a cottage for three or four hours and translated a book of logic as a text-book for Kingswood School—he had remarkable powers of detachment and concentration. Having crossed the sands he stayed at an inn in Caernarvon, then made for the Moel-y-don Ferry, four miles further on, at Port Dinorwic. Once he misjudged the distance and called across the water for a boatman, but with no result. Rain came on and he sheltered in Llanfair-is-gaer Church, which is still used for worship. On another occasion when delayed, Jenkin Morgan, the schoolmaster of Rhos-y-Meirch, came along and took him home for the night.

Wesley visited Anglesey sixteen times and as he often had to wait, sometimes for days, for the Irish packet, he travelled and preached in many parts of the island. Once on arriving outside Holyhead, hearing that the boat had already sailed, he was not in the least perturbed. "Never mind," he said with a laugh, "perhaps we may catch it yet." And he did, although it had sailed the previous night and had gone half-way to Ireland, the wind having driven it back into Holyhead harbour.

Accompanied by an interpreter he preached at Rhyd-y-sbardun, Llanddaniel, Llanfihangel, Clwch Dernog and Glan-y-Gors. He attended a Welsh service in Llangefni Parish Church of which he understood nothing and remarked: "O what a heavy curse was this confusion of tongues!" Birds and beasts, he added, understand the language of their own species. "Man only is barbarian to man, unintelligible to his own brethren." But though the country people spoke no English, he was amused to hear so many oaths from Welshmen in good broad English! The house where he stayed with William Jones at Trefollwyn is now a barn.

Travellers in those days needed great patience. Once after waiting nearly a week for a boat he made this humorous comment: "I never knew a man make such poor lame excuse as these sea captains did, for not sailing. It put me in mind of this epigram:

> There are, if rightly I methink,
> Five causes why a man should drink,

which, with a little alteration, would just suit them:

> There are, unless my memory fail,
> Five causes why we should not sail:
> The fog is thick, the wind is high;
> It rains; or may do, by and by;
> Or any other reason why."

I explored Holyhead on the day I stepped off the Irish boat—a plain clean town open almost on every side to the sea and full of invigorating air. But little trace remains of Wesley's visits. The old Wesley Chapel is now a laundry, with Wesley Terrace adjoining. Where is the inn where he had trouble with a notorious Caernarvonshire character, Captain Griffith, a clumsy, overgrown, hard-faced man whose language was worse than Billingsgate? The Irish boat had run into a storm and after two days had returned to the harbour. Wesley improved the occasion by preaching to a rich and well-dressed company, but found them unresponsive and was glad afterwards to spend the evening with "some plain honest Welshmen". That night at the inn, Griffith with others arrived the worse for drink, burst open the door, struck the landlord, and demanded: "Where is the parson?" The landlord, to secure Wesley's safety, had locked him in his room and the intruders withdrew. Later they returned, but the Captain was taken unawares by the landlord's daughter who drenched him from head to foot with a pail of water, the door was locked behind him, and he was a prisoner. The inn where this may have happened, and where Dean Swift stayed, stood on the site of the new car park in Swift Square.

The present dock and breakwater did not exist in those days. The harbour was at the end of the present Promenade, and traces of an old quay can be seen at Porth Defarch, where the path runs along the cliff to the remains of a custom shed.

We must visit the ancient collegiate church of St. Cybi—a sixth-century foundation, rebuilt a thousand years later, and restored in the nineteenth century. Its vicar, Thomas Ellis, sent a message to Wesley saying he would take it as a favour if Mr. Wesley would write some little thing, to advise the Methodists not to leave the Church, and not to rail at the clergy. Wesley willingly complied and immediately sat down and wrote a pamphlet *A Word to a Methodist*, which the vicar translated into Welsh, printed and circulated. The conduct of his curate, however, was very different, for when Wesley announced that he would preach as soon as Evensong was over he deliberately prevented him by keeping the children so long at their catechism that Wesley was obliged to abandon his service.

Sometimes Wesley travelled by way of North Wales, but not of course along the modern highway, and there was no coastline of crowded resorts. He followed the old coach road through St. Asaph and Bettws-yn-Rhos which brought him down the steep hill to Conway Ferry, where there was then no bridge, nor at Menai. Traffic, including coaches, crossed the river and the Menai Straits by ferries, which led to delays, sometimes to fatalities, as at Conway when a mail coach sank. The Bangor ferry was at the narrowest part of the Straits, near the point where the drovers with loud cries urged their cattle and pigs into the water, making them swim to the opposite shore. They were noisy occasions, as the heavy animals splashed and bellowed their way across and landed, shaking their dripping flanks.

Houses now stand on the field where he preached at Mold, known as Coetiau Moch, off Clay Lane, near the parish church.

He stayed at a farmhouse, Plas Bach, Glan Conway, now derelict. He found Conway Castle overgrown, but the noblest ruin he ever saw. He describes the turnpike road overhanging the sea at Penmaenmawr, which can still be seen above the new tunnelled motorway. When he first used this route it was but a narrow and dangerous path, but had been widened by 1774 when Dr. Johnson travelled along it.

In later years Wesley made the journey by stage coach from Chester via Halkyn, Holywell, St. Asaph and Abergele, staying at Kinmel in one of the pleasantest inns in Wales. In 1789, at the age of eighty-six, he made his last journey to these parts, travelling from Shrewsbury to Conway, by way of Llangollen and Llanrwst—seventy-eight miles in a single day, reaching Holyhead the following day. He returned a month later from Ireland to Parkgate. Only two years remained of his long and eventful life which spanned the century, during which, in an age of slow and laborious travel, he had made at least forty-seven journeys through Wales.

CHAPTER SIXTEEN

IRELAND — DUBLIN — CASTLEBAR — CROAGH PATRICK — BALLINGRANE—HOME OF AMERICAN PIONEERS—CORK—NORTHERN IRELAND—THE GAYER FAMILY—CHROME HILL—TANDARAGEE—WICKLOW—THE HAPPY TRAVELLER

IT'S A LONG way to Tipperary, but Wesley took it in his stride. On the boat from Holyhead we are still in his wake, but our journey is easy compared with the twenty-six hours he took to cross to Dublin, when more than once he was driven back into Holyhead Harbour.

There was no mistaking the greeting as I landed at Dun Laoghaire at seven o'clock on a chill March morning: "Good morning, Father, and thanks be to God for a foine morning and ahll." It was indeed a fine morning and a good Irish welcome, even if the title was misplaced. It warmed the heart on a cold day and in a land thick with churches. The sunlight was touching the sea with gold and shining upon the Wicklow hills. The little town was hardly astir and a church lifted its spire above the quiet streets like a symbol of the morning.

Wesley travelled the road from Dun Laoghaire, and once at least, when no carriage was available, walked it, taking two hours to reach the city, but on his first visit he landed in Dublin at St. George's Quay. It was a Sunday morning, the church bells were ringing and, his host not having met him, he left his luggage at an inn and attended matins at St. Mark's, and the same evening, by invitation of the curate, Moses Roquier, of Huguenot origin, he preached in St. Mary's. In 1935 the Dublin Methodist Council placed in the church a handsome brass plate recording the occasion. Canon Emerson, the present rector, tells me that the pulpit now in the church is not the one used by Wesley, also that in 1947 a bi-centenary service was held there commemorating Wesley at which the Archbishop of Dublin preached. But in Wesley's day the archbishop, Dr. Cobbe, raised objections, and Wesley on learning of this lost no time in riding ten miles out of the city to "Newbridge" to see him.

27. Brock House, near Preston—"the house of a friend" as Wesley called it

28. Wesley greatly favoured the octagon design for chapels. *Above*, the old "Totum Kirkie" at Arbroath, and, *right*, the chapel at Yarm, Yorkshire—the oldest Methodist octagon chapel in the world

Left, Heptonstall chapel in Yorkshire, which has hardly been altered since Wesley's day

Opposite St. Mary's in those days, in Jervis Street, was the residence of Mrs. Katherine Wesley who had recently died, widow of Garret Wesley, M.P., of Dangan Castle, who having no children of his own had offered to adopt Charles Wesley as his heir. But Charles had just settled in as a scholar of Westminster School and the offer was declined. The young cousin adopted in his place became the first Earl of Mornington and grandfather of Arthur Wellesley, Duke of Wellington.

Bethesda Chapel in Dorset Street, in the same parish, was the scene of several of Wesley's services. For a time it was used by Sandemanians, then reverted to parochial use until some fifty years ago when services were discontinued. A picture of it (as it was) appeared in the *Proceedings* of the Wesley Historical Society, March 1942.

On his second Sunday in the city Wesley worshipped in St. James's church and in Christchurch; in the meantime he preached in a Lutheran chapel which was situated on the east side of Marlborough Street, near the corner of Abbey Street, and he lodged at No. 15, Francis Street with William Lunell, a Huguenot banker of the firm of Lunell and Dickson. The narrow three-storied building, with an office below and an attic with a gable, no longer exists, but there is a sketch of it in the Public Record Office. Here on one occasion G. F. Lampe, the musical composer, of Covent Garden, and his wife met Charles Wesley.

During his fortnight's stay Wesley saw most of the sights of the city including Trinity College and Phoenix Park. St. Stephen's Green was different in those days. He would see a great change today, where wide roads run out to attractive suburbs with rows and squares of well-preserved Georgian architecture, reminding us of Bath, and fine shops and hotels. Trinity College is like a Cambridge college transplanted to the banks of the Liffey; and the Green itself is an oasis in the heart of the city.

Facing the Green is the Mother Church of Irish Methodism, erected after Wesley's death, flanked by the Connexional office, and by the gateway of Wesley College, founded in 1845, which has five hundred pupils, is co-educational, is one of Ireland's foremost public schools, and numbers Bernard Shaw amongst its old boys, who said it was a bad school but the best in Ireland.

It was in Dublin that one of his preachers, Samuel Bradburn, solicited Wesley's help in a love affair, which Wesley settled with characteristic dispatch. Bradburn had won the heart of a Miss Elizabeth Nangle, but her guardian, Mrs. Karr, had refused consent. Wesley wrote to her and she replied in polite and general terms that she would be guided by him, but implying that he would wish to please her in the matter by not intervening. Wesley, however, took this as her full consent, informed the happy pair that all was settled, invited them and Mrs. Karr to breakfast and, before the latter realized what was happening, had begun the marriage ceremony.

A plot of land was leased in Whitefriar Street where the first Methodist chapel in Ireland was opened in 1752. Attached to it were two houses for ministers, a free school, a book room, an orphan house for girls, and an almshouse for twenty-four widows, each of whom received free bedding, coals, candles, and a small weekly allowance. It was supported by collections and charity sermons. Wesley frequently visited it. He wrote: "One thing I cannot but particularly wish, that all their rooms may be kept as clean as possible." When the lease expired the Carmelite Friars built a school on the site, but a new home was acquired in Grantham Street, and when that area deteriorated it was transferred to a commodious villa in the suburbs—Eastwell in Palmerston Park, where, under modern conditions, the Irish Methodist Conference carries on Wesley's philanthropic work.

During his many visits to the city he frequently worshipped in St. Patrick's Cathedral, sometimes assisting in the Communion Service, and led his converts there for the Sacrament in such numbers that the Communion vessels were inadequate and larger chalices were procured which are still in use. He preached regularly on Oxmanton Green, and in Gravel Lane Chapel, now Blackhall Place. No. 46, Charlemont Street, where he also stayed, is still standing, though it was then half a mile out of the city in rural surroundings.

On one occasion he was summoned to the Court of Conscience by a man who had fed his horses on his passage from Parkgate, and who had demanded ten shillings; Wesley had paid him half a crown. The man lost his case and was sharply reproved.

At Moira, in County Down, Wesley preached in the churchyard and was more than once the guest of Lord and Lady Moira at Moira House in Dublin. Lady Moira was a daughter of the Countess of Huntingdon, and when Wesley was denied the use of the church Lord Moira sent a bellman round to summon the people to service. The mansion at Moira is demolished, and Moira House, with its top storey removed, is now the Mendicity Institution, and offices cover its once lovely grounds. Wesley described its octagon room as more elegant than any he had seen in England—twenty feet across, with a single window from floor to ceiling inlaid with mother of pearl.

He penetrated every county except Kerry, and we find the same pattern of untiring activity. He records the country seats he visited, the scenes he admired, the castles and cathedrals he explored. He was a great sightseer and nothing escaped his observant eye. His passion as an evangelist was combined with the zest of a tourist, and in his twenty-one visits, many of them of four months' duration and together totalling five and a half years, he found Irish scenes and the warmth of Irish life irresistible. Nowhere, he says, had he found a more kindly or warmhearted people.

But he also had setbacks. There was calumny and persecution; inns, as at Rathcormack, which turned him from the door; churches closed against him, as at Ardstraw, where the church door was locked and its key hidden; bogholes, as at Sligo, in which his horses floundered and his carriage was immobilized; riots, as at Cork, where the military protected him; also quagmire roads and never-ending rain. The over-all picture, however, is of triumphal progress. Never since the days of St. Patrick had Ireland known such flaming evangelism or greeted a more fervent apostle. The soldiers to whom he preached in Athlone Barracks declared "there was something superhuman about him".

As in Cornwall he preached in the main street, the market, the town hall or assembly rooms of almost every principal town and village. It would be tedious to record every place to which he came or every spot in which he spoke. The Rev. R. Lee Cole, the Irish Methodist historian, has very usefully listed the parish churches in which he preached or worshipped. When a church was denied him, Wesley would call for a chair and preach in the open street. He slept in mansions and mud cabins. Sometimes in the latter, as at Castlecaulfield, the rain seeped through the thatched roof on to his bed. He preached in meadows and orchards, stables and haylofts, riding schools and on barrack squares. He was specially popular and always at ease among soldiers.

His old chapel can still be seen at Castlebar—a plain building with a single gable and an inscription on its outside wall: "This Chapel was built for the Methodists under the Patronage of Charles, Lord Lucan. The Rev. John Wesley, M.A. laid the first stone May the 21st, 1785. 'And this stone which I have set up for a pillar shall be God's House.' Genesis, Chapter 28, verse 22." The manse, which is a continuation of the building at the rear, was built in 1805 and was vacated two years ago, since when a visiting minister travels twenty or thirty miles for a monthly service. The Earl of Lucan and his family had previously heard Wesley preach in the Court House. While in the neighbourhood he climbed Croagh Patrick (or Mount Eagle, as he called it), following the pilgrim's path, "the pilgrim way to the clouds". With two friends, leaving their horses at the foot, he made the ascent of two thousand, five hundred feet, in two hours, in a burning sun.

In Ballingrane, fifteen miles from Limerick and two from Rathkeale, is the ancestral home of Barbara Heck who with her cousin, Philip Embury, was the founder of Methodism in North America. The house, Fort View (formerly Ruckle Hill), still stands (Plate 30*b*), and until recently was in the possession of Mr. and Mrs. Julius Sheppard, direct descendants of Sebastian Rückle (or Ruttle), the father of Barbara Heck. Its present occupier is Mr. Walter Ruttle. With six thousand Lutheran refugees Sebastian had been driven out of the Palatinate, and fifty families of them had been sent to County Limerick where they formed a strong religious community. The walls of the house are eighteen inches thick, the heavy oak door has an iron key, the kitchen with its whitewashed beams and stone floor was unchanged until four years ago, but the rest of the house has been remodelled and has an added storey. Outside is a neat yard with flowers and a well-trimmed hedge. Wesley's pear tree was blown down in a storm about seven years ago and only its stump remains. From this tree hung the famous cow's horn (Plate 30*a*) which is now in the Embury–Heck Memorial Church, near Ballingrane. Wesley gave young Paul Rückle sixpence for blowing it to call the men from the fields to the preaching service under the tree.

If we did not know the story we should never associate this enchanting spot, near the winding Shannon and the mountains of Limerick and Kerry, with the foundation of Methodism in New York. The ancestors of Barbara Heck lie in the quiet graveyard, and a heap of stones in a meadow are all that remain of Philip Embury's birthplace. Wesley many times visited the room in which Barbara was born and was distressed when he came and found that she and others had emigrated to America, little dreaming of the strange providence that would transplant the spirit of Ballingrane across the sea. No memorial marks the site of Embury's cottage or of the chapel he built at Courtmatrix, but a bi-centenary pilgrimage was made last year to Ballingrane, and plans are on foot to mark and preserve what remains of Methodist origins in this neighbourhood. Americans often come here. Mrs. K. E. Brookfield, another direct descendant of the family, has given me interesting details. Ireland may not have an Epworth or a Trewint, but it has its Ballingrane.

Donegall Square Methodist Church in Belfast has a beautiful memorial window which is a vivid reminder of the link between Irish and American Methodism. Its centre light depicts Christ commissioning His disciples. To the right of it we see Barbara Heck in the costume of the day, with books and ink symbolizing her industrious nature, and a view of the landing of the Ballingrane emigrants in America. The left-hand light shows Embury conducting the first service in his home, with his carpenter's bench behind him, and Barbara exhorting him to build a church, which is depicted in the background.

In the Dunraven demesne at Adare, near Limerick, is an inscribed stone near the east window of the ruins of the Franciscan abbey, marking the spot where Wesley preached, and where an open-air service is held early in June each year. Adare had once been a flourishing town, but Wesley found only huts and ruins and the remains of its three abbeys, two of which have since been restored. For thirty-seven years he came regularly through this fertile land of the Golden Vale, past the mansion by the river of the Earl of Dunraven with the text carved upon its parapet: "Except the Lord build the house, they labour in vain that build it," and through the wooded lanes to Ballingrane.

Further north we reach Farragh in Co. Longford where Wesley stayed with an old friend, Mr. Gosselin, and preached in his hayloft. Descendants of the family owned the house until last year when it was sold to the Land Commission, and is probably scheduled for demolition.

In Carlow he preached on the Barrack Field which is now

the Fair Green and the site of a recently completed cattle market; also in the Sessions House which subsequently became a corn exchange and is now the parochial hall, known as the Deighton Hall.

His visit to Rathcormack, where he preached several times in the parish church, led to the following bold reply from its friendly vicar to the Bishop of Cloyne's request that Wesley should no longer be allowed to preach in the church:

> I confess that Mr. Wesley has preached (though seldomer than has been wished) in my Church, and I thought that a Fellow of Lincoln College, Oxford, who is admitted to preach before the University there, and has preached in many churches in London, and other parts of England, as also in Dublin, might be permitted to preach here also . . . Religion, my Lord, is now at a very low ebb in the world, and we can scarce see the outward form of it remaining. But corrupt as the world is, it is thought better that the devil should reign than that Mr. Wesley should preach, especially in a church.

It was at Rathcormack that Wesley heard for the first time the Irish funeral howl—a dismal inarticulate yell at the grave by four shrill-voiced women hired for the purpose, and not one to shed a tear.

In Cork, which he visited many times and which became a vigorous centre, there were violent scenes on one occasion, when the mayor gave orders to his sergeants and the town drummers to beat their drums outside the preaching house. "Are there not churches and meeting-places enough?" he said. "I will have no more preaching; and if Mr. Wesley attempts to preach, I am prepared for him." The upshot was that the congregation on leaving the building was roughly handled and the premises were wrecked (for the third time). Wesley escaped injury and rode on to Bandon, while the mob burnt his effigy near Daunts Bridge. A few days later Wesley was back in Cork, only to find the town drummers again ready with their drums. But this time he had the protection of the Highland Regiment from the barracks who provided him with an escort and prevented further disturbance.

He was no less active in Northern Ireland. The Market House and the Linen Hall[1] were among scenes of his preaching in

[1] It was the old Brown Linen Hall in Donegall Street, now a warehouse.

Belfast, which in those days had a population of only 8,500 compared with Dublin's 150,000. At Londonderry he worshipped in the cathedral, and dined with the bishop on boiled beef and "an English pudding". Mr. M'Geough of Armagh proved a good friend, for when Wesley was refused the use of the church he said, "Then he shall preach in my drive." This was at Drumsill, and the square-backed wooden chair which he used there is preserved at The Argory.

He wrote to a preacher stationed in Armagh, provoked by his indolence or by the state of the Irish cabins: "I shall now tell you the things which have been more or less upon my mind ever since I have been in the North of Ireland," and after exhorting him to be more serious and zealous continues:

> Be cleanly, In this let the Methodists take pattern by the Quakers. Avoid all nastiness, dirt, slovenliness, both in your person, clothes, house, and all about you. Use all diligence to be clean. Whatever clothes you have, let them be whole; no rents, no tatters, no rags . . . another fruit of vile laziness. Mend your clothes, or I shall never expect you to mend your lives. Let none ever see a ragged Methodist. Clean yourselves of lice. Do not cut off your hair, but clean it and keep it clean. Cure yourself and your family of the itch; a spoonful of brimstone will cure you.

This outspoken letter throws light on the habits of the century, when in a primitive countryside it was hard to keep clean, and Wesley's insistence on hygiene is not so odd as it sounds. He also abhorred laziness and chose to walk the few miles from Londonderry to Brickfield to show the indolent brick workers "how to use their own feet". His own powers of endurance were remarkable. He was once in the saddle almost continuously from 5 a.m. to 11 p.m., was awakened at 2 a.m. the next morning, and at four o'clock was once more on his way. On another occasion, at the age of seventy-five, he drove sixty-eight miles, from Snugborough to Ballinrobe, with the same pair of horses, which was hard on the animals, but was unavoidable as all the inns he passed were full.

At Lambeg, about three miles north of Lisburn, he was the guest of Mr. Edward Gayer, Clerk of the Irish House of Lords. Mrs. Gayer had attended his service and Wesley said he would call on her, but Mr. Gayer had no use for Methodism, and she and her daughter were greatly perturbed, fearing her husband's displeasure, and made it a matter of prayer. In due course Wesley set out for her home at Derriaghy and in the avenue leading to it met a stranger and inquired if Mrs. Gayer lived there. The stranger replied: "Yes, she is my wife," and was so impressed by Wesley that he invited him for dinner. So all was well. The same day Wesley preached in his house, where a prophet's chamber was afterwards set apart for his use whenever he came that way. At a later period he was nursed by Mrs. Gayer when he was seriously ill.

This was a time of political upheaval and national tension; the Industrial Revolution was creating great social problems and there was a real danger of revolution. In the American colonies discontent at being taxed and ruled without representation in the English Parliament produced a situation that was bound to come to a head, and the stubbornness of George III and the weakness of his Prime Minister, Lord North, did nothing to avoid the impending crisis. In April 1775 the pot boiled over and hostilities broke out at Lexington. It was civil war, not a war between two nations, and although the bulk of the British people supported their Government, there was a strong minority who spoke out against such fratricide, including John Wesley, not the least perhaps because he had visited America and appreciated the viewpoint of the colonists there.

It was on one of his visits to Ireland, in the very year of 1775, following an extensive preaching tour, that he arrived at Armagh on June 10. It was from here that he wrote his famous letters to the Earl of Dartmouth, Secretary of State for the Colonies, and to the Prime Minister urging them to bring the war to an end.

> My Lord, he wrote to the Prime Minister, I would not speak, as it may seem to be concerning myself with things that lie out of my province. But I dare not refrain from it any longer; I think silence in the present case would be a sin against God, against my country, and against my own soul . . .
>
> I do not intend to enter upon the question whether the Americans are in the right or in the wrong. Here all my prejudices are against the Americans; for I am an High Churchman, the son of an High Churchman, bred up from my childhood in the highest notions of passive obedience and non-resistance. And yet in spite of all my long-rooted prejudices, I cannot avoid thinking, if I think at all, these, an oppressed people, asked for nothing more than their legal rights, and that in the most modest and inoffensive manner that the nature of the thing would allow. But waiving this, waiving all considerations of right and wrong, I ask, Is it common

sense to use force toward the Americans? . . . You see, my Lord, whatever has been affirmed, these men will not be frightened. And it seems they will not be conquered so easily as was at first imagined. They will probably dispute every inch of ground, and, if they die, die sword in hand . . . They are enthusiasts for liberty.

Three days after writing this letter Wesley reached Mr. Lock's farm at Cockhill near Cranagill and here, feeling ill, he lay on the grass and fell asleep in the orchard. When he awoke, he preached to a large company of people; the next day he went to Grange near Loughgall and then through Portadown to Lurgan and finally to Tandaragee. He was now far from well. His strength was entirely gone and he could not preach. But he pushed on, knowing of the one place where he would be nursed back to health—at the home of Mr. and Mrs. Gayer. On reaching here, he completely collapsed and was unconscious for several days.

Some years ago a pilgrimage was made to Derriaghy House when the owner, Mr. Alexander Withers, showed the visitors the room in which Wesley lay more dead than alive, and the yew tree under which he preached twice.

To continue the story of the Gayer family, Mary Gayer, the daughter, married Richard Wolfenden and went to live at Lambeg House near the parish church. Later, this house, which still stands, was renamed Chrome Hill and in its grounds are two large beech trees growing into one another and known as "Wesley's Tree" (Plate 30*c*). There is a tradition that these two trees, as saplings, were interwined by Wesley as a symbol that Methodism and the Church of Ireland would unite and grow together—a hope that was not realized.

Six times Wesley preached on the prehistoric mound at Clones called the Danish Fort. At Portstewart is the old thatched cottage by the roadside at Agherton where Dr. Adam Clarke lived as a boy; his story is one of the most romantic of the early Methodists. Before he was twenty he walked to Londonderry, took a boat to England, made his way to Bristol on foot to join Wesley, and became a powerful preacher, a scholar of national repute, and an eminent linguist and theologian. Though he moved in distinguished circles his proudest boast was that he was a Methodist preacher. His memorial (an obelisk) can be seen in Portrush.

Only a few houses remain at Terryhoogan, a village between

Scarva and Tandaragee, where Wesley came so often that a room was built for his accommodation. It was well that he was a small-sized man, for it was only nine feet long, seven feet wide and six feet high. And he joked about its "marble walls" which, along with the floor and ceiling, were of mud. Its sole furniture was a clean chaff bed. In the neighbourhood is "the lone house" referred to in his *Journal*. He preached many times in Tandaragee, a lovely town on the hillside, also in the old graveyard on the road to Scarva, where an annual Wesley commemoration service is held.

The Rev. Dr. T. E. Warner when serving as senior Church of England Chaplain to the R.A.F. in Ireland wrote: "I spent Easter 1954 at the Rectory, Tandaragee. As I walked about these grounds I began to think myself back into the years 1778 and 1787. I had a quiet holiday on that 'fruitful hill' so dear to the heart of Wesley. And I could see him now here, now there, but especially on the 'shady walk' and round about the ruins of that home where he was always welcome. I, too, love Tandaragee."

The present rectory lies a couple of hundred yards from the hilltop on which the old rectory stood. He traced the "shady walk", taking a spade and starting to dig, following the line of it from an old courtyard wall down the east side of the field, through a swamp and up under the hill to where it came out on the road near the quarry. Was this the lovely avenue? It had moss-covered roots of trees, and there were foundations of an old gate lodge almost opposite where the former rectory stood. Here were the shady walks and lawns that Wesley knew, now overgrown and returning to a rough heath. "On Easter Day," Dr. Warner continues, "as I held the three-century-old chalice in my hands and remembered that from it hundreds of newly-converted 'tasted that the Lord is gracious, in those days of the Son of Man', when Terryhoogan boasted a Prophet's Chamber . . . two centuries were but the twinkling of an eye."

It was at Terryhoogan that Wesley met Robert Strawbridge, a lively farmer of County Leitrim, who later emigrated to America and became another pioneer of American Methodism. He settled in Maryland where, at Sam's Creek, he built a log meeting house—possibly the first Methodist preaching house in America.

The talking robot which attracted Wesley's attention in Lurgan, and which anticipated the gramophone, has not survived.

Stuart's *History of Armagh* refers to it. "At Lurgan Wesley was entertained by Mr. Miller, a very ingenious gentleman, who had executed a piece of mechanism, unique and almost unparalleled in the world. This was a wooden figure, in the form of a man, which uttered articulate sounds, by means of internal valves and tubes of a most ingenious and singular construction. It called the hour and it repeated sentences." Miller, finding no purchaser for it and embarrassed by the crowds which flocked to see it, dismantled it. His son, Dr. Joseph Miller, resided in the house called The Wilderness on the Belfast Road.

On arriving at the King's Arms, Monaghan, Wesley was threatened with arrest by the Provost who was on the look-out for three strangers in connection with a recent rising, but fortunately letters which Wesley carried enabled him to establish his identity. Apologies were made and the Provost wished him a good journey.

In Moy Church we find a reminder of those days in a tablet to John Smith, a pioneer Methodist preacher "called out to preach by John Wesley 1766. In 1774 he was waylaid near Clogher and cruelly beaten, with difficulty he reached Charlemont where he died a martyr's death. His dust lies in an unknown grave in Legar Hill." When this tablet was unveiled in 1933 a letter was read from the late Lord Baldwin, whose great-grandfather, James Macdonald, had been a convert of John Smith, and was one of upwards of twenty young men who entered the Methodist ministry under his influence.

The Downpatrick Chapel to which Wesley came—the second oldest Methodist chapel in Ireland—was demolished some years ago and replaced by another. At Carrickfergus the old Court House is now the Town Hall and the Borough Council sits in the Assize room where he preached. He worshipped here in St. Nicholas Parish Church. Swanlinbar is interesting because of its curate, James Creighton, who when Wesley first came there was sceptical about Methodism, but afterwards became his assistant at City Road, London, and was present when he died.

Sligo recalls an interesting story. Entering an inn after preaching in the Cornmarket, Wesley encountered a shrill-voiced landlady about to turn a strolling actor and his wife into the street. Seeing the preacher, she dropped her angry tone. "I have kept him for a fortnight," she said, "and never seen the colour of his money." "Who is this gentleman?" inquired Wesley. She replied, "He is one of those you preach against. I wish you could preach him out of the town." Wesley turned to the victim of her anger and gave him a guinea, saying, "You serve the stage. Would I could teach you to serve a better Master." "Who is your master?" asked the actor. Wesley replied, "God is my Master. Return Him thanks, on your knees in private, in public at all times, in your principles and in your practice." And to the angry landlady he paid fifteen shillings to cover the actor's debt, saying, "May God forgive you!" and departed. "Forgive me, indeed!" she exclaimed. "Only yesterday he was preaching everybody to the devil that encourages the players, and today he was the first to do it himself."

Between Wicklow and Rathdrum we come to Glenealy Parish Church which stands on a rock above the road. According to tradition its erection was a direct outcome of the growth of Methodism in this neighbourhood, and Wesley himself drew a rough draft of a suitable building, basing his design on St. John's College Chapel, Cambridge. The Tighes, who were the local landowners and great friends of his, adopted his design. The little church is built like the choir of a cathedral, with pews facing each other across the aisle, the back rows with oaken recesses and canopies.

Mention of the Tighes brings us to Rosanna, near Wicklow, a pleasant mansion in an extensive park, still inhabited, formerly the home of Mrs. Tighe, a lady of large fortune and deep piety, who was a good friend to the Methodists, and where Wesley stayed, and preached in its great hall. "Even our Bedroom Candle sticks were of solid silver," wrote a London Methodist who stayed there. The house was well-ordered, with nineteen indoor servants. "The Porter, an old man, does little but read his Bible. Indeed, a Bible is to be found in almost every place you put your head in." And the letter continues, "Horses enough in the grounds to mount a little regiment. Breakfast at 10. Dine at 5. Tea about 7. Supper at 10. From 1 to 3 the ladies ride in their carriage. She has a little cottage three miles off in the mountains." But there was a fly in the ointment. She has a son "who has not the right use of his understanding. A pious young clergyman acts as his tutor." She also "has a little school of seven girls whom she boards, cloathes and educates at her sole expense and afterwards fortunes them out into the world £40 dowry to each". He adds that the house was well barricaded with shutters that were musket-proof against rebels; this at a time when people were dragged out of their homes as they dined, and piked in a field. It was Mrs. Tighe who commissioned Romney's well-known painting of Wesley.

Back in Dublin we come to his last visit. Eighty-six and the crossing from England had taken twenty-nine hours! Seasick and suffering severely from cramp, he landed, again on a Sunday morning, and went straight from the boat to Whitefriar Street Chapel and preached, with five hundred at the Communion service. A prolonged and bitter controversy in the Irish press followed because he had allowed one of his preachers to assist him; the time had not yet come when Methodist preachers administered the Sacrament.

Two years earlier, on May 2, 1787, *The Glasgow Mercury* had the following item in its column of Irish news:

> We hear that the Rev. Mr. Wesley, who arrived a few days ago in this city (Dublin) intends visiting most of the principal towns in this kingdom, with his usual celerity, though in the 84th year of his age. This gentleman may be truly considered as a prodigy of the present century, who at this advanced age rises every morning at four o'clock, preaches twice, frequently three times, and travels forty or fifty miles a-day, and what is most extraordinary, after all this labour, remains a stranger to weariness.

And now, two years later, he was still the untiring traveller. "He rides easily, whom the grace of God carries."

He revisited Lord and Lady Moira in Dublin, preached in Bethesda, attended St. Patrick's Cathedral taking several hundred Methodists with him to Communion. He agreed to Methodist services in church hours on condition that the Methodists attended the cathedral on the first Sunday in every month. He was, says Robert Haire, a great Anglican as well as a great Methodist. On Easter Day he preached three times, then travelled for the last time throughout Ireland, as far as Wexford and Waterford, revisiting Rathcormack and Cork, and places in between and far beyond. He was taken ill at Limerick and had thoughts of returning to London, but resumed his tour, dining in the barracks at Sligo, "hobbling on" to Annandale, preaching for the last time on the great earthwork at Clones, and staying with his friend, Alexander Knox, at Londonderry.

After preaching in the Court House in Wicklow he returned to Dublin by the lovely road through the Glen of the Downs. "I enter now," he records, "on my eighty-seventh year. I now find that I grow old: 1, my sight is decayed, so that I cannot read small print, unless in a strong light; 2, my strength is decayed, so that I walk much slower; 3, my memory of names, whether of persons or places, is decayed, till I stop a little to recollect them."

But his work was not yet done, and two years of travel still remained. He prepared a sermon on "Why has Christianity done so little good in the world?" He presided over his twentieth Irish Conference. (Among its *Minutes* we find this injunction: "Except in extraordinary cases, every preacher is to go to bed before ten o'clock.") He was treated with great respect by the nobility of the city, and was received in honour at the cathedral, and placed near the Dean with his preachers in conspicuous seats.

He preached his last Dublin sermon in the New Room (probably Gravel Walk). A crowded Communion service followed. A great company gathered at the quay to watch his departure, where he gave out a hymn, and knelt down and prayed that God would bless them, their families, the Church, and especially Ireland. Some fell on his neck and kissed him. Then he went aboard. And the last they saw of him were his hands uplifted in prayer as his boat moved down the river.

APPENDIX I

WESLEY IN AMERICA

FOR TWO years Wesley lived in America, sailing from Gravesend for the new Colony of Georgia on October 21, 1735 (though, delayed by storms, it was not until December 10 that the boat left Cowes Roads), and returning on February 1, 1738. He was thirty-five years old, newly-ordained, and he went as chaplain to the Colony. He landed off Savannah on February 6. "About eight o'clock in the morning," he records, "I first set my foot on American ground. It was a small uninhabited island, over against Tybee." Here he held his first service in America, calling his fellow passengers to prayer. Though his duties were mainly confined to Savannah he visited other parts of the area including South Carolina. On his journeys down the coast and into the undeveloped interior he slept often in the open, lived on bear's flesh, crossed flooded rivers and preached to the Indians, enduring the arduous life of a pioneer missionary. But circumstances and his own temperament were against him, and the enterprise proved disappointing, which accounts for his early return to England in a mood of frustration. General Oglethorpe, the founder of the Colony, did not encourage his work among the Indians, and Wesley's pastoral discipline provoked antagonism. He found himself in a queer and mixed community, full of gossip and intrigue, of which in the end he became a victim. His friendship with Sophy Hopkey, one of his most promising pupils and parishioners and niece of the chief magistrate, bordered on romance and was encouraged by Oglethorpe, who wished to retain him in the Colony, but ended painfully and led to bitter misunderstanding. It was followed by a tactless action on Wesley's part, on a point of Church order, which led to a public outcry and he hurriedly left the Colony.

But it was not all loss. In Georgia he published his first hymn-book (Charleston, 1737), which was the first hymnal ever issued in America, and of which only two copies are now known to exist. And from Georgia he sent his stirring challenge to Whitefield: "Only Mr. Delamotte is with me, till God shall stir up the hearts of some of his Servants, who, putting their lives in His hands, shall come over and help us, where the harvest is so great, and the labourers so few. What, if thou art the man, Mr. Whitefield?" And Whitefield records: "On reading this my heart leaped within me, and as it were echoed to the call . . . I at length resolved within myself to embark for Georgia." The result was enormous gain both for America and England, for Whitefield evangelized the New World, and Wesley, on his return, stirred the heart of Britain. It was also on his Georgian journey that he encountered Moravian missionaries who influenced so profoundly the course of his life. During a storm at sea on his outward journey he had been impressed by their calm demeanour. "Were you not afraid?" he asked. "I thank God, no," replied their leader, "our women and children are not afraid to die." And a conversation in Savannah with their pastor, August Spangenberg, affected him deeply. "Do you know Jesus Christ?" inquired the Moravian. "I know He is the Saviour of the world," replied Wesley. "But do you know He has saved you?" asked Spangenberg. "I do," answered Wesley; but in his *Journal* he recorded: "I fear they were vain words." Here is the genesis of his Aldersgate experience. Out of Georgia also came his first *Journal* which he published on his return to England: *An Extract of the Rev. Mr. John Wesley's Journal From his Embarking for Georgia To His Return to London.* For sheer interest this is by far the best section of the *Journal*. There is a springtime freshness about it; the style is clear, the story vivid.

Among commemorative tablets in Savannah is one on the site of the old Court House recording that he preached there, and another in Christ Church (Episcopal) which reads:

To the Glory of God
In Memory of
JOHN WESLEY
Priest of the Church of England
Minister to Savannah 1736–1737
Founder of the Sunday-School of this Church.
Erected by the Diocese of Georgia.

Some claim that this was the first Sunday-school in the world. On St. Simon's Island in the churchyard of Christ Church is the Wesley Oak under which he is said to have preached to the Indians. Nearby is the ruined Fort Frederica built by Oglethorpe and now a national monument. There is a Methodist centre here, Epworth-by-the-Sea, on the site of Hamilton Plantation where Charles Wesley once served as Oglethorpe's secretary. Bethesda Orphanage in Savannah, founded by Whitefield in 1737, is the oldest in America and is still functioning. The spot is appropriately marked on the beach of Cockspur Island where the Wesley brothers first landed, in 1736. Charleston has strong Methodist associations—the only American city visited by the Big Five: the two Wesleys, Whitefield, Coke and

29. Fonmon Castle in Wales. Wesley wrote he would visit it "once a year for so long as my life is prolonged". His host's descendant still lives there

Below, Llanlleonfel Church near Garth where Charles Wesley was married by his brother

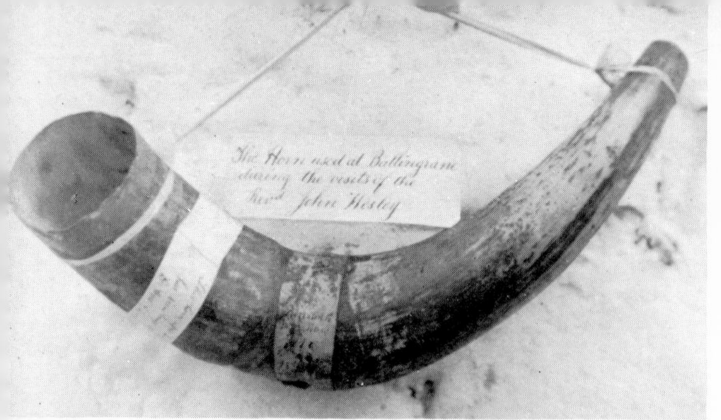

30. *Left*, the horn used at Ballingrane in Ireland to call men in from the fields to hear Wesley preach

Above, an old photograph of Barbara Heck's home, Fort View, Ballingrane. "Wesley's pear tree" can just be seen on the right (it no longer stands) and the two elderly ladies are grand-nieces of Barbara Heck

Right, there is a tradition that these two trees at Chrome Hill near Lisburn were intertwined by Wesley

Asbury. And Lake Junaluska in N. Carolina, an American headquarters of the World Methodist Council, has a large collection of Wesleyana.

Elsewhere, in New York, John Street Methodist Church, containing Philip Embury's old pulpit, stands on the site of the first Methodist building in America (1768), and close by, at No. 120 William Street, a plaque marks the scene of the old Rigging Loft —a sail-maker's attic rented for worship by the first New York Methodists. Before that, services had been held in Philip Embury's house, No. 10 Augustus Street. We have already seen how Methodism was brought here by Irish immigrants. Barbara Heck, finding a group engaged in card playing, had seized the pack and thrown it into the fire, then had rushed to her Cousin Embury and implored him to preach. "How can I preach?" he said. "I have neither house nor congregation." "Preach," replied Barbara, "in your own house and to your own company." Which he did, making his own pulpit, and New York Methodism began with a congregation of six including a Negro servant. The first Methodist building in the world to be called a church was an unfinished Dutch church in Philadelphia, purchased by the Methodists in 1769. It is called St. George's, is part of the National Park, and Dr. Elmer Clark tells us it is the oldest Methodist chapel in America. It houses a museum and library, and John Dickins, an old Etonian and one of Wesley's preachers, who opened a Methodist publishing house at his own expense, is buried at the rear. The first American Conference met in Philadelphia in 1773. Whitefield's remains lie under the altar of the old South Presbyterian Church, Newburyport. In Washington, Dumbarton Avenue Church traces its origin back to 1772 and Lincoln often worshipped in the present building which was erected in 1849. During its use as a hospital in the Civil War Walt Whitman was among the patients nursed there. Washington also has two equestrian statues of Methodist leaders, one of Asbury, unveiled by President Coolidge; the other, just erected, of Wesley, and already referred to (page 71).

Maryland competes with New York in its claim to be the scene of the first Methodist preaching in America, for it was here that Robert Strawbridge, another Irish immigrant, preached at Sam's Creek in 1764 and built his log cabin meeting-house. Its site is marked in New Windsor, and his house is now a Methodist shrine. But this by no means exhausts the number of places of historic interest for the Methodist traveller in America. The new nation and the new Church grew up together. The circuit riders, among the heroes of history, certainly among the saints and martyrs, followed the trail of the settlers, ministered to their scattered and lonely flocks, baptized their children and buried their dead. They set up their altars in every new township, and in barns, log cabins and camp meetings preached the Gospel to a community that would otherwise have had no spiritual provision. When no man cared, they pioneered. Here in the providence of God was the justification of Wesley's phrase, that he took the *world* as his parish.

On the motion of John Dickins at the Conference held on Christmas Eve, 1784, in Lovely Lane Chapel, Baltimore (erected 1774), the American Societies first took the name of the Methodist Episcopel Church—the first Methodist Episcopal Church in the world. The site is marked at Merchants' Club, 206 E. Redwood Street.

It was the refusal of Dr. Lowth, Bishop of London, to respond to Wesley's sensible request to him to ordain suitable men for work in America that compelled Wesley in desperation to ordain his own preachers for the purpose. Lowth replied, with apparent indifference (or irresponsibility) that there were three clergymen already in America! "But what are three," cried Wesley, "to watch over all the souls in that extensive country? . . . I mourn for poor America, for the sheep scattered up and down therein." But Lowth was obdurate and his refusal altered the shape of history. Today there are thirty-seven Methodist episcopal areas in America covering 570 Methodist Districts, with upwards of 30,000 ministers and 10,000,000 members. Methodist colleges and schools in America, including eight universities, embrace nearly a quarter of a million students. And 229 Methodist medical and welfare institutions, including seventy-five hospitals, serve annually one and a half million people. Enough, in all conscience, to make the Bishop turn in his grave.

APPENDIX II

WESLEY IN GERMANY AND HOLLAND

IN JUNE 1738, immediately following his Aldersgate experience, Wesley visited Germany on a pilgrimage to the Moravian Settlement at Herrnhut. He sailed from Gravesend to Rotterdam and travelled by way of Amsterdam (which favourably impressed him) and Cologne—"the ugliest, dirtiest city," he said, "I ever yet saw with my eyes. Its cathedral—a huge mis-shapen thing." He spent four nights journeying down the Rhine, reaching Mainz, and Frankfurt where, not having passes, he and his party were halted at the city gate until rescued by a local burgher—the father of his friend, Peter Böhler. They moved on to Marienborn and were the guests of Count Zinzendorf, the head of the Moravian community. The next stage included Weimar, Jena, and Halle where for two hours they were refused admission and at length were admitted into the Orphan House founded by A. H. Francke, on which both Wesley and Whitefield modelled their own Orphan Houses, and to which much of the orphanage work of the nineteenth century in Great Britain can be traced. Next came Leipzig, Dresden, and finally Herrnhut on the border of Bohemia which was Zinzendorf's main centre and original Moravian settlement and the chief aim of Wesley's journey. After twelve days they returned via Cologne and re-embarked at Rotterdam, reaching London on September 16.

Forty-five years passed before Wesley, in June 1783, revisited Holland, celebrating his eightieth birthday in Utrecht. It was in the nature of a summer holiday and he calls it "my little excursion". His party included his friend, Robert Carr Brackenbury, and his niece Sally. They sailed from Harwich, landed at Hellevoetsluis, took a coach to Brielle and a boat to Rotterdam. Their tour, which lasted three weeks, included The Hague, Delft, Haarlem, Zeeburg, Amsterdam, Scheveningen and Zeist.

Three years later he paid his third visit to Holland, again in the company of Brackenbury, sailing from Harwich on August 9, 1786 to Rotterdam where he preached in the Episcopal Church. Again, it was a happy occasion, during which he revisited old scenes and friends. He liked Amsterdam and loved the people. "Taking boat," he says, "we went at our ease through one of the pleasantest summer countries in Europe." And again, of a Dutchman who sent a coach to meet his boat, "he received me with the courtesy and cordiality of an old Yorkshire Methodist."

The diary of Sophie V. La Roche (*Sophie in London*, translated by Clare Williams) gives lively glimpses of Wesley in Holland and on the homeward voyage. "A venerable old man, and very understanding, who speaks well of everything and at the immense age of eighty-three enjoys complete good health . . . After the dinner-bell had sounded we assembled, and the Methodists straightway gave us proof of their stern practices, for when we had taken our places Wesley began to pray. The good language-master was holding a discussion by the window, and was not at once aware of the prayers, when suddenly Wesley reproached him in a most violent manner. . . The poor man was very embarrassed; and old Wesley found it difficult to resume his sermonizing, as the rest of us said we would be glad of a meal."

The twenty-two travellers, delayed at the inn by rough weather, while waiting for the Harwich boat, were thrown closely together. "We teased Miss du Moulin because she had been given a bedroom behind strict Mr. Wesley's apartment . . . We attended the short sermon and chanting of the psalms which Wesley and his disciples had arranged in his apartment, and promised to breakfast together. Charming du Moulin had to turn in early so that Wesley could shut his door." The food was poor and complaint was made, but not by Wesley. "On board ship the captain and sailors all paid Wesley great respect . . . Wesley sat and read Virgil, with spectacles, in an Elzevir edition. Heavens! I thought, if the Methodists' principles keep the sight as clear as that to the age of eighty-three, then I wish I had been educated in their sect . . . Yesterday he preached a very fine sermon about the need for death and the danger of life, which was very well chosen and adaptable to the storm." Wesley's record of the same occasion reads, with unconscious humour: "When we had been twenty-four hours on board, we were scarce come a third of our way. I judged we should not get on unless I preached, which I therefore did, between two and three in the afternoon, on, 'It is appointed unto men once to die.' " They landed at Harwich on July 4.

APPENDIX III

LIST OF PLACES BY COUNTIES

ENGLAND

BEDFORDSHIRE
Bedford
Everton
Luton
Sundon
Wrestlingworth

BERKSHIRE
Buckland
Wytham

BUCKINGHAMSHIRE
Fleet Marston
High Wycombe
Stony Stratford
Winchendon

CAMBRIDGESHIRE
Ely
Grantchester
Harston
Melbourn

CHESHIRE
Alpraham
Altrincham
Boothbank
Bunbury
Chester
Knutsford
Macclesfield
Mellor
Mow Cop
Neston
Parkgate
Sale
Stalybridge
Stockport
Styal

CORNWALL
Altarnon
Busveal
Camborne
Carines
Carharrack
Cubert
Falmouth
Goldsithney
Gwennap
Hea Moor (Penzance)
Helston
Kenwyn
Laneast
Launceston
Methrose
Newlyn
North Tamerton
Port Isaac
Rosemurgy (Morrah)
St. Endellion
St. Gennys
St. Ives
St. Just
Tresmeer
Trewellard
Trewint
Truro
Week St. Mary

CUMBERLAND
Alston
Cockermouth
Gamblesby
Penrith
Whitehaven

DERBYSHIRE
Bakewell
Bolsover
Bongs
Buxton
Chapel-en-le-Frith
Chesterfield
Chinley
Crich
Derby
Hayfield
New Mills
Ockbrook

DEVONSHIRE
Crediton
Crockernwell
Cullompton
Devonport
Exeter
Fremington
Plymouth
Sticklepath
Tavistock
Tiverton

DORSET
Bourne
Bridport
Charmouth
Corfe
Langton Matravers
Poole
Preston
Sturminster Newton
Swanage
Weymouth
Winterbourne Whitechurch

DURHAM
Charters Haugh
Gateshead
Lamesley
Low Fell
Middleton-in-Teesdale
Monkwearmouth
Newbiggin-in-Teesdale
Sunderland
Whickham

ESSEX
Colchester
Little Easton
Maldon
Tilty

GLOUCESTERSHIRE
Brimscombe
Bristol
Buckland
Cheltenham
Cirencester
Coombe Hill
Gloucester
Gotherington
Gretton
Kingswood (Bristol)
Randwick
Stanley
Stanton
Stroud
Tewkesbury
Winchcombe

HAMPSHIRE
Fordingbridge

HERTFORDSHIRE
Bishop's Stortford
Royston

HUNTINGDONSHIRE
St. Neots

KENT
Bexley
Bickley
Canterbury
Eynsford
Gillingham
Maidstone
Newbourne
Rolvenden
Sevenoaks
Shoreham
Southborough
Tunbridge Wells

LANCASHIRE
Blackburn
Bolton
Brock
Chipping
Darwen
Flookburgh
Kent's Bank
Liverpool
Manchester
Nelson
Preston
Rochdale
St. Helen's
Southport
Ulverston
Walton-le-dale
Warrington
Westhoughton
Wigan

LEICESTERSHIRE
Ashby-de-la-Zouch
Donnington Park
Leicester
Markfield

LINCOLNSHIRE
Boston
Epworth
Gainsborough
Grantham
Haxey
Owston
Raithby
Sleaford
Spilsby
Winterton
Winthorpe
Wroot

NORFOLK
Diss
Great Yarmouth
Hempnall
Thurlton

NORTHAMPTON-SHIRE
Northampton
Whittlebury

NORTHUMBERLAND
Allendale
Alnwick
Berwick-on-Tweed
Blanchland
Cambo
Felton
High House
Hindley Hill
Horsley
Keenley
Morpeth
Newcastle-on-Tyne
Plessey
Prudhoe
Wooller

NOTTINGHAMSHIRE
Newark
Nottingham

OXFORDSHIRE
Ascot
Bampton
Blackbourton
Cuddesdon
Finstock
Holwell
Oxford
Pyrton
Shipton-under-Wychwood
South Leigh
Stanton Harcourt
Witney
Wood Green

SHROPSHIRE
Broseley
Ironbridge
Madeley
Shrewsbury

SOMERSET
Bath
Brean
Ditcheat
Shepton Mallet
Taunton
Washford

STAFFORDSHIRE
Bilston
Bloxwich
Burslem
Great Barr
Leek
Newcastle-under-Lyme
Tipton
Walsall
Wednesbury
West Bromwich
Wolverhampton

SUFFOLK
Lakenheath

SURREY
Godalming
Leatherhead
Mickleham
Reigate

SUSSEX
Ewhurst
Horn's Cross
Rye
Winchelsea

WARWICKSHIRE
Birmingham
Blake Street
Quinton

WESTMORLAND
Ambleside
Appleby
Huttongate
Kendal

WILTSHIRE
Bemerton
Bradford-on-Avon
Devizes
Pewsey
Salisbury
Seend (Melksham)
Wilton

WORCESTERSHIRE
Broadway
Dudley
Honeybourne
Oldbury
Pebworth
Stourport
Worcester

YORKSHIRE
Barnsley
Beverley
Bingley
Birstall

YORKSHIRE (cont.)
Bishop Burton
Bradford
Bramhope
Bramley
Bridlington
Eccleshill
Filey
Foggathorpe
Fulneck
Grassington
Guisborough
Halifax
Harrogate
Hawnby
Haworth
Hebden Bridge
Heptonstall
Hipperholme (Brighouse)
Honley
Hotham
Howden
Huddersfield
Hull
Hunmanby
Ilkley
Kirkstall
Leeds
Lepton
Market Weighton
Middleton (Pickering)
Netherthong
Northallerton
Osmotherley
Otley
Pickering
Pocklington
Poppleton
Rawdon
Reeth
Ripon
Robin Hood's Bay
Rotherham
Rothwell
Selby
Sheffield
Skipton
Stanley
Stanbury
Swinefleet
Thirsk
Thorne
Thorpe Hesley
Todmorden
Wakefield
Wentworth
Whitby
Yarm
Yeadon
York

CHANNEL ISLANDS

Alderney
Guernsey, St. Peter Port
Jersey, St. Helier

IRELAND

ANTRIM
Belfast
Carrickfergus
Chrome Hill
Lambeg
Portrush

ARMAGH
Armagh
Lurgan
Tanderagee
Terryhoogan

CARLOW
Carlow

CORK
Bandon
Cork
Rathcormack

DOWN
Downpatrick
Moira

DUBLIN
Dublin

LIMERICK
Adare
Ballingrane
Rathkeale

LONDONDERRY
Londonderry
Portstewart

LONGFORD
Farragh

MAYO
Castlebar
Croagh Patrick

MONAGHAN
Clones
Monaghan

SLIGO
Sligo

TYRONE
Castlecaulfield
Moy

WESTMEATH
Athlone

WICKLOW
Glenealy
Rosanna

THE ISLE OF MAN

Ballaugh
Castletown
Douglas
Kirk Braddan
Lezare
Lonan
Peel
Ramsey

THE ISLE OF WIGHT

Yarmouth

SCOTLAND

Aberdeen
Arbroath (Angus)
Banff
Dalkeith (Midlothian)
Dalwhinnie (Inverness)
Dumfries
Dunbar (East Lothian)
Dundee
Edinburgh
Gatehouse-of-Fleet (Kirkcudbright)
Glasgow
Inverness
Portpatrick (Wigtown)

WALES

ANGLESEY
Holyhead
Llangefni
Trefollwyn

BRECON
Brecon
Builth
Garth
Maesmynis
Trevecca
Watton

CARMARTHEN
Carmarthen
Llanelly
Trecastle

CARNARVON
Bangor
Carnarvon
Conway
Llanfair-is-gaer
Penmaenmawr

FLINT
Mold

GLAMORGAN
Cardiff
Cowbridge
Fonmon
Fontigary
Oxwich
Porthkerry
Rhossili
Swansea
Wenvoe

MERIONETH
Dolgelly

MONMOUTH
Bedwas
Devauden
Lower Machen
Newport

MONTGOMERY
Llanidloes

PEMBROKE
Haverfordwest
Henllan
Llwyn-y-Gwair
Narberth
Nevern
Newport
Pembroke
Spittal
Tenby
Trecwm

INDEX OF PLACES

The figures in bold type refer to Plate numbers

INDEX OF PEOPLE